ALL YOUR
BASE
ARE
BELONG
TO US

ALL YOUR BASE ARE BELONG TO US

HOW FIFTY YEARS OF VIDEOGAMES CONQUERED POP CULTURE

HAROLD GOLDBERG

 THREE RIVERS PRESS > > > NEW YORK

Library of Congress Cataloging-in-Publication Data

Goldberg, Harold.
All your base are belong to us: how 50 years of videogames
conquered pop culture / Harold Goldberg—1st ed.
p. cm.
Includes bibliographical references.
1. Video games—History. 2. Video Games—Social aspects. I. Title.
GV1469.3.G65 2011
794.8—dc22
2010036095

ISBN 978-0-307-46355-5
eISBN 978-0-307-46356-2

Book design by Maria Elias
Cover design by Kyle Kolker

Printed in the United States of America

1 3 5 7 9 10 8 6 4 2

First Edition

For the Rzepecki Family, who always had game

CONTENTS

You are likely to be eaten by a grue.

If this predicament seems particularly cruel,

consider whose fault it could be:

not a torch or a match in your inventory.

Does it descend from there, adventure to nightmare?

Did I battle a snake? Was the treasure intact?

Or did the TRS-80 in my brain get hacked?

—"It Is Pitch Dark" by MC Frontalot

• • •

Mechanic: Somebody set us up the bomb.

Operator: Main screen turn on.

CATS: All your base are belong to us.

CATS: You have no chance to survive make your time.

—Dialogue from Zero Wing, the Toaplan/

Taito game for Arcade and Sega Mega Drive, 1989

• • •

When trouble looms, the fool turns his back,

while the wise man faces it down.

—Kenji Kasen in Grand Theft Auto III, written by Dan Houser

• • •

We all make choices, but in the end our choices make us.

—Andrew Ryan in BioShock, written by Ken Levine

INTRODUCTION

I am Nightmare. I am Nightmare in the deepest darkness and I am Nightmare even when the brightest halogen burns. I am Nightmare when life is tough, and real people around me die. I am Nightmare when I am completely angry at life and need to lash out.

I, as Neil Gaiman says, am a dark and stormy Nightmare. I have the voice, frightening, growling, ready to attack, like Mercedes McCambridge as the demon Pazuzu in *The Exorcist*. I carry the sword, the long, heavy magical blade called SoulCalibur. Within my chest is a jagged maw. It is forever open to reveal a blood red beating heart engorged after devouring the countless souls whose bodies I chopped and cut with the burdensome SoulCalibur. Always, I wear a black iron mask for I am awesomely ugly and evil. So don't mess with me. You will not survive. Give me more souls. I need to snack.

In real life I am thin and bald, sometimes cute but never handsome. I have Crohn's disease and am often half-sick. In my life, I would not punch you or cut you or even insult you (at least, to your face). I would be respectful, understanding, and nice, if somewhat cynical. Inside, I would despair and worry. But when I am Nightmare, I am nearly invulnerable. I feel alive and optimistic, full of life, healthy and strong.

I know one thing. Sick or not, sometimes I can't stop playing. Time ticks away, the half hour, the hour, the whole evening, and then, it's three a.m.; I'm in the zone, just as I am when writing. Normally, I like to savor a game rather than manically tsunami through it. But I remember spending hours just nosing around in BioShock, the scariest, best game of 2007. At the beginning of the first level, which evokes the first episode of TV's epic *Lost,* I was tossed from a crashing plane into the ebony ocean, where what seemed to be the skyscraper-tall fires of Hades burned all around me. Panic came over me, and then, a feeling that did not mimic real life, there was beauty in the danger. To gawk at the fireworks that played off the grim, foreboding water, I kept swimming even though the gasoline-induced flames kept shooting deep into the defenseless body that was the night sky. Dream. Reality. Beauty. Nightmare. Give me more.

Briefly as I play, I even feel immortal.

I am not the only one.

You probably have felt some visceral connection to videogames as well, no matter how old you are. In the dank confines of the arcade or the corner dive when the lights were low, you were the plumber who saved the dainty princess in Donkey Kong. As your fingers ached and your joints stiffened, you were the one who couldn't stop playing Tetris. You even had visions of blocks falling softly as snow as you slept. In front of a nineteen-inch TV, you went long and completed the Hail Mary in Madden football. As Master Chief you saved humanity from the gross aliens of the Covenant.

You know it is just a game, a videogame on a plastic disk that bears the computer bits and bytes, endless numbers that meet with a chip to turn you into Nightmare, or Mario or Sonic or Master Chief. But within that disk is magic as big and entertaining as any movie or TV show. And when that disk spins, it is a Sufi dervish who makes celestial pictures and sounds that are an extension of you and me. So forget this sordid keep-up-with-the-Joneses life, with its e-mail spam, inane tweets, bills, mortgages, and recessions. Down the rabbit hole we go to control it all as the hero, for in every videogame there is a hero. We admit it. We are junkies who must save the world. But we're game.

Believe it or not, we've been gaming for more than fifty years. Man, how it's grown, prospered, and evolved. The videogame industry in the United States is now a $20-billion-a-year juggernaut, surpassing movie, music, and DVD sales—combined. Just one game, the Houser brothers' Grand Theft Auto IV, earned $500 million in its opening week, far outpacing the movie industry's biggest force, James Cameron's *Avatar,* which earned less than half that amount. Forty-two percent of Americans have videogame consoles. If you add computer games, 68 percent of us are gamers. And the average age of today's gamer is thirty-five. Almost half of online gamers are female, and they play games with competitive zeal and attitude. And videogame consoles are now the guardians of the living room beyond games. They play DVDs. They stream movies from Netflix. They connect to Facebook and Twitter. *That's* entertainment.

And videogames have correspondingly become an unstoppable force in popular culture, one that constantly influences other forms of entertainment. From *30 Rock* to *South Park,* videogames are the subject of crucial plot points and full episodes. Even more important, they have changed the way blockbuster action films and TV programs are shot. Cars that blow up in *Transformers* roll toward you, coming at you like they're alive, like something out of Need for Speed or Burnout Paradise. Car commercials feature the characters and monsters in World of Warcraft. Beverage ads are informed by Grand Theft Auto. Sonic the Hedgehog and Pikachu are featured balloons in the Macy's Thanksgiving Day Parade, flying high and proud next to Spider-Man and Buzz Lightyear. Mark Ecko designed a full line of clothing devoted to Halo. And the phenomenon is worldwide. You can even buy a box of Pokémon-branded milk in Thailand.

How and why did this happen? As a journalist, I've watched the growth for two decades now. I've seen the cycles come and go. I've seen the Nintendo dominance end and begin again, more powerful than before. But as the trends come and go, I keep thinking about the big riddle of videogames: How did we get here? How did videogames rise to take over popular culture? I've watched in amazement as the videogame industry, like that Energizer bunny, keeps going and going. How does it get bigger every year, even as mainstream media continue to turn up their noses at videogame culture? (And isn't that utterly idiotic? Why aren't games reviewed alongside books, movies, and pop music?)

Those questions have always fascinated me, but another process—that of an individual game's creation—only really captured my imagination when I worked for two years as editor in chief of Sony Online Entertainment. There, I was witness to the fascinating if sometimes daunting way games were made. I helped with the words to many games and I helped test them too, including the massively multiplayer online role playing game of elves and ogres, EverQuest, often called EverCrack because of its insanely addictive nature. I was absolutely intrigued by the creation of games, utterly entranced by even the smallest nugget about, yes, *how* they were made, but even more, *why* they were made. There was nothing better than being inside that womb of knowledge. I felt the same way at VH1, where I wrote the daily GameBreak blog and worked on Viacom papers full of techspeak to help the company soldier forward during the casual game revolution. After those experiences, when a game struck me as ingenious—a cut or two above the rest—I wanted to know all about it and the people who imagined it. Questions for the game makers would drop into my head like those constantly falling blocks in Tetris. What could the game have become if you didn't have to worry about sales? What did you fight to retain when those heavy-handed executives from the megacorporation chimed in with their say? Overall, why did the game work? Why did it tickle and charge my neurons, axons, receptors, and thalamus, making me completely and utterly bliss out? Was it because the game itself was a triumph of the craft or because I could feel comfortable living in the game's world? Was my nerdy perception exactly on par with the game makers'? Or did the game permit my own imagination to grow and flourish in ways that I previously believed only books and music could? And finally, when a game was really terrific, when it grabbed my heart and soul just like Alice Sebold did with *The Lovely Bones* or Joseph Conrad with *Heart of Darkness,* why could I not stop playing?

There have been other books about videogames, books that talk about facts, money, and technology, books that personalize the experience of gaming, books that detail trends, books that simply tell you how to play a game. I've read many and have enjoyed some of them. But there have been few books that, to rephrase Robert Frost, began with delight and ended in wisdom, few books that led me to feel those completely exciting aha moments of creation and camaraderie, of theorizing and implementation, of process and panic, of wild success and looming deadline doom, that I know from experience go into making the finest games. Most of all, there have been none that convincingly told me how we got here.

That's what I've tried to capture in these pages. You will find out how the world of game making profoundly affected those artists and craftspeople who made Super Mario Bros., Pong, Myst, Spore, EverQuest, BioShock, Shadow Complex, and more—and not always in a positive way. Each of these changed videogames forever, and the untold facts, fascinating anecdotes, and heretofore buried details about these pieces of popular art tantalized me. But I also wanted to explore the larger question: How in the pantheon of games did each of these help the medium evolve enough to keep you and me excited for all these decades, these crazy fifty years?

I don't try to look at every moment of videogame history in

these pages. And I won't I look at every great videogame franchise. For that way lies madness . . . and redundancy. Instead, I've chosen to detail some moments of supreme discovery and utter failure by the brilliant inventors and craftspeople who gave innovation, personality, and even drama to an industry that altered my life (and, when you think about it, made a big difference in yours, too).

If you know games, you know what I mean. If you don't, I hope that, in the course of reading these chapters, you will feel it like I so often feel it, with surprise, pleasure, panic, awe, goose bumps, and exhilaration.

THE PRELUDE

FIRST BLIPS ON
THE SCREEN

On a freakin' cold, windy fall Friday, the 7:39 a.m. commuter train rolled through Queens, frozen wheels squeaking and moaning. I passed indistinguishable tall apartment complexes with ratty balconies like something out of Gears of War. As the city morphed into the equally indistinguishable suburban sprawl of Long Island, bleary-eyed reverse commuters checked their BlackBerries, ready for the week to end.

But forget their sour faces. I was going to visit the Brookhaven National Laboratory, where Dr. William Higinbotham made the first videogame—more than fifty years ago. Higinbotham's Wikipedia entry doesn't reveal much about the origin of his game, Tennis for Two. Mainly, it tells readers that his son, William Higinbotham Jr., thinks his father didn't want to be remembered primarily for creating a game. The party line was that he really wanted to be remembered for his work in nuclear nonproliferation. Fair enough. But that begs the question, Why did Higinbotham take time to make a game at all? No one forced him to design relays and transistors in such a way that he could hook them up to a big $200,000 Systron Donner 3300 computer, which his instrumentation department had used mainly for multifarious mathematical calculations. Not the government, not the lab, not his department. No, Higinbotham did it himself with the aid of lab technician Bob Dvorak. They took three weeks to make it work and two more days to work out the bugs. So what was it about the scientist that made him want to entertain others by making a game on a five-inch screen?

Higinbotham most likely did not know that at least two attempts at videogames had already been made. In 1948, Greenville, South Carolina, physicist and TV pioneer Thomas T. Goldsmith teamed up with Estle Ray Mann to patent and make a very rudimentary experiment that shot missiles—well, light rays that mimicked missiles—across an oscilloscope's screen. The Cathode Ray Tube Amusement Device used eight vacuum tubes and a radarlike display. But Goldsmith was more interested in the Washington, DC, TV station he owned and in producing the classic *Captain Video* TV series, so nothing ever came of the patent. Four years later, Cambridge PhD candidate Alexander S. Douglas became enamored with a giant, seemingly unwieldy computer created for the university. With its hundreds of vacuum tubes emitting firefly-like light within a dingy laboratory, the Electronic Delay Storage Automatic Calculator looked like something out of the 1931 movie *Frankenstein*. Douglas was entranced with the computer and added a tic-tac-toe game called Noughts and Crosses to his thesis about how humans interact with computers. It was the first computer game to use primitive graphics and can still be downloaded from the Web today.

Yet neither of these games made the step forward that's needed to create a satisfying communal gaming experience: the ability to hang out, play together, and maybe even understand your friends better from that play.

Two hours later, I found myself sitting in the Energy Department shuttle from the Ronkonkoma train station to the forested 5,300-acre property of the Brookhaven National Laboratory. Around me, a half dozen young scientists, all bearded, all bespectacled, listened to the youngest's idea for a new medical imaging technique. As the scientists chattered, the shuttle turned onto the grounds themselves. Dozens of wild turkeys lurked on the grass, their blue snoods ugly as they gobbled.

Brookhaven is full of old one-story wooden buildings and drafty barracks from its days as an army encampment in the 1940s. But around the campus, there are a few new buildings of soaring, un-dulating glass, twenty-first-century designs that look like they were informed by architect I. M. Pei. Inside one such building, public re-lations people tied helium-filled balloons to metal folding chairs and railings as old and young employees and visitors gathered around to look at a greasy old Magnavox Odyssey, the original PlayStation with the Gran Turismo racing simulation, a Wii with Wii Sports Bowling, and a few other mementos from videogame history. But an essential jewel was found where a smaller crowd of curious employees gathered. There it was on a folding table, a few more helium bal-loons heralding its birthday. It was merely an ancient oscilloscope, its graphics board on display within a Plexiglas box. The instrumenta-tion people had cheated a little to re-create the device. Gone was the six-foot-high Donner analog computer. Instead, Tennis for Two was attached to a Dell desktop hidden by a tablecloth. They had linked this re-creation to a fancy big screen, high definition TV—as if you needed such a thing to enhance its old-fangled graphics.

The visuals were rudimentary, merely a green dot on the screen and a small block in the middle to represent a net. There was a welded stainless steel box to take into my hands, upon which was a single button to press and from which heavy wires led to the sig-nal box. The primitive thing appeared otherworldly on the fifty-inch Samsung screen. That was when my nerd heart started beating, my mouth grew dry, and I found it somewhat difficult to take air. It was as if Tennis for Two were a living, breathing celebrity, an old-time star slightly Botoxed up to make it appear new again. And that green color was seductive. Green symbolizes everything videogames are made of, the life-and-death struggle, the yin and yang of heroism and evil, for green in various cultures means hope, rebirth, death, and envy. The color meant immortality in ancient Egypt (Osiris, the god of the afterlife, had skin tinged with green). It is the suit color of Shigeru Miyamoto's Link from The Legend of Zelda, the color of the camouflage gear of Metal Gear's ultra-macho Solid Snake. Green is perfect for games.

In videos presented online, Tennis for Two seemed to have a bright green tinge, but perhaps because of the streaming sunlight in the new Brookhaven building, the bouncing ball now had a rich jade hue, the color of a shining emerald. Each time the ball made its way to my side of the scope, I pressed the plastic button on the old-fashioned controller and the magnets in relays clicked loudly. I was able to angle the shots by twisting a plastic knob that aimed the blip on the screen.

Just before a few members of the press arrived, Higinbotham Junior, slightly wary but affable, stood before the game with Charlie Dvorak, the son of the lab technician who had actually made the machine full of circuits, capacitors, relays, and a mishmash of wires. Both were around fifty years old, and both had a look of pride and occasional glee as they played Tennis for Two. As they volleyed the dot, it left handsome trails on the screen and the relays clicked and clacked. Dvorak asked, "Can you imagine if your father patented this with my father? Things would be a lot different. We'd be on easy street. We'd be millionaires living in Montana somewhere."

Higinbotham Junior was dressed in a striped gray flannel suit with a striped tie. He, too, had worked at Brookhaven in various positions for more than eleven years. But he was somewhat of a rebel, who never went to college. In the economic downturn of 2001, Brookhaven let him go. He now worked at a Staples store on Long Island. Still playing, and without looking at Dvorak, he was pragmatic. "Nah. The government would have owned the patent. Even if he had the patent, my father would still be at Brookhaven. He would still be working here. Money wouldn't have changed his life's goal and that was working here and with the Federation of Scientists."

At lunch, Higinbotham Junior passed over a multipage document listing his father's achievements. Nowhere on it was the game. Sitting back in his seat, he said, "My dad liked the game a lot. But in a way he cheated. He saw in the oscilloscope instructions that you could manipulate the dot on the screen. In his mind it became a tennis ball. It took just a few hours to go from point A to point B, to an interactive game." Then he said it again. "The thing is, he didn't want to be remembered just for the game."

Whatever he wanted his legacy to be, it didn't stop Dr. Higinbotham from engineering version 2.0 of the game on a larger, seventeen-inch screen, one that added play on the moon and on Jupiter, including a fairly precise modeling of the gravitational pull of those celestial bodies.

With its expensive germanium transistors, the game was state of the art in 1958, a time when technology was speeding forward rapidly in many industries. The world itself was infected by space fever. Sputnik went 60 million miles as it orbited Earth; the world was entranced. The Cold War had frozen relations with the USSR, and Nikita Khrushchev became its cunning, fist-pounding premier. Americans were mired in a heavy fear and paranoia about a coming nuclear war. On January 13, 9,235 scientists, led by the father of molecular biology, Linus Pauling, took out ads in newspapers, begging the United States to put a permanent halt to its nuclear testing. One of those scientists was Dr. William Higinbotham, the head of the Instrumentation Division at the Brookhaven National Laboratory.

Higinbotham had worked on the Manhattan Project, and like many scientists who worked on the project, he was plagued by guilt when the bomb was used on Hiroshima.

To understand why Higinbotham made the game, you have to look into his personality. On May 18, 1958, just months before he created Tennis for Two, *Parade* magazine profiled Higinbotham in a three-page article entitled "A Scientist You Should Know . . . Wonderful Willie from Brookhaven." Like many *Parade* profiles, the story was a puffy feature. But it spoke volumes about the five-foot-four, 125-pound personality who invented an electronic bombsight, one of the first digital computers, and who helped to create the Atomic Energy Commission. Not mentioned in the *Parade* story was that, as the chairman of the anti-bomb Federation of Scientists, Higinbotham was considered to be a communist sympathizer by paranoid, self-serving senator Joe McCarthy. Because Higinbotham had given his life to science and the government, the label haunted him.

He forgot about any woes, though, when he was with his family. *Parade* said, "He's an electronics expert who can play the accordion, call a square dance and 'do anything with an egg.' To his lawn mower, he would attach a sulky and to that, two red wagons to take his kids around the yard." As much as he was a scientist, he also longed to entertain. He would lead his band, the hilariously named Isotope Stompers, down the road at Brookhaven during festivals, playing Dixieland jazz. Making the simple game was another way to let off steam. In his role of government scientist, Higinbotham was the maker of the trigger that set off the nuclear bomb. In his role as Brookhaven entertainer, he was someone who could give pleasure beyond the passive but tangible joys of listening to music. His real gift was one of interactivity. His experiment allowed people to become one with a machine. Hands on and gloves off, they competed, they won or lost, and those excited folks told other people of their newfangled adventure.

In Higinbotham's own unpublished notes, he lamented that at Brookhaven's Visitors' Days, the main exhibits were typically "picture or text displays or static instruments or components. . . . It occurred to me that it might liven up the place to have a game that people could play, and which would convey the message that our scientific endeavors have relevance to society." The tube on the oscilloscope was not that different from the tube on a TV, except that its screen showed patterns and not pictures. When Higinbotham opened the instruction booklet to his new computer at Brookhaven, he noted that it "described how to generate various curves . . . using risitors, capacitors and relays." The booklet explained how to show bullet trajectories, wind resistance, and a bouncing ball. "Bouncing ball?" thought Higinbotham. "That sounds like fun."

Some of the more persnickety game fans do not consider Higinbotham's work to be a videogame. After all, it did not use a video signal, the kind of electric impulses that became images on the old cathode-ray analog TV sets. It did not display pictures that you could recognize. It did not connect to something in the living room. To the naysayers, what Higinbotham made looked like nothing more than the display on an early heart monitor. Yet while Higinbotham's oscilloscope didn't technically display video, by "alternating the computer's output with the transistor's switching circuit," he certainly did create what looked and played like the videogames that would become available to everyone more than a decade later. Who cares if you couldn't display it on a TV?

In September, the curious stood and waited for hours in long lines during Brookhaven's ninth annual Visitors' Days to play Tennis for Two; even though Brookhaven's official press release made no mention of the game, word of mouth had spread quickly, almost with the speed of today's Internet gossip. It was more than just fun. Once those lines of people played and enjoyed, it marked the beginning of videogame history.

Higinbotham proved a few things with Tennis for Two. People enjoyed playing together while looking at a screen. As they went at it, they made the communal noises of primal togetherness that you make at a sporting event. They hooted, hollered, and laughed. They imagined they were playing on the courts. And then they went home and talked to others about this brand-new thing they had witnessed. That enthusiasm lasted when Higinbotham made version 2.0 the following year; people continued to queue up, indicating that the market for such games was already in place. Willie Higinbotham, the scientist/entertainer, had stumbled upon the future. And the future was games.

Meanwhile, a determined but self-effacing engineer was hard at work on a game machine that would work when hooked up to a television set. His name was Ralph Baer. A few of the old-timers at Brookhaven believe that Baer took a trip there to see Tennis for Two years before he came up with the idea for a brilliant invention that would mark the videogame's debut as a commercial enterprise.

1.

A SPACE ODYSSEY

In 1966, Ralph Baer, a short, bespectacled man with a deep, radio-quality voice and a sharp wit, had been a successful engineer for thirty years, overseeing as many as five hundred employees at Sanders, a large New Hampshire manufacturer whose primary contract was with the United States Defense Department. Much of Baer's work revolved around airborne radar and antisubmarine warfare electronics. In the late summer of that year, he was sitting on a step outside of the busy Port Authority Bus Terminal in Manhattan, waiting patiently for a colleague and about to head to Madison Avenue for a meeting with a Sanders client. Manhattan's traffic ebbed and flowed and taxis honked and the passing parade went by. Suddenly, Baer began furiously writing notes with a number 2 pencil on a spiral-bound yellow legal pad. It was like some spirit, some videogame ghost, was doing the writing.

When he was done, he had a title page and four single-spaced pages of notes. His brainstorm produced a passel of ideas for an ingenious "game box" he initially called Channel Let's Play! In that detailed outline, he described Action Games, Board Skill Games, Artistic Games, Instructional Games, Board Change Games, Card Games, and Sports Games, all of which could be played on any of the 40 million cathode-ray-tube TV sets that were ubiquitous in America at the time. He even detailed add-ons, like a pump controller that would allow players to become firemen and put out blazes around a virtual house displayed on-screen.

It wasn't the first time Baer had come up with an idea for games on TV. Fifteen years earlier, in 1951, he worked at another defense contractor, the Loral Corporation, and suggested a rudimentary checkers game. But he didn't think about games on TV again until that day in 1966, probably because his boss at Loral thought a game inside a TV was a ludicrous idea.

Let's Play! was a much grander and more complex idea that would take a lot of time, manpower, and money to create properly. On that summer day in Manhattan, Baer didn't know how much time or money. But Herb Campman, Sanders's chief of research and development, believed in the concept and gave Baer a budget of $2,000 for research and $500 for materials. Baer, a complete work addict, would soon be on his way to becoming the father of videogames.

Little has been written about how Baer's early life informed his later work. In fact, Baer was infected by the invention bug when young, not long after his family left Cologne in the 1930s. As a kid growing up in Germany, Baer didn't realize the war was coming. He played with a stick and a hoop outdoors. At night, he and his sister performed puppet shows in their bedroom, laughing and laughing as they transported themselves into worlds of their own creation. The childish plays took Baer's mind off the schoolkids who bullied him and hit him in the face for being a Jew. After packing their possessions into a half dozen three-by-four-foot wooden crates, in August 1938 the teenage Baer and his family fled Hitler's Germany for New York City, via a ship that docked in Rotterdam. Many of his Jewish relatives weren't so lucky and were killed. Baer was too young to comprehend the danger; as the ship steamed toward Ellis Island, he spent most of his time in a swimming pool or playing Monopoly with his sister in the game room. Even then, games intrigued him.

The family settled into a courtyard apartment near the Bronx Zoo, and Baer worked at a factory for $12 a week, putting buttons onto cosmetic cases. In the winter, the sixteen-year-old made his first invention: a machine that sped up the process of making leatherette goods. He got the engineering bug when he saw an ad for a correspondence course that read "Big Money Servicing Radios. Be a Genuine 'Radiotrician.'" Baer was so excited about this new radio technology that he began to have dreams about resistors, coils, and capacitors. In a small store on Lexington Avenue, he listened to the radios he fixed, hearing the news of the Blitz on London and the invasion of Poland by the Germans.

By April 1942, Baer was an engineer in World War II as well, learning to prepare roads and bridges for infantry grunts and armored troops. He also laid and removed mines by gingerly digging around in the earth with a bayonet. Life as an engineer turned to life overseas in Bristol, England, teaching military intelligence courses, where he led classes for GIs on subjects such as recognizing German uniforms, ranks, organizational affiliations, and weapons handling. In Tidworth, he and his team created a military intelligence school that trained 120,000 Americans. Part of the school was an immense exhibit hall that included a huge cache of German weapons and vehicles. Ensconced in an industrial hangarlike edifice, the museum was featured in the November 3, 1944, issue of *YANKS* magazine. In his spare time, Baer secretly wrote a comprehensive manual on weaponry. He kept inventing, even fashioning AM radios from German mine detectors.

The organizational skills Baer learned in the military would serve him well as he began work on his videogame machine. Too, his experiences in the army imbued him with a self-confidence and talent for communication that helped him open up to those above him in rank. He may have been a nerd who cared more about technology than girls, but he was a surprisingly charismatic nerd who didn't hide away a good idea when he truly believed he had one; he had chutzpah.

His design skills improved as he worked on radio equipment in college in Chicago, and on radar equipment and amplifiers at Transitron, a small company in what is now New York's Tribeca neighborhood. Soon, Baer was chief engineer and then vice president at Transitron; he moved up the ranks because he was able to get things done quickly and accurately. By the time Sanders Associates made him a chief engineer, he was more of a manager than an inventor. Yet he yearned to get his hands dirty.

The $2,500 Baer received from his boss for developing Let's Play! may not seem like much now. But in 1966, the sum was enough to purchase a new car, was one third of the amount most Americans earned yearly, and was more than half the cost of the average home. Baer had two men assigned to the project to do the hourly work. Bill Harrison, a hip-looking, conscientious engineering associate, built the prototypes. Bill Rusch, a cranky, temperamental powerhouse who had studied at MIT, came up with the idea of a "machine-controlled ball that would interact with player-controlled 'paddles.' " Both men were already on Sanders's payroll.

The project was top secret and time-consuming, so much so that

Rusch brought a guitar to work so he could blow off steam—leading some curious wall-listeners in the company to believe that Baer was working on some sort of technologically advanced musical instrument, perhaps for the Beatles. But Baer's boss, Herb Campman, didn't care about rock 'n' roll. He gave Baer the money for a sensible reason: He felt the company could eventually make games that would work well in training the military. He was not wrong.

Baer and his wife, Dena, would occasionally canoe in the Merrimack River and walk hand in hand through the Manchester, New Hampshire, snow as it fell. They loved the quaint town. But the weather could be as hostile as the tundra-like blizzards that fell in Capcom's treacherous Lost Planet. The heavy snows just made Baer work harder. The game box became a consuming project that bordered on obsession. Inventors are like that: zealous to the exclusion of others. It was that way with surveyor George R. Carey, who had the idea for an early TV, the tectroscope, in 1877. It was that way, too, with the twenty-two inventors who tried to make a practical lightbulb after Humphry Davy created incandescent light in 1802, more than seventy-five years before the compulsive Thomas Edison and his team made a bulb that could last twelve hundred hours.

By the time Baer, Harrison, and Rusch were deep into it, the trio had tested many prototype machines, drably named TV Games #1 through #7. To the untrained eye, the inner workings seemed like a vision of chaos. The insides of even the later prototypes looked like a mass of angel hair pasta swirling in a pot of boiling hot water.

Yet the machine worked like magic. It hooked up to a TV's antenna terminals and used the frequencies of channel 3 or channel 4. On the screen were what Baer called "spots," little white squares that could be moved around smoothly like a puck on the ice. Attached were two metal boxes that had knobs for vertical and horizontal manipulation. TV Games #1 used four vacuum tubes. There were no circuitry chips; they were luxuries that were too expensive at the time. And there were no transistors. Although Higinbotham used them in his tests, Baer didn't yet trust transistor technology. But when the box was switched on and that spot moved on-screen for the first time, it was quite the eureka moment. Baer didn't jump up and down or wave his fist in the air. But inside, he was thrilled and amazed.

What the primitive contraption would do was extraordinary. It would make the television an extension of you, the player. It would let you interact with a square on a black-and-white screen, and if you had even the lamest imagination, it made you believe you were volleying at tennis, aiming carefully as a brave marksman, even playing hero to the innocent as you saved lives.

While the design work proceeded apace, there were continual roadblocks. Worker bees would be called off the project, assigned to work on some secret, pressing defense initiative. At the same time, Sanders executives sometimes seemed aloof and uninterested. In addition, the machine itself became unwieldy. One of the early prototypes was completely impractical, with a chassis that was as large as a kitchen sink. It also looked like something out of high school shop class.

On June 14, 1967, Baer showed Herb Campman a shooting game with a toy gun rigged up with a light mechanism, which interacted with the TV screen. Campman and Sanders's patent lawyer was impressed enough to call a meeting with the company president and the stodgy board of directors—the next day. Baer had seven games he wanted to show on a color TV set: chess, steeple chase, a fox-and-hounds game, target shooting, a color wheel game, a bucket-filling game, and that firefighter game in which you'd whale on a pump handle like you were trying to get water from a well. If you did it right, water would get to a window in a house. If you failed, the house would go up in flames. On the night before the demo, Baer frantically searched for a script explaining the seven games that he'd recorded circus-barker-style on a sixty-minute Mercury cassette tape. Though he found the tape quickly, Baer was still apprehensive. He tossed and turned in his bed. But he was ready.

The big bosses filed into a dreary conference room on June 15. There was whispering and conferring and the raising of eyebrows during the demonstration. Bill Harrison noticed that Sanders himself was completely uninterested. He was gossiping about a competitor with another colleague. But, ultimately, the suits seemed impressed. Harold Pope, the affable company president who'd come up through the ranks as an engineer, didn't quite know what to do with what he had seen. Pope's command to Baer was "Build us something we can sell or license."

"Build us something we can sell" was a grim declaration that would irk Baer during the next several years. Compared to figuring out how to sell it, getting the console to work properly was the least of his worries. Because gossip had begun among Sanders employees, Baer made sure the work in his ten-by-twenty-foot lab was treated as a top secret project. He told Harrison, "I don't care if people in the company think we're making some kind of guitar. I just want to get the job done without a lot of questions from people who aren't involved." It was like the first rule of Fight Club. Baer told his team in no uncertain terms, "You don't talk about TV Games."

In February 1967, the three created the Quiz Light Pen, which, when attached to TV Games, could be used for an educational instruction and game show–like experience. "Just point it at the screen and click a button to make it work," announced Baer in impresario mode as he spoke to the camera in a primitive half-hour black-and-white instructional video, which showed how aiming the pen at small boxes on the screen could be used to answer multiple choice questions. Maybe it could even be used for a game show, thought Baer, like *Jeopardy!*

The inventiveness didn't stop there. In a memo stamped

"Company Private," Baer also made plans for a steering wheel for racing games and a device that would let you make artistic drawings on the TV screen. There was a baseball game and a strange ESP-like number guessing game. There would be a peripheral for a golf game that included a putter. There was skeet shooting, soccer, and horse racing, too. And there was a cool, addictive version of a Ping-Pong game, the game that people would play the most. (It was also a game that would soon be ripped off, become more popular than Baer ever imagined, and herald a very nasty lawsuit.)

Admittedly, these games were all done with "spots," not high-quality artwork. To make the games feel more real, the team designed plastic overlays that, through static electricity, stuck to the TV screen. They looked like Howard Johnson restaurant place mats but were somewhat transparent. There was no masterful artwork to the overlays, but the best of them resembled the most dramatic back glass art on pinball games of the day. The first joysticks included were two controllers that had horizontal and vertical abilities and knobs to add English to the ball, somewhat like Tennis for Two (which Baer said he never saw at the Brookhaven National Laboratory).

More ideas for technology and games spewed forth, and so did some manna from heaven: $8,000 more from Sanders's Campman. The goal in early 1968 was to beef up the console's circuitry to make it a leaner, meaner machine. Rusch was also able to make those all-important square spots circular, even star-shaped. Initially, Rusch preened, thinking he had done something as historic as translating the Dead Sea Scrolls. Baer was totally enthused, too, until they found a problem with the spots. They moved randomly when they weren't supposed to. They ran up or down or to the side like feral animals. Sometimes, they'd even change their shapes. Baer decided to stick with the square spots, even though Rusch put up a fuss. This was a constant cycle between the two. Baer would try to mend fences with

Rusch. He'd seem OK for a while. Then he'd go off the rails and get angry again.

Inventing was natural to Baer, Harrison, and Rusch; as engineers, they got it. But Baer lay awake at night thinking about the company president's dictum. Over and over, he asked himself, "How do we sell this? We're a defense contractor. We can't manufacture this. We don't have the infrastructure. Do we license it to someone? How do we do that?" To complicate matters, he still had no business plan whatsoever. By mid-June, management was unyielding; they demanded precise details. The business plan questions kept coming with far more frequency.

Baer racked his brain. His first plan was to involve the nascent cable TV industry. Cable TV, available in the United States since the late 1940s, was in the doldrums. Americans didn't want to pay for television programming unless mountains interfered with their over-air signals. In the late sixties, people were more than content with innovations in network television—like the first Super Bowl, Gene Roddenberry's *Star Trek* (which dealt with societal issues in a science fiction way), and the ever naughty *Smothers Brothers Comedy Hour* (on which British mod-rockers the Who went wild and maniacally destroyed their instruments).

Baer believed his TV Games idea could give the cable industry a "shot in the arm." To Campman, Baer suggested, "We could create the action, and the cable company would provide colorful backgrounds for our games" from their studios. Especially since the plastic layovers Baer and his team had been able to create were graphically unimpressive, the plan had merit. Cable companies could provide an almost photographic level of detail for backgrounds.

The TelePrompter Corporation, the people who now make the machines from which newscasters and others on TV read, also outfitted sixty thousand families with cable TV. They were the country's biggest cable provider at the time. After some prodding, one of the founders, Hubert "Hub" Schlafly, agreed to meet with Baer in New Hampshire. Schlafly so thoroughly enjoyed the games experience that he suggested to Irving Berlin Kahn, the company's president, that he better get up to Nashua because something important was happening there. A week later, an impeccably dressed Kahn arrived from New York in a stretch limo. After that, there was a series of excited, hopeful meetings with TelePrompter executives in New York City. But a recession had hit the nation, and TelePrompter wimped out: They claimed to be out of money when it came to new projects. The same sour outcome occurred after initially optimistic meetings with Manhattan Cable and Warner Cable. Who knows how much more quickly today's downloadable games would have become popular had Baer's cable deal been given the green light back in the early 1970s. Conceivably, a company like TelePrompter might now be as vital as Sony or even Nintendo in the videogame industry.

If Baer's dealings with the cable companies were disappointing, he hadn't endured anything yet. When the TelePrompter deal fell through, Campman unceremoniously ordered an end to the flow of money for the game console. Other projects needed work, and Baer hadn't proven the viability of TV Games as a business. It wasn't until the late 1960s that Baer was able to convince Campman to add some more research and development money and reassign engineer Bill Harrison to the project. Harrison's first order of business was to go shopping at Sears to purchase a plastic toy gun. But he wasn't going to play cops and robbers. With a mini-flashlight-sized lightbulb and a transistor amplifier, Harrison refashioned the toy into a weapon that worked when aimed at an object on the TV. Even more valuable was Harrison's savvy when it came to circuitry, which allowed him to reduce the number of parts in the latest prototype by about 50 percent. But the box looked somehow unadorned. Baer asked Harrison to go out to the store to get some self-adhesive kitchen cabinet liner that made the box look a little better. While the liner had a cheesy, basement rec room look, it inspired a generally catchy name, the Brown Box. Like the adhesive, it stuck.

In 1968, there were more than one hundred TV makers in the United States alone. Baer got the idea to phone each of them to see if one would consider manufacturing TV Games. He had some help: Sanders's director of patents, Louis Etlinger, was a smart New York lawyer with a folksy demeanor that made people believe he was from the sticks. Etlinger made the cold calls and charmed his way into setting up appointment after appointment with major corporations. But it was Baer who had to sell the idea, based on his demonstrations with Harrison. While Baer was an erudite speaker, he didn't have a salesman's swagger. In one early meeting, a buyer from Sears felt their numerous retail stores would be mobbed by kids who wanted to play the system in the store, but wouldn't buy it. The Sears buyer felt that the stores would be forced into the role of babysitter for hordes of screaming brats. Baer sorely needed a Madison Avenue marketer to help him from that point on. But there was no budget for a show-person who would come to meetings armed with talking points and glittering generalities.

The meetings with RCA were typical of the constant challenges and failures that Baer faced time and time again. In April 1969, RCA began serious negotiations to license the Brown Box. But these fell apart when the megacorporation began playing dirty pool. After months of waiting, the contract finally arrived.

"It's no good," said Etlinger.

"What do you mean?" asked Baer.

"It leaves Sanders with next to nothing."

"That's it, then?" asked Baer.

"That's it," responded Etlinger.

When Bill Enders, one of the RCA executives who was ear-nestly gung-ho about the Brown Box, became the vice president of

marketing at Magnavox, he engaged in extensive, detailed talks with
Sanders through Baer and Etlinger. By mid-July, the two (along with
Bill Harrison) were jetting to Magnavox's corporate headquarters
in Fort Wayne, Indiana, for the most significant demonstration of
Baer's life.

As showtime approached, the weather didn't cooperate. The
Midwest had been besieged by rainstorms since Independence Day,
and the area around Fort Wayne had seen water rise to emergency
proportions. The city of 178,000 was situated in a floodplain, and
loyal residents had to take the good with the bad. Baer wondered
if the high waters amounted to a bad sign. As he drove, he thought
he was traveling in some surreal, *Night of the Hunter*–like land of
religion. He saw revival tents everywhere. He wondered to himself,
"If Magnavox's engineers are this religious, can they make a good
product?"

When he and Harrison set up the machine at the end of a highly
polished oak table in a fancy conference room, they were nervous and
on edge. Once the presentation began, Baer saw a room full of bored
executives who were probably more concerned about eating dinner
and getting to the bar for a drink than with listening to a pitch about
what they most likely considered to be a throwaway toy.

Yet there was one person who nodded his head, his eyes focused
and bright. After Baer did his dog and pony show for about twenty
minutes, showing each game and each peripheral, the executive actually seemed to be downright thrilled.

"We're going to do this, and we're going to commit a million
dollars to it," proclaimed Gerry Martin, Magnavox's vice president
and general manager for console product. The formerly sullen executives nodded their heads and exchanged huzzahs like the finest
yes-men money could buy.

The Sanders trio was flying high. But they didn't celebrate.
They had been dealt too many disappointments, so they held back

until the contracts arrived. One night, Harrison and Baer were on the road and stopped into a greasy spoon diner. They had a thrifty meal, saved the receipts, and talked a lot about how great it was to be doing what they wanted to do. That was the extent of the celebration for the first videogame device ever made for consumers.

It took Magnavox another eight months to begin work on the project in earnest at their Morrison, Tennessee, manufacturing plant. For the Brown Box to hit store shelves in time for Christmas, Magnavox engineers had to break their backs working overtime as the deadline approached. They had proved their mettle as far as Baer and his team were concerned. Meanwhile, Sanders was doing poorly in the recession, and Baer became concerned about the future of his job. To make matters worse, he heard some disturbing news from Magnavox. For cost reasons the company axed the golf putt add-on and the fireman game with the pump, which would have required a higher retail price tag. There had also been heated discussion about whether or not to make the Brown Box work with four players at once, but this, too, never made it past the planning stages. Adding circuitry for color spots on the TV screen was also nixed. Only those overlays remained.

"You know the one thing that bothers me," Baer told Harrison in their small office.

"What's that?"

"The fact that it won't be in color. Color would make a big difference."

Harrison nodded. That was all he could do.

Just as sad was that once Magnavox licensed the idea for TV Games, Ralph Baer didn't have much say in anything that happened, not even in the product's new name, Skill-O-Vision. To Baer, the moniker sounded like a cheap sideshow penny arcade game.

By mid-October 1971, Magnavox felt they had a potential hit on their hands. Market surveys were held over a period of four days at the company's retail stores in Los Angeles and Grand Rapids. Eighty-nine percent of those who played Skill-O-Vision for a couple of hours liked it "very much." Even though just eighty-two people participated, a laughable number by today's standards for surveys, there was a certain tempered glee in the interoffice memos that circulated to key executives in Magnavox enclaves around the country. On October 15, one executive wrote with barely muted enthusiasm, "The price of $75 presents no barrier."

When Magnavox became involved in Ralph Baer's project, they took over in the way a giant wave totally engulfs a small shell on the beach. The change of the name from TV Games to Skill-O-Vision was kind of a move sideways. The latter recalled Hollywood producer Mike Todd's Smell-O-Vision, a dated technique of adding scents to movies that never really took off. When the name was changed to Odyssey, it was an inspired move, to a name that Baer thought really sang. It sounded like the beginning of a mysterious, futuristic adventure. Additionally, the look of the box was quite beautiful for the time. That fake brown wood grain was gone. Added were pieces of sleek white and black plastic and a box that looked like something out of Stanley Kubrick's *2001: A Space Odyssey*. Nonetheless while TV Games wasn't a sexy name, it did say exactly what the console would do. The name Odyssey did nothing of the sort.

The inventor's input became even less valuable to Magnavox as the launch date approached. Baer himself was transferred between two divisions within Sanders, and he began to suffer from depression. After a hernia operation in February 1972, he languished in a hospital room, saturnine and in some pain. Then Campman and Etlinger arrived with Cheshire cat smiles on their faces. They unrolled a long sheet of paper that bore an oversized facsimile of a check for $100,000, the first payment from Magnavox for licensing. It didn't matter that the check went into Sanders's bank account. Baer felt valued again, and his doldrums lifted in moments. In the second or two it took for a blip on the Odyssey to cross the screen, Baer felt happier and years younger than his age.

When Baer attended the press presentation for Magnavox products at a restaurant in Central Park in late May, he beamed like a proud father. Everything was hyperreal, from the heady smell of spring flowers to the excited looks on journalists' faces in the room. But he wasn't introduced as the inventor of the Odyssey. He wasn't introduced at all. To Baer, it mattered little. He was struck by the splendor of the finished machine. As he left and walked through the park, he was flying high.

The Odyssey hit the stores backed by a fairly odd marketing plan. Consumers were somewhat bemused by a Frank Sinatra commercial touting the machine. After all, Sinatra had retired from the music business in 1971 because his career was doing so miserably at the time. His recent movies (like the awful western comedy *Dirty Dingus Magee*) were failures, as were his recent albums; although critically acclaimed, the album *Watertown* had sold just thirty thousand copies. (Ol' Blue Eyes didn't release his landmark comeback tune, "New York, New York," until 1973.) Kids, the target audience, didn't care about Sinatra; kids then liked the Beatles' solo efforts, Elton John, David Bowie, and Stevie Wonder. Magnavox's pitch was considered completely uncool. Worse, the Sinatra commercial indicated, perhaps intentionally, that the system would work only with Magnavox televisions. In reality, it worked with any TV that had a rabbit ears connection in the back and a picture tube large enough to hold the overlays. Despite the confusion, people paid for one hundred thousand Odysseys at $100 each during the 1972 holiday season.

The stylish magazine and newspaper ads were perhaps better selling tools. They were artfully detailed and packed with juicy information, so exciting that the games seemed to jump off the page and proudly dance in midair. Even the copywriting sang like the best of

Madison Avenue poetry: "With Odyssey, you participate in television. You're not just a spectator. The fascinating Casino Action of Monte Carlo, the excitement of Wimbledon, the thrills of a heated game of football—can all be duplicated right in your own living room."

Yet the Odyssey did not reap the expected rewards. Each machine cost Magnavox almost $50 to make. The 350,000 made and sold between 1972 and 1975 cost approximately $15 million. Testing the unit with consumers added at least $1 million. Sinatra's fee added another million. Magnavox's receipts came in at only $20 million. Baer postulated that the returns of some defective products ate up much of the remaining profits. He tried to convince the company of the need to release more and more games to support the machine, perhaps the first time the razor-and-blades economic theory was applied to videogames. In other words, the Magnavox system should have been sold like a Gillette razor, cheaply, and forward-thinking games should have been sold like blades, where the real profit lay. As the years passed, Baer wrote impassioned letters to Magnavox, suggesting new games. He told Magnavox of numerous Odyssey knockoffs around the world, but the company didn't immediately pursue these ripoff artists in court. There were plans to sell a kind of Magna-Odyssey, a fattened device that included a seventeen-inch color TV and an impressive cabinet for $424. Baer was brought in to try to figure out what to take out to get the price down appreciably. But the Magna-Odyssey was never released. Like many ideas at Magnavox, it became severely bogged down by company posturing and politics.

Through most of the brainstorming and all of the hoopla, Baer was relegated to the sidelines, like an aging football star aching to be sent in for a big play. Yes, he and Sanders had licensed the rights to a mammoth corporation. And Sanders certainly received monetary rewards for the contract into which they had entered. But Baer was not just a "company man" who didn't care about anything more than his weekly salary or about becoming rich from his videogame inventions. In fact, he did think about asking for more money and getting himself a lawyer on a few occasions. He was never told exactly how much money was coming in from worldwide licenses of his game technology and from where; Sanders feared he would sue for more money. They tried to keep all sales data from him. But he saw the total projected on a big screen at Sanders's monthly meetings. He knew he could have gone to court. He was sure he could have won. But he chose not to, feeling as he did that he still had much more inventing to do.

Still at Sanders after the release of the system, Baer (along with engineers Larry Cope and George Mitchell) continued to hatch numerous game ideas. He developed the first detailed concept for an arcade game loosely based upon ABC-TV's *Monday Night Football*. It was a complex game that involved offense, defense, coaching, and a joystick that let you move in eight directions. Mitchell and Baer took their machine on the road to Kenner, Bally, Coleco, Ideal, and Mattel, but they couldn't drum up any enthusiasm. Bally in Chicago was the worst. In the meeting Baer saw a group of well-dressed people who looked very grim, uninterested in his idea and generally angry with him. He was glad to get out of there.

Occasionally, he peppered Magnavox with ideas for new games, not the least of which was Run Silent, Run Deep, based on the World War II submarine warfare movie starring Clark Gable and Burt Lancaster, from United Artists. Magnavox always balked. For Centronics' Gamex division in Las Vegas, Baer designed the display portion for the first electronic casino blackjack game, along with a horse racing gambling game called Photo Finish. Just as the manufacturing process was about to commence, all work stopped: Word was that certain unsavory characters had strongly suggested that Gamex get the hell out of Dodge. While the lead engineer was hired

away to Bally in Chicago, most of the others ran for the hills like
Sonic the Hedgehog on speed. The mob controlled much of Vegas in
those days, and their grip only began to let up after the FBI's massive
assault on gambling crime in the late 1970s. That was too late for
Gamex and, by default, Ralph Baer.

But Baer wasn't done. To Campman's joy, he created videogame training exercises for the military. Later, with two cohorts, he
invented the Simon memory game, a popular toy that used flashing light sequences. Milton Bradley's marketing of Simon was sheer
Madison Avenue genius, and included the adver-poem: "Simon's
a computer. Simon has a brain. You either do what Simon says or
else go down the drain." Also in the seventies, after a panicked call
from Coleco about the Telstar, Baer helped to get a nasty bug out of
the three-game console in which Coleco had invested $30 million.
The Telstar was emitting too much interference for the FCC to approve its distribution to toy stores. Baer added a simple resistor to
the inside that fixed the problem. Baer did this even though he knew
Coleco's game system was very like the Odyssey and thus a competitor to his baby.

The Telstar was just one of many consoles obviously influenced by Baer's creation. But throughout this roller-coaster ride with
Magnavox and beyond, Baer did his best to keep calm and to look
on the bright side. His struggle to bring videogames to every home
with a television set was undoubtedly a superhuman feat, the Alan
Moore/Watchmen kind, which required years of stamina in the face
of unremitting disappointment as doors constantly closed in his face.
The business travails involved in touting his invention would have
broken lesser people.

Ralph Baer remained strong because he knew in his gut that
games would soon become part of our collective consciousness. His
game machine didn't become an overnight hit. But the ideas he put
forth when he first proposed TV Games are still the basis of games

today. The sports games he outlined and prototyped would become billion-dollar industries in themselves—when made by others a decade or so later. His brainstorm for multiplayer online games also became a billion-dollar industry—three decades later. His idea to incorporate cable TV as a distribution medium would become reality thirty years later, when broadband cable allowed games to be downloaded onto the newest consoles. And that light gun that shot at the screen was not so terribly different from the wireless controllers and guns of today. So back in the seventies, Ralph Baer was the Seer, a quiet Nostradamus. Every idea he laid out on paper came to fruition in the future.

Yet in the very near future, one of Baer's visions would be imitated and reproduced in disturbingly familiar, and spectacularly successful, form. Someone on the West Coast wanted to beat the Seer at his own game by popularizing his own version of Baer's Ping-Pong game. This small company honcho with an expansive need for success was a savvy, calculating giant of a man who Baer felt was the ultimate bloviator. "He's a plain old shit. A real son of a bitch," Baer would say.

SO EASY, A DRUNK
COULD PLAY

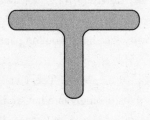

DEPOSIT QUARTER
BALL WILL SERVE AUTOMATICALLY
AVOID MISSING BALL FOR HIGH SCORE

-Instructions seen on the first
Pong arcade game, September 1972

Nolan Bushnell was a dreamer who dreamed big dreams. In his dreams, he imagined the finest things that money could buy: expensive cars and massive homes and the prettiest girls. Yet his greatest dream surrounded a game so simple, so utterly straightforward, so easy to learn that even a stinking drunk in a bar could learn to play it.

The testing ground for Pong, the very first arcade game, was a newly opened bar in the Silicon Valley. Andy Capp's Tavern in Sunnyvale, California, wasn't the kind of place where fights would break out every night. But the hole, named for the surly British comic-strip slacker, was shadowy and dark. Cigarette smoke swirled so thick that it rivaled the fog that rolled in over the Santa Cruz Mountains. You might bring your girlfriend to Andy Capp's, but not on a first date.

The story goes this way. After designer Allan Alcorn made Pong's circuitry and Ted Dabney crafted its case, a lowly sawed-off plastic milk jug was placed inside beneath the coin slot, to collect quarters. Pong was put in a truck and delivered to an anteroom in Capp's that also included a pinball machine. Then the drunks played. Not only did they play, they lined up to play. Their egos wouldn't take being beaten by a machine. They fed so many quarters into the slot that the machine jammed up. Then the bar's usually genial manager, Bill Gattis, phoned Bushnell in a booming voice that carried the length of the bar.

It's a wonderful creation story for Atari, but it might not be exactly true. Loni Reeder, Bushnell's longtime assistant, claims the tale was a well-crafted myth. "The Atari guys (and I don't remember if Nolan personally went over there along with the guys or not) went to Andy Capp's and stuffed the coin box to the point that the machine wouldn't work—then just sat back and waited for the bar to call to say the game wasn't working." Reeder says the fabrication was completely in keeping with Bushnell's "carny" personality.

Whatever the true story, the age of the videogame arcade was born.

Nolan Bushnell was a master showman from the get-go. It wasn't just an act; it was part of his very phylogeny. More a smart, calculating marketer than a brilliant game designer, Bushnell was born in Clearfield, a northern Utah town created because people flocked to the region to work at a cannery factory in 1907. Bushnell was the epitome of a strapping young lad, more than six feet tall before his thirteenth birthday. His Mormon father was a successful cement contractor whose motto was said to be "Work hard. Play hard." Which is exactly what the younger Bushnell did through much of his life. He loved to play practical jokes with a science twist. One night, he went out into a field and, in a feat that was part Ben Franklin and part P. T. Barnum, attached a battery-operated light to a kite. As it flew high and proud in the night wind, some residents briefly believed the light was an alien spaceship. At Clearfield High, he honed his skills on the debate team and was entranced by board games that required strategy, like Clue. His charming nerdiness bloomed at the University of Utah, where he spent way too much time in a then state-of-the-art computer lab playing Spacewar!, the fascinating precursor to the more well-known Asteroids.

Spacewar! was created by Steve "Slug" Russell and his engineering school friends at MIT as a lark in February 1962. On the then-futuristic, enticingly round screen of a massive PDP-1 computer, two green dots representing spaceships flew in zero gravity. They shot at each other on the ebony background of a star-filled galaxy. Players captained the ships by sitting at a panel and moving switches up and down. It was a transporting, transformative experience, and for players like Bushnell, it was a vision of the future, a future in which you could be Buck Rogers or Flash Gordon in your own imaginary science fiction universe. In Spacewar!, you even had to avoid planets that rushed in your direction as you tried with all the energy your brain and body could muster to annihilate your opponent's ship. Viewing the minimalist screen with such early graphics, Bushnell's neurons fired thousands of excited messages to his axons and millions of vesicles struck his synapses. Spacewar! was it for Bushnell. He just couldn't get it off his mind. When he lost his tuition money in a card game and went to work as a barker and weight guesser on the midway at Utah's giant Lagoon Amusement Park (where everyone from Count Basie to the Rolling Stones played), he schemed about it. He thought about it when he was rejected for a job at Disneyland because he didn't have enough engineering experience. He began work on what he called Computer Space when he toiled at Ampex, which made tape recorders, recording tape, and an early VCR, as a research designer for $12,000 a year. He didn't like the gig much, feeling that the only way to make real money was to become an entrepreneur who made his own games for an audience that had yet to be targeted or mined.

At Ampex, Bushnell and straight-shooting former navy man Ted Dabney got to know each other during lunches. They ate their brown bag ham sandwiches, turned over a wastebasket, put a Go game table on top, and played the strategy game almost daily. When he created the oddly named Syzygy, his first company, in late 1971, Bushnell's vision for games was all he could talk about. Syzygy would be primarily based around pinball arcade routes in the Bay Area and a deal to make double-wide pinball machines for Bally in Chicago. Videogames weren't exactly an afterthought, but they certainly wouldn't be the primary cash cow in those early months of existence.

Superiors like Charlie Steinberg, a future Ampex president, thought Bushnell had gone mad and tried everything to rid him of the idea of starting his own company. He wanted to keep Bushnell at Ampex as a career man. All this made Bushnell even more obsessed with forging his own path. When he had trouble with his wife and the two divorced, a prime reason was that Bushnell was spending too much time on his plan for world domination through games.

It has been widely written that Bushnell began work on his first arcade machine in 1970 in his daughter's bedroom. Soon, the story goes, there were pieces of wood, wires, tools, and parts of a black-and-white TV set strewn about everywhere. The work proceeded with such passion and zeal that Bushnell's child had to sleep elsewhere in the house. In fact, Bushnell worked on the game in his partner Ted Dabney's daughter's bedroom. It was young Terri Dabney who had to bed down in the master bedroom, which she shared with her parents. In that cramped inner sanctum filled with a child's stuffed animals, the two inventors spent countless hours burning the midnight oil. The elder Dabney, a balding beanstalk of a man with a mustache, horn-rimmed glasses, and a penchant for plaid shirts, worked hard to make a charily crafted, handsome cabinet for Bushnell's Computer Space that looked somewhat like an arcade version of Munch's *The Scream*. It certainly appeared alien. Inside it was, as in Baer's prototypes, a mess of wires. But a small Texas Instruments computer was in there, too.

After it was made at Nutting Industries, where Dabney and Bushnell consulted, the machine was sent to pinball arcades in the region. However, the black-and-white Computer Space was ahead of its time and deemed too tricky for an industry that was just being born. It needed a joystick, not those confusing buttons, to make it easier to play. Yet the game had a tantalizing pitch line: "A simulated space battle that pits computer-guided saucers against a rocket ship that you control."

Computer Space wasn't the key to the kind of Ali Baba–type riches Bushnell knew were within his grasp. Only three thousand machines were made and fewer than a thousand were distributed. Few at the penny arcades and bars wanted to play. The fact that the saucers made an annoying, high-pitched whine when they emitted laser beams probably didn't help the game's popularity. Yet the fifties retro futuristic machine made it to the silver screen to be forever part of the B-grade science fiction message movie *Soylent Green*. In its thirty seconds of fame, there was much sexual innuendo as a giggling and ravishing Leigh Taylor-Young begged her much older gift giver to "come on and play" Computer Space. Then she begins to kiss him. It was the kind of scene that led a young moviegoing nerd to fantasize.

Bushnell and Dabney each put $250 into their Syzygy company, but a California roofing contractor already bore the odd moniker. Undaunted, Bushnell changed the name immediately. He loved Go, the strategy-oriented game from ancient China—everything from the way the smooth stone game pieces felt to the way the board looked. So for his company's name, Bushnell settled upon a word from Go, the game he loved so much: Atari. The definition is the equivalent of the word "check" in chess but also means "you are about to become engulfed."

The twenty-seven-year-old's first employee was a former Ampex engineer, twenty-two-year-old Allan Alcorn. Alcorn was a genial, hefty award-winning high school football player with a carefully trimmed beard. Obsessed with learning, he was an engineering whiz with a bachelor of science degree out of the University of California Berkeley, who worked his way through college by fixing TVs while the older guys in the local shop got drunk and played cards in the back room. Alcorn, who grew up on the corner of Haight and Ashbury, enjoyed the San Francisco psychedelic music scene, and fell in love with computers in college. But he had a mischievous side and almost got in trouble for hacking into and using a college professor's access, which was very expensive at the time.

Bushnell impressed Alcorn with a free lunch and his turquoise Buick station wagon. He offered Alcorn a $1,000-a-month salary, which Bushnell hoped to pay from the contracts he was aggressively seeking. Alcorn's pay was $200 less than he made at Ampex, but the package included a generous 10 percent of the company. At their meeting, Bushnell started telling Alcorn of all the contracts he had suddenly amassed. In actuality, he had only *planned* on getting those deals. Alcorn took it in stride, understanding that there was something entrepreneurial about Bushnell that made him utter the most outrageous things. While some were offended by that, Alcorn saw it as a talent. In their small office lab in one of the shabbier districts of

Santa Clara, Bushnell walked back and forth and gestured with his hands as he told Alcorn, "I want to make a game that any drunk in any bar can play. Simple. Simple enough for a drunk to play."

Alcorn thought the idea was simplistic, not simple. He had believed that their first project was going to be a spiffy driving game, maybe with sleek-looking cars. After all, Bushnell had originally recruited the computer expert by saying he was doing a racing game for Bally in Chicago. Alcorn also dreamed of doing something computer-based that was a bit more of a challenge. The arcade game the Atari founder proposed was primitive, not cutting edge: It included no computer whatsoever. Instead, it would just use old-fashioned TTL logic, a series of transistors and resistors with a different circuit for each function of the game.

"Get started on this. We want to make it for the arcade and then for the home. So keep the costs down." Bushnell gave Alcorn some tortured, haphazard schematics to help, and Alcorn complained, "What the heck is this? I can't read these."

"Look, everyone's on board with this," said Bushnell. "I'm almost sure I have GE on board. Just do this and more will come out of it. Everything's going great. Don't worry, because we're on our way."

"OK, boss, OK." Bushnell's magical enthusiasm continually won Alcorn over. The boss's most valuable quality was to make people believe in him and in his sweeping vision. During the gestation of Atari, Alcorn loved listening to Bushnell as he espoused his grand hopes. Alcorn, who didn't come from money, looked to the Utahan as a philosophizing mentor more than a peer in engineering, because Bushnell's design chops were middling. But as he listened to the founder's big plans, Alcorn began to dream big dreams himself. Just as important, he worked extremely hard on the three-month project, although years later, he thought, "It's got one moving spot. It's got scoring digits. It's got basically one sound. It's the de minimis of a game. It's really lifted from what Nolan saw in the Magnavox Odyssey game."

But at the time, Alcorn hadn't seen or played Baer's tennis game—the Odyssey wouldn't appear on retail shelves until later that fall—nor was he aware of Bushnell's early knowledge of the device. Bushnell sometimes stated to the press that he never saw the precursor to Pong. But Baer, the ultimate stickler for detail, had squirreled away a signed attendee log that proved that Bushnell viewed a demonstration of the invention—along with Baer's table tennis game—on May 24, 1972, at the Airport Marina in Burlingame, California. Atari was formed a month later, on June 27. A pattern was forming: Bushnell was being inspired by (or possibly taking) ideas for games he had seen and even loved in the past and trying to distill them for a mass audience.*

Yet whether the boisterous founder was unconsciously motivated by Baer's idea or blatantly pilfered it ultimately didn't matter when it came to marketing the game and getting it out to arcades beyond the Bay Area. With Pong, Bushnell, Dabney, and Alcorn were stepping into a shaky car for a wild roller-coaster ride that no videogame could ever imitate, even today. Something inside Bushnell needed to ride that ride more than anyone. He wanted so badly for Atari to show "Jack and the Beanstalk"–like growth. At night, he schemed: "If we do this right, it could take off. But if this really takes off, I'm not certain we're prepared."

Early in the gestation of Atari, Bushnell, who many thought wasn't a good manager, sent a lucid eight-point document to the

* In fact, Bushnell and Atari were involved with a lawsuit brought by Magnavox for patent infringement, which included Baer testifying before Judge John Grady in Chicago's Northern Illinois Federal District Court in early June 1976, long after Pong's release. The suit never made it to trial. Bushnell and Atari settled with Magnavox on June 10 and Atari became an Odyssey licensee.

engineering staff. There was no joking and no spin; it was serious business in which he laid down the law. Bushnell's one-page charter, as he called it, asked the slim staff to build four or more Pong machines by December 31, along with a Chicago-style coin box for those machines; to add more staff for emergency projects; to design packaging for Doctor Pong for dentists' offices; and to create packaging for a possible home version of Pong. At the end, he wrote, "Statements concerning our manufacturing capacity are inapplicable to the above design schedule."

The pragmatic Alcorn wrote back, "Is the fact that we have no money a reason not to do this?" Manufacturing costs were indeed huge bugaboos.

Bushnell quickly replied with a handwritten "NO!!!" and sent the memo back.

Once it hit the arcades and was distributed beyond the borders of California's Bay Area, Pong took off around the country. From town to town, Bushnell preached his gospel of selling machines. At the peak of Pong mania, there were thirty-five thousand of Atari's machines in the United States. Each machine brought in an average of $200 weekly, a staggering amount. Merely carrying the quarters from a machine on Atarite Steve Bristow's Berkeley arcade route was a pain in the, well, back. Seven days of quarters could equal one hundred pounds from each machine.

With each phone call and pitch he made, Bushnell refined his amazing gift of gab along with his trademark shooting-from-the-hip style. Beyond the bs, he kept learning more tenets of the fine art of human manipulation. He enjoyed taunting the competition, and he wasn't above spreading impressive rumors about Atari's future products that were downright false. He wasn't a snake oil salesman, because what he sold was tangible entertainment. But he wasn't afraid to exaggerate like the best of salesmen. Because they didn't trust

Bushnell, both Midway and Nutting Associates refused to manufacture Pong for Atari.

The word "no" rarely daunted Bushnell. It was like a fly to be batted away. Though he had no infrastructure for it, Bushnell decided to have Atari itself begin to make the machines, from 1972 onward, with a local Wells Fargo bank on board. First, he began to search for larger digs. Then the few folks who made up Atari went to an unemployment office in Santa Clara and randomly hired a slew of slackers who were down on their luck, to build machines and try to meet an ever-increasing demand. The workers were Hells Angels, parolees, addled high school dropouts, alternative-minded hippies, and drug addicts, who earned $1.75 an hour and who were put on an assembly line of sorts for up to eighteen hours a day in an old roller skating rink on Martin Avenue. Employees were found just about everywhere. Ted Dabney picked up a hitchhiker and ended up hiring him.

One day during a deadline crunch, Dabney saw Bushnell smoking some ultra-fragrant skunkweed with the "potheads and hippies." He was livid, furious. "Nolan!" cautioned Dabney, "you can't smoke that stuff with those guys."

"Why not?" asked Bushnell, calm from the pot.

"Because we have machines to make. We have orders to fill. We can't afford getting busted by the cops. It would ruin us."

"OK, I won't smoke it on company property." To Dabney's dismay, Bushnell still got stoned with the workers—away from the office. Over time, a few employees would move up the ranks to become engineers. And some would be found in the bathroom, shooting up with needles.

Atari's new home had the feel of a carnival midway. It was ensconced within a skating rink so expansive that the young Alcorn even tried revving up and riding his Triumph 650 motorcycle on the polished floors (which resulted in a minor spinout due to a layer of dust on the floors). Bushnell kept returning to the unemployment office until Atari had more than seventy employees who ultimately made about a dozen machines daily—if they weren't too stoned. It wasn't as if Atari was a dope lover's paradise. The line workers worked hard. But there were constant parties, rampant hooking up, and nasty next-day hangovers. Despite the pot-churned hazes, Bushnell made some wise decisions. He paid his suppliers immediately, and there was rarely a shortage of parts in the office. And distributors understood Pong; there was beauty in its simplicity. Some bought the machines by the hundreds.

But mainly, there was something intensely instinctive about playing Pong in a bar that went beyond enjoying the Odyssey at home. Like the pinball and other penny arcade games that came before Pong, the game coaxed adults, not kids, to play it. It vied for your money along with booze, the jukebox, and pinball. Like the sexy new thing in town, its video screen constantly beckoned. Its distinctive sound was familiar and persuasive, extraordinarily mimicking the thwack of a paddle smacked against a plastic ball. And, like a voyeur looking into a window, you had to peer into the game's hooded cabinet to engage the mystery within. Everything about Pong was alluring, even the way it sucked quarters from your pocket as it dared you to master it. Once you became its master, you could brag about your achievement throughout the tavern—which men and women did constantly. And it wasn't cheap. Pong broke the coin-op barrier with its quarter-per-game charge; at the time, pinball still gave pinheads three games for one quarter.

Pong became super popular super quickly. Like the seventies pop songs by ABBA, it went beyond being successful, earning the company $3.2 million in profits in 1973. It was a superstar on its own, a machine so ubiquitous, forty companies made knockoffs. At Atari, the new executives' emotions ran the gamut from feelings of angry woe to nervous distress; they found it difficult to meet ever increasing demand for the arcade machines. There were so many demands on Bushnell's time that he didn't push hard to hasten the patent on the arcade game. So the knockoffs and rip-offs continued. By the time the trend peaked, there were well over 100,000 Pong-inspired arcade games across the United States. Probably fewer than a third of them were made by Atari.

Bushnell wanted it all, and that need for world domination ate at him. He even had a licensing deal in Japan. But Atari Japan ended up being a heavy weight upon his shoulders. So many arcade machines were stranded at customs at the docks that it was driving him nuts. Bushnell's golden rule was, Do it and then fix it if it needs fixing. But the Japanese fiasco was difficult to fix. (Eventually, he ended up selling it for $500,000.) And at home, the company just did not have enough cash on hand to expand in any kind of robust, meaningful way.

Ironically, not long after Pong became a huge hit, Atari was inching toward the dark precipice of bankruptcy. Even though they were cranking out new coin-operated arcade games along with double-wide pinball machines like Superman, Atari was by no means run with the military-like prowess and might of a Sanders Associates, which allowed Ralph Baer to research and develop the Brown Box over the course of many years. Bushnell's management style was, in the words of the Big Bopper, loose like a long-neck goose.

Still, he knew what he had to do with Ted Dabney. Beyond the maddening challenges of managing a new business, Bushnell and Dabney, once very close friends, began to come to blows. Dabney felt Bushnell was not just a fibber; he was sure in his soul that Bushnell was scurrilous and morally bankrupt, the kind of guy who would say anything to anyone just to make a buck. For his part, Bushnell found that one of Dabney's relatives was dipping into the Atari coffers, taking literally tons of quarters from the local Berkeley routes that were so zealously guarded and coveted by Steve Bristow, a soft-spoken guy who sometimes carried a hatchet to guard himself should someone jump him while he was carrying $1,500 worth of quarters in his car. Much worse in Bushnell's mind was that Dabney had no brain for manufacturing, which was the position the older engineer was forced to take on for the burgeoning company. On an early evening in June 1973, Bushnell came into Alcorn's office/workshop, worried.

Bushnell didn't mince words. "I want you to stay on. But I have to fire Ted."

Alcorn was stunned. Not Ted. Ted is a founder. Ted is cool.

Bushnell continued. "He doesn't know what he's doing. He—"

At that point, Dabney entered the room, and Bushnell peppered him with questions about manufacturing. "How many machines will be made today? How much will they cost?" Dabney, an engineer, not an MBA, didn't have the answers. Nor had he seen the possibility of the axe falling. He was shocked and appalled. After the bullying interrogation by Bushnell, it became clear to Alcorn that Dabney couldn't handle the job.

Dabney was incensed when Bushnell approached him with a $250,000 buyout and nothing more. After a short, terse conversation, he took the offer. As he left the building, Dabney paused to look back for a moment. Then he revved up his car and got the hell out of there. In a way, Dabney was relieved. He'd been harboring mixed feelings about his participation in the company for some time. He felt Bushnell was hiring minor leaguers to run Atari, and he was hiring them without Dabney's input. Sometimes, he felt that Bushnell was a "stupid idiot."

As he sped faster, he reasoned, "I've begun to feel I am important. That's a terrible feeling. I'm glad I left before it got hold of me. Bushnell is the kind of guy who would sell his soul for money. That's what he's doing. I'm getting out before I sell mine." One of the original minds behind Atari was gone. This generally good man

who tempered Bushnell's grandiose ideas with devil's adv[ ]
esty didn't care that the not-so-distant future would be f[ ]
of videogame gold.

After Pong took off, Bushnell settled into remaking and spinning off his hit with a kind of banal alacrity. It was as if beyond Ping-Pong, he didn't think arcades really had legs as a new form of entertainment. There was Gotcha, SuperPong, Pong Doubles, QuadraPong, Space Pong, even a faux dog house–encased Snoopy Pong (based on the stalwart beagle from Charles Schulz's *Peanuts* comic strip) for physicians' offices, which was renamed Doctor Pong and Puppy Pong lest it incur the litigious wrath of the popular franchise's powerful lawyers. Other companies around the world kept producing Pong clones, frantically trying to cash in. The law of diminishing returns had to kick in at some point soon. But that time had not yet come.

By 1974, Bushnell was almost out of cash, due partially to the bad investment in Japan. GranTrak 10, the arcade racing game that Alcorn really wanted to do when he was first hired, cost too much money to build and was a failure. The poorly paid, exhausted workers on the line were quietly revolting because they hadn't had a raise. Machines beyond GranTrak 10 were being sent out to arcades—and they didn't function properly. Atari had become a mess due to growing pains and lackadaisical management.

For the first time in the history of his new company, Bushnell began to worry hard. Games with four joysticks like Tank ("Cannon fires, shells explode!" said the flyer) fared better than GranTrak 10. But making a new coin-op game every four to five weeks was taxing and full of irritating deadline pressures. Atari had become a sword of Damocles hanging sharp and ready over Bushnell's head. He couldn't sleep. He had headaches. He went from believing he was a god who had all the answers to thinking his ideas might not have legs. And he couldn't stop pushing Pong as his salvation. He went full steam ahead with plans for a console version of the game to be played in the living room.

The Pong home player was nicknamed "Darlene" by the wolves in the company, in honor of a stunning Atari office assistant with a pretty face, large breasts, and a twenty-inch waist. The nerds might not have been able to coax Darlene into bed, but they sure could objectify her into the status of goddess as machine. At first, no one was interested in the home version, even when the game was shown to retailers at New York City's famous and chaotic Toy Fair. Part of the Toy Fair debacle was due to Bushnell and his people being wet behind the ears. Their space for Toy Fair wasn't in the building on Broadway and Twenty-third Street where most business was done. It was far away (in the Jacob Javits Convention Center). Few stopped by. Of those who did, none were interested in making a deal.

Bushnell kept plugging away, making cold calls to any company he could think of that might consider it. It was then that a savior appeared. This rescuer wasn't ensconced in the arcade industry. He wasn't even in toys or electronics. Tom Quinn, a six-foot-four redheaded Irishman who was rarely seen without a suit, worked as the senior buyer for Sears' sporting goods section. He believed that Sears had done fairly well by selling the Odyssey. Even though Magnavox had made many missteps in marketing the machine, he felt that Sears could do good business selling the Pong console. For the first meeting at the Atari offices, Quinn arrived early, at 8 a.m., the proverbial early bird ready to catch the worm.

Bushnell, who rolled into the office much later, initially blanched at Quinn's request for exclusivity—even though Sears was the only game in town. Since no other companies were buying, Alcorn packed up the prototype of the home unit in a big protective case and traveled to Chicago. There, he looked like a gawking tourist as he regarded the foreboding 110-story Sears Tower, then the world's tallest building. That particular stop of the Atari dog and pony show didn't go well at all. The wooden box and its mass of wires was plagued by interference problems during the demonstration. A nervous, sweating Alcorn had to take the assembly apart and do some emergency mending right on the spot. One of the creaky old executives from the Deep South frowned upon the mass of wires inside the prototype. "Son," he asked Alcorn, "how you gonna get that dang bird's nest of wires in there to hook up to a silicone chip?"

"Silicone?" thought Alcorn. "It's *silicon*. If this is what we're up against, there's no hope." But Quinn was still game, more enthused than ever, despite the demonstration's glitches. He immediately contacted Bushnell.

"If we go with this, how many can you give us?" asked Quinn.

Bushnell barely skipped a beat. "I can get you seventy-five thousand units."

"That's not enough," said Quinn, explaining that Sears cut a wide swath with its nine hundred retail stores. Additionally, there would be an enormous number of sales generated through its popular catalog. Sears would throw in free advertising to sweeten the deal. "But we still want exclusivity for one year."

Bushnell's eyes widened. He salivated. Exclusivity no longer mattered. They had one shot, and that one shot was Sears. "So, how many?"

"Not seventy-five thousand. One hundred and fifty thousand."

Bushnell was enthusiastic, but he kept his cool. Inside, his synapses were firing like he was about to have sex with the most beautiful woman on earth, maybe even Darlene. Soon, though, he had qualms. He thought, "How in the world can I produce so many thousands of consoles with nearly no capital?" It was then that Quinn went from savior to hero. He said Sears itself would help with the manufacturing. Later, Quinn again stepped up to make an early video in Sears's TV studio, advertising the machine, with a female quiz show host bearing the juvenile moniker of Ima Douche; Quinn himself was a game show contestant. The video was a smash with retailers, so much so that Sears held a place for the console in their coveted catalog, even though it was past their deadline for including a brand-new, full-color page for the merchandise. Said one Sears wag to Alcorn in the company cafeteria, "You know the last time—the only time—we held up the catalog? That was with Marvin Glass slot car racing. We had fifty thousand of them. And none of them—not one—worked." The pressure was on.

Tom Quinn had made an audacious, ambitious gamble. If he failed, he would be without a job—and he would likely have a hard time finding another. Bushnell had bet it all too, but he wasn't about to worry, at least not publicly or in meetings. For Bushnell it was more guts than business acumen. Bushnell told everyone that Sears would be Atari's savior. And he claimed Atari was going to make big money for Sears as well.

Even before the console was released, the very thought of Home Pong had people lining up at Sears stores—just to put their names on a waiting list. Atari was, in the parlance of *The Jeffersons*, movin' on up. Home Pong was a fast-selling holiday phenomenon. By the end of 1975, Atari had raked in $40 million in sales from the rabid fans who bought more than 150,000 consoles. And that was just from one retail entity, Sears. Pong was a bona-fide cultural phenomenon, and was even part of an Al Franken skit on the seventh episode of the hottest show on TV, *Saturday Night Live*. It was also the only arcade game a young Barack Obama ever played.

Bushnell had created not one, but two revolutions in gaming. When Pong emerged, it started the arcade revolution. Suddenly, the arcade machine was an essential accoutrement in every bar and bowling alley. Pong was more popular than pinball. Not only was it the first arcade game to make money, it was *so* exciting to play. The heart rate increased just as the on-screen ball sped up. As you stood there, your spastic body moved so much, it was like a workout in itself. People would plan to go out to the local bar just to play Pong. So Pong sold booze for the mom-and-pop tavern. When a few more iconic games, like Space Invaders and Pac-Man, were released, the smarter moms and pops started video arcades, which became as essential to American culture as the movie theater.

With arcades established, Atari went on to prove that an at-home market existed too. Pong in the home made people forget TV programs for a while because Pong was its own TV program, one *you* could direct. Higinbotham had proved there was consumer curiosity for games. Baer proved the working concept could be made on an assembly line. But Bushnell had made games into a viable commercial enterprise.

As he saw the phenomenon grow, Bushnell certainly wanted to manufacture more variations of Home Pong. And there were other games to publish, and bigger, better consoles to make. The world was his own to control, just like a Pong machine. And since he'd made that world, he knew how to win every game. But Bushnell needed more money to make Atari bigger.

Today, you can turn over a flat rock in the Silicon Valley and a hundred venture capitalists will slither out. Back in the seventies, one man was pretty much the only game in town. Enter Don Valentine, a dour, plaid shirt–wearing venture capitalist who looked like an all-American astronaut. The smart, slow-speaking Valentine had short hair, a no-nonsense attitude, and always chose his words carefully. By 1967, Valentine was already something of a legend in the Silicon Valley, having cofounded National Semiconductor after a successful career in marketing at Fairchild Semiconductor. The

1972 start-up of Capital Management (today called Sequoia Capital) allowed Valentine, an inquisitive man who had many interests, to branch out beyond the magic material that is used for microprocessor chips and transistors. The company's tagline said it all: "The entrepreneurs behind the entrepreneurs." Ironically, Valentine was thrifty bordering on being cheap. He drove a practical Mercedes diesel station wagon, and when the Atari kids visited his mansion, they had to wear sweaters because the heat had been turned down. When his family spent extra cash on a customized license plate, Valentine chided them for wasting money.

Bushnell met repeatedly with Valentine, stating that Sears's exclusivity would end in late 1976. Then, they could sell Home Pong to, well, everywhere, to the multitudes and beyond. The sky was the limit, said the Atari boss. Bushnell also made it clear that Atari had amassed $3 million in profits in 1975. Atari was ready to break out, said Bushnell, if only the capital were there for infrastructure like a new factory to produce a new generation of consoles—consoles that could play more than just a tennis game.

Valentine was fair, but prone to anger. He had a fit when, on the day before closing the venture capital deal, Bushnell asked for twice as much money because Atari's net worth had skyrocketed. But when Valentine saw the numbers prepared by Atari's legal and business team, he agreed to the extra cash. He even showed up with a car full of champagne. Valentine being Valentine, it certainly wasn't Dom Pérignon.

Because Valentine was in, everyone from Time, Inc., to Fidelity Investments came on board. In Atari's coffers was a total of more than $4 million with which to make interactive entertainment even better than it already was. It was a heady, adventurous time indeed. The floors of Atari buzzed with the energy of Santa's workshop— with the aroma of pot thrown in to add a Cheech and Chong essence to the mix. Workers roller-skated or skateboarded from place to place. Employees' dogs were brought to the offices as barking companions who got them through crunch time. Workers would play with the dogs like they were kids again. But the sense of childlike wonder wouldn't last very long at all.

3.

HIGHEST HIGHS,
LOWEST LOWS

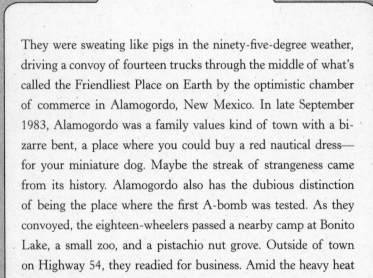

They were sweating like pigs in the ninety-five-degree weather, driving a convoy of fourteen trucks through the middle of what's called the Friendliest Place on Earth by the optimistic chamber of commerce in Alamogordo, New Mexico. In late September 1983, Alamogordo was a family values kind of town with a bizarre bent, a place where you could buy a red nautical dress—for your miniature dog. Maybe the streak of strangeness came from its history. Alamogordo also has the dubious distinction of being the place where the first A-bomb was tested. As they convoyed, the eighteen-wheelers passed a nearby camp at Bonito Lake, a small zoo, and a pistachio nut grove. Outside of town on Highway 54, they readied for business. Amid the heavy heat of the desert, its gnarly scrub bushes, and the occasional noisy rattlesnake, the heavy equipment crawled into the Alamogordo landfill. Reporters were kept away. So were the local townspeople. What was thrown in the dump and unceremoniously buried in the desert and then poured over with concrete epitomized all that was wrong with Atari. Atari was trying to bury their failure and with it, one of the most foolish, most expensive videogame licensing deals of all time.

Two years before, in 1981, Warner Bros. CEO Steve Ross had made a deal with Steven Spielberg regarding an E.T.: the Extra-Terrestrial videogame. Ross, whose empathy served his salesmanship well, loved movies more than anything, especially movies that made him money. Although he liked and even played games, it was in the film industry that his true loyalties lay. Spielberg would be assured of $23 million in royalties just to sign on the dotted line. If the game did well, he would receive even more. If the game tanked, the director would be off the hook. Spielberg looked up to Ross as the ultimate father figure, so much that he filmed a short, expensive homage for his sixty-fifth birthday. It starred Spielberg, Quincy Jones, Chevy Chase, Clint Eastwood, and the top Warner movie executives, as hobos. Very much like Frank Capra's *It's a Wonderful Life* (which was Ross's favorite movie), the film pointed out, George Bailey style, how bad off Ross's pals and associates would have been without their magnanimous CEO. Spielberg and Ross would have done anything for each other, and the Atari licensing contract for the E.T. game looked an awful lot like a case of one hand washing the other—at the expense of the videogame company's future.

Because the E.T.: the Extra-Terrestrial game deadline was nearly impossible to meet, Atari designer Howard Warshaw was between a rock and a hard place. If the game had been on the shelves in tandem with the movie's summer release, it might have fared better, even though it was a buggy game with poor graphics and audio. As it stood, the *E.T.* phenomenon was waning when the cartridge premiered in late 1982. Atari manufactured four million cartridges. Only 1.5 million were sold, and that may be a liberal estimate when

coupled with the fact that many of the games were returned due
to their overwhelmingly crappy quality. Eventually, the games hit
bargain bins for 10 cents each, and even then, few bought them. So
millions of E.T. game cartridges were unceremoniously dumped,
crushed, and buried in Alamogordo. From plastic dust they were
born and to plastic dust and desert sand they returned.

In 1975 that plastic hadn't been worthless at all. It was precious gold
to the principals of Atari, and it would only become more valuable
as the decade progressed. Atari's arcade business was still thriving,
and Home Pong exceeded sales expectations, and demand exceeded
supply. Alcorn hired an unkempt and unshaven Steve Jobs, who in
turn asked his best friend, the diffident genius Steve Wozniak, for
help with what would be one of Atari's most popular additions to its
ever expanding library. Without telling Alcorn, Bushnell asked Jobs
to help him streamline the innards of a brick-breaking arcade game
called Breakout. Bushnell wanted to save money because the chips
used in each arcade machine were still pricey at the time. He coaxed
the brazen, odoriferous Jobs with $750 and a $100 bonus for each
chip removed from the prototype. Wozniak, who worked with Jobs
simply because it was fun, was fascinated by the challenge and didn't
sleep at all while he worked on it. In less than three days, he cut
the chip number from seventy to twenty. Alcorn was amazed by this
miracle of engineering. But he was also pissed off at Bushnell, who
was doing what he always did, throwing a lot of utter crap against the
wall to see what would stick—without Alcorn's approval.

Wozniak pocketed $375, but Jobs kept the remainder of the
$5,000. When Wozniak discovered what Jobs had been paid, his
hacker heart, which had led him to work on Breakout for art's sake,

was broken. Wozniak never really trusted Jobs completely again—even though they went on to create Apple together.*

Breakout was indeed a tour de force of design—even though Wozniak's work was ultimately scrapped because many at Atari didn't understand how to replicate the genius design on a mass production level. Still, breaking bricks with an oddly and slowly bouncing ball was one thing. When the ball sped up and the paddle became smaller, your heart seemed as though it would break out as well, right through your rib cage. Just when you believed you could beat it, that dastardly internal computer chip that seemed so superhuman would beat you into submission. Breakout did so well in the United States, Namco came calling to license it in Japan.

When the Atari team arranged to meet the Namco president, Masaya Nakamura, in Japan, the head of the company was late to the gathering. As the Atari executives, still not much older than teenagers, sat around shooting the breeze in the president's fastidious office, they felt so loose and confident that Steve Bristow positioned himself behind Nakamura's desk. Comfortable in the power broker's chair, he brazenly put his feet up on the finely polished desk. When Nakamura entered, he said nothing, but his face grew red as he steamed inside. He had that "Get the fuck out of my chair" look on his face. After the meeting, Namco partnered with Atari. But Namco suspiciously soon requested that Bushnell stop all overseas shipments of Breakout because the game wasn't a hit. The Japanese company reported selling fewer than fifty machines. In reality, the game was a breakout success for Namco, placing the company that started with coin-operated mechanical horse rides on a department store rooftop, in the mid-1950s, near the top of the Japanese arcade

---

* Two interviewees told me that Wozniak was very shaken and hurt by what Jobs did to him. In his *The Ultimate History of Video Games*, Steven L. Kent quotes Wozniak as saying, "I knew he [Jobs] believed it was fine to buy something for $60 and sell it for $60,000 if you could do it. I just didn't think he would do it to his best friend."

scene. Throughout Japan, massive pachinko parlors had their gambling machines removed, only to be replaced by Breakout clones. Japanese businessmen flocked to these parlors, often using them for betting illegally. Though they couldn't prove it, everyone at Atari was certain Namco was behind the Breakout clones. And it wasn't only Namco that was a thorn in Bushnell's backside. Dozens and dozens of companies were knocking off clones of Atari games.

Beyond that annoyance, others were beating Atari's 2600 console to market with gaming machines that were high tech for the time. A company called Fairchild released the Channel F in August 1976, beating Atari by over a year. Imagined by future Intel founder Robert Noyce and engineered by Jerry Lawson, the Channel F introduced the idea of cartridges to home videogames. Its large, palm-sized Videocarts featured rudimentary graphics and barely recognizable characters made of pixels. But the primitive artwork gave life to characters and saucers in lurid living color. Beyond chess, the finest of these was a bowling game with cinnamon red pins and an alley that returned your ball. If the ball didn't speed from left to right and back again before you rolled it, and if there was no beeping when pins were hit, it would have been a very accurate simulation. You could even play the Fairchild F via a telephone connection and via a partnership with a syndicated TV show called *TV POWWW.*

But Coleco's Telstar was the most successful pre–Atari 2600 console, bringing in nearly $100 million in sales to the Connecticut company. Between 1976 and 1978, the variants of the console were so numerous, a game head would look at the systems as a wolf looks at a flock of sheep, salivating. The oddest addition was 1977's Telstar Arcade, a seemingly haphazard mishmash of plastic that looked something like a triangular umbrella holder with places for a Wild West pistol, a steering wheel, and a gearshift. It made you think you were about to play as Clint Eastwood in a futuristic cowboy racing game.

While the 2600 wasn't the first to market, Bushnell was still

seen as a videogame god among men. After Home Pong sold 150,000
units, the *New York Times* dubbed him "The Man with the Golden
Touch" and alluded to him with the same respect Silicon Valley tech
wizards did: They called him King Pong. Every member of the team
was excited about launching the 2600 in the fall of 1977. It was Atari's
biggest design idea yet, a comparatively inexpensive gaming console
that used far fewer chips than most of the competitors. But Atari
was out of money. Its millions weren't nearly enough to accomplish
the three things Bushnell aspired to do: keep manufacturing Atari's
home version of Pong, make more double-wide pinball machines for
Bally, *and* create the microcomputer multi-gaming console that for a
time bore the code name of Stella. It was not named after the current office hottie, but after a turquoise blue ten-speed bike that sat
up against one of the carrels and was owned and pedaled each day
to the office by Atari engineer Joe Decuir. Stella, with its eight-bit
graphics processor, became the Atari 2600, proudly nicknamed the
Video Computer System (VCS).

Despite the potential of this new invention, and in addition to
imitators that seemed to grow and flourish like so many Elvis im-
personators, Bushnell had to deal with a poor economy that put a
dent into video arcade sales across the country. Only Midway with
Sea Wolf truly thrived in 1976. When you stepped up to the fancy
metal periscope that hung from the Sea Wolf cabinet and heard the
underwater-like sonar sounds, it made you feel like you were a heroic
undersea gunner who would save the world from attack. Many quarters were spent trying to torpedo the swift-moving PT boat that sped
across the screen.

The year 1976 saw unemployment in the United States rise to
nearly 8 percent. As the economy slumped and inflation skyrocketed,
a weakened President Ford tried desperately to steer the country
toward better days with the specious WIN (Whip Inflation Now)
program. Swiftly emerging from the wrecked economy wasn't to be.

Bushnell, Valentine, and Atari's board of directors had dreamed of taking Atari to the stock market and of amassing unimaginable fortune while producing popular and artistic games for the VCS. They even had the prospectus ready. They had dolled themselves up in business suits and traveled to Wall Street to speak to prospective underwriters. But there was no money to be had. The IPO turned into a no PO. Bushnell and the board determined, after a tense, sometimes acrimonious meeting, not to go public.

It was then that Bushnell decided to sell Atari.

Yet there were no immediate takers. Quaker Oats and MCA didn't believe the dancer had legs, especially with the economy the way it was. Disney, which was a conservative, family outfit, thought Atari was too radical, with unsustainable success. Bushnell was getting nervous and so was the board. But like the undaunted, fascinating talker he was, he interested Warner Communications—upon the urging of Don Valentine, who was one of Warner's largest shareholders. If Warner chose to purchase the videogame company, Valentine would get a huge finder's fee.

By late summer, Bushnell had been in contact with Warner Bros. CEO Steve Ross, the smart, greedy, show-biz-loving entrepreneur who had turned his family's funeral parlor business into gold before striking greater lucre with music and movies at Warner. While the dashing Ross liked to tell the press that he got the idea to purchase Atari after he couldn't pull his kids away from Atari's arcade games at Disneyland, Ross really had been talking with Bushnell prior to this fabricated eureka moment. Ross certainly knew how to charm. He flew Bushnell and Valentine to New York on Warner's corporate jet. Clint Eastwood and his waifishly fetching girlfriend Sondra Locke were on the plane too. Eastwood and Locke were perfectly chatty with Bushnell and feigned interest in Atari. Eastwood even made Bushnell sandwiches. On the ground, there was a suite fit for a king in midtown Manhattan, and the screening of Eastwood's upcoming Dirty Harry film, *The Enforcer*. The starstruck Bushnell felt special, accepted, appreciated beyond his niche. There were drinks and conviviality and all-night negotiations. By the time the early September sun rose over the East River, Bushnell had agreed to sell the company for approximately $28 million. Later, Bushnell would say that he sold the company for far too little and called Warner's people "incompetent" executives who committed company suicide and homicide.

He was both right and wrong. In December 1978, there was an ugly argument between Bushnell and Warner executives. Bushnell felt in his heart that the Atari 2600 Video Computer System, the $199 console that shipped with a Combat game, was not high tech enough to continue selling well. Yet upon release in October 1977, the machine sold 250,000 units, and the next year 550,000 units. Warner expected to manufacture a second run that produced a million more systems. To outside eyes, 800,000 consoles sold within two years seemed like a huge amount. But due to production and marketing costs, the VCS was not making money. Though he had sold the company, Bushnell was still a part of Atari, and he had something to say.

"The market isn't holding. Stop making it. Stop selling it. Forget it!" Bushnell told the startled suits. "We've got to make a newer, better machine. Let's sell the 2600 for cheap and do something with better graphics and better games. Prepare for the future. That's the only way to go. The only way."

The executives looked like they'd had the wind knocked out of them. It was as if the 2600 itself had grown boxing gloves and sucker punched them repeatedly. Steve Ross felt an ache in the pit of his stomach, and as a master of the universe, he found that feeling unknown and unwelcome. Though he didn't trust Atari as a long-term play, he genuinely liked the idea of Atari as a new kind of entertainment and he appreciated the ingenuity that went into each cartridge. He even played the games well into the night in his tony East Hampton mansion.

But that day, that confusing day, made him angry. "What the fuck is going on here?" Ross asked. Swearing was unusual for the CEO. His ticker wasn't what it once was, and he would have a heart attack in just a few years.

Manny Gerard, the most senior Warner vice president who dealt directly with Atari, tried to calm Ross. He urged Ross to stay the course with the older machine, at least through the holiday season. His wait-and-see approach proved lucrative in the long run. The 2600, because of the variety of games available, began to sell like bottled water during a heat wave. During 1979 and 1980, videogame fans bought more than three million VCS machines. The knockoffs of Space Invaders and Pac-Man together sold an astonishing fifteen million copies. But it wasn't just the thrill of playing familiar arcade games without constantly adding quarters. It was the idea that they could be played in the home on your own TV set with your friends—at any time. And you didn't have to dress up or spend money on beer to play. The console features themselves weren't so savagely amazing. It was the games that led people to buy in droves. And in the stores, Atari had the brand name that was the most familiar and most up-front. While the competing Fairchild Channel F console was the first to have cartridges, it never had the essential licensed hits, nor was it seen to be as hot as the familiar Atari brand. Atari was gaming nirvana, endless, eternal fun, the highest happiness you could find in entertainment. It was games like Superman, where you changed in a phone booth and flew over tall buildings in a single bound, your cape waving confidently in the wind as you saved the world. Later, it was Yars' Revenge (comic book included) in which the David-like flying insect Yar, angry about the destruction of planet Razak IV, mandibled carefully or shot cannons adamantly through a vast rainbow-colored boundary. Beyond, he faced off with a brown Goliath named Qotile who bore a looming, repulsive alien visage. It creeped you out royally.

After the confrontation with Warner, Bushnell showed up to the Atari offices infrequently, feeling strongly that the layers of corporate politics at Warner were destroying his baby. He was soon fired. Then came the sad exodus. The designers, the soul of Atari, became restless. While Bushnell had given them cushy offices and sexy secretaries, most of their salaries now hovered below what the market would bear. Moreover, they weren't getting credit for the games the way the cast and crew did in each movie's credits or the bands and their sidemen did in the liner notes of records. Nor did they receive a percentage of the profits, even though Atari was making hundreds upon hundreds of millions as one of the world's fastest growing companies. And despite all his faults, Bushnell's influence was missed. Bushnell understood games. The suits at Warner didn't; they came from staid industries like clothing and shoes. They knew diddly-squat about a technology product that did something to the senses beyond giving the wearer a sense of pride. In fact, they knew little about the world of entertainment in general. So between 1979 and 1981, the vast majority of Atari's original designers left to form their own companies, like Imagic and Activision, the latter of which is still a mighty company to this day. Like those aliens being shot as they fell from the night sky in Space Invaders, Atari was being decimated.

Still, some essential designers remained. Though it wasn't easy, they would do their best to make the quality games for which Atari had been known before the purging. For example, Tod Frye, a former Berkeley carpenter, was in love with computers and games. Even while in high school, on punch cards for a giant HP 2000 Timeshare computer Frye made a text-based adventure game about dealing drugs. It was a well-thought-out simulation in which you managed your resources to become a better pusher. It wasn't a strange game to make in a Bay Area enjoying the drug culture of the seventies.

The opinionated Frye, along with a handful of other designers, was bold enough to bring some literate and almost literary games to Atari. He dreamed up the Swordquest series, an early action role playing game that integrated various forms of pop culture, like comic books, with philosophy, like *The I Ching*, into game play. While Swordquest didn't sell like the popular arcade ports of the time, it set a kind of standard. Games that were based on deeper thought and philosophy could occasionally stand out if given tender loving care. But Frye was best known for designing a maligned version of the bestselling Pac-Man arcade game for the Atari 2600.

Frye began the Pac-Man project when his boss called him into a meeting and announced that two games required attention post-haste. Both Pac-Man and Defender had to go out the door in a matter of months, and both Frye and Larry DeMar were up for the gigs. DeMar worked on the brain-curdling Defender arcade game with former pinball machine designer Eugene Jarvis. Earnest and thoughtful, DeMar didn't believe Pac-Man could be made on the 2600. He told Frye that every dot on the screen that the pizza-shaped character hungrily chomped was considered an additional graphical element, which would eat up precious memory. When DeMar chose to help design Defender, Frye took on the monumental task of squeezing Pac-Man onto a cartridge, even though the cartridge might not have enough free data to do the landmark game justice.

As with other employees ensconced in the crunch-time depths of Atari's offices, Frye's work was sometimes fueled by pot and then cocaine, partly because the Pac-Man deadline was extraordinarily tight, partly because it was simply part of the try-anything culture of debauchery at the time. Some have written that Frye threatened to quit unless he received a bump in pay to do the game. But Frye did nothing of the kind. He simply wanted to do the job. He told

others, "I just want to trip out on the technology." Frye loved coding the game, and the art of programming moved him. He slept in
the office to meet the deadline. Every night, he dreamed in code.
Sometimes, he solved problems while he slept. When he was awake,
he was embracing of Atari up-and-comers, like the teenage Mark
Cerny, who was working on Marble Madness for the arcades, the
first physics-based game, one in which you nervously guided a ball
with surgical precision through maze upon maze. During their rare
breaks, Frye invited Cerny into his truck, tossed him a beer, and put
the Atari office culture into perspective. Sometimes Frye bitched a
blue streak; sometime he philosophized. But it all made the young
Cerny feel part of the gang, not an outsider. (Cerny would become
such a vital force in videogames that he would be inducted into the
industry's Hall of Fame decades later. But without Frye's friendship
amid the ulcer-inducing politics of Atari, he might have given up on
games altogether.)

When Pac-Man was released, it was plagued by an annoying
flicker. Frye told those who would listen around the office that the
four ghosts (humorously nicknamed Blinky, Pinky, Inky, and Clyde)
who chased Pac-Man were supposed to be transparent. Whatever
the case, Frye was one of the first game designers to get a piece of the
action with management's new "enhanced compensation package,"
something developers at the company had lobbied for incessantly. It
was only about .30 of 1 percent of each $30 cartridge, about 10 to 15
cents on each game. Atari made twelve million units, and each cost
about $2.50 to make. They sold seven million copies of the game and
earned about $15 per cartridge. Still, executives at the company con-
sidered it a disappointment. Frye also complained that if you were a
writer, you'd get at least 5 percent in royalties. He didn't receive anything near 5 percent. Still, the cranky programmer earned a million
dollars from Pac-Man royalties alone in 1982.

Sadly, Frye failed to report the income properly to the feds, an understandable mistake for a young programmer still very green when it came to life experience. The IRS got to him, eventually discovering an illegal tax shelter Frye's accountant had created, and came down on him hard.

At least in a small way, Atari had tried to do right by some of its employees (like Frye) with a royalty package. But it was already too late. Atari became known in the industry as a game maker that would cut corners on its games. The problems with Pac-Man sales proved that in-house designers and programmers, even good ones like Frye, weren't being given enough time to complete even the best games. And employees were still leaving in droves. The games were symptomatic of a larger problem: half-assedness across the board. Atari was cracking from the inside out. Corruption and stealing by high-flying sales representatives around the world was becoming more and more prevalent. The current president, Ray Kassar, flew to New York City in a private jet, his preferred means of travel. Armed with a presentation for Warner executives that was full of Greek god–like hubris, Kassar estimated that Atari would earn $2 billion a year and bring in revenues of $6 billion by 1986. He was betting wildly, believing that Atari could sustain the huge profits of 1982, during which the company brought in $2 billion in revenue for Warner. Kassar was never without a limo, and he was flying so high that Atari's 1982 fete for salesmen was held in Monte Carlo, not the usual staple, California.

In late August 1982, one Warner executive discovered that hundreds of thousands of games were sitting, undistributed and unsold, in a Milwaukee warehouse. But Warner executive Manny Gerard, who was often the most boisterous and self-confident of the entertainment company's honchos, palliated the situation for everyone, including Steve Ross. He constantly reminded all those within earshot that Atari had a lock on 80 percent of the market. Ross wasn't so sure. Now more than ever, he considered Atari a flash in the pan.

So Ross quietly had begun selling nearly sixty thousand shares in the company when it hovered in the stratosphere at nearly $60 a share.

On December 8, 1982, after horrible earnings were reported to the public, the stock plummeted. As in the tale of the Terraces of Purgatory in Dante's *Divine Comedy*, the avaricious, the slothful, and the gluttonous were purged—most of them. No eyes were sewn shut, and no one had to lie prostrate on the ground, but new Atari owner Jack Tramiel, formerly president of Commodore International, butchered the staff from two thousand to a few hundred. Tramiel, a Pole who was formerly a taxi driver, had worked his way up the ladder through sheer cutthroat tenacity. At Atari, he began to focus the remaining staff on making the Atari 1040ST. It could play games, yes, but also would supposedly rival the popular Apple II PC. Tramiel, who had remade his image into a dashing fellow who was cut from cloth finer and fancier than many of Atari's fascinating nerds, was nonetheless a follower, not an innovator. He was doomed to fail because he was playing catch-up.

Atari's brain drain was embarrassing, but the executives at the company refused to notice. Meanwhile the top minds, now at Activision, created stellar games for the Atari consoles with an entrepreneurial energy not seen since Bushnell, Dabney, and Alcorn had come together to form Syzygy. Activision not only pushed the envelope; it invented a whole new genre with designer David Crane's quickly but not haphazardly designed Pitfall!, a captivating game in which you played Harry, a Tarzan-like adventurer who swings from the trees and dashes through caves in 255 screens of constant mayhem. You became breathless as you avoided giant, scorpion-ridden holes and famished crocodiles, all the while searching for thirty-two treasures—in a frantic twenty minutes.

That success was upsetting for Atari, which had become a place where deadlines came and went without being met. Worse, software was pushed to market before being refined and perfected, à la the

E.T. discomfiture. But Atari was hardly alone in its failures. In the wake of the gaming gold rush Atari had created, crapware was released *hundreds of times* by dozens of companies, so much so that the gamer couldn't really trust the hype that preceded a game's introduction. There were too many consoles and too many games released by too many companies to sustain a boom. In addition to Channel F, for example, there were machines from Bally, Mattel, Emerson, Tandy, and Coleco. In fact, Coleco left the industry entirely. Imagic decided not to go public on the day before its IPO. Many of the consoles and games that remained languished on shelves and in warehouses. Dozens of the little guys with tiny staffs of a dozen or less were forced to shutter their doors, although Activision and a handful of other companies stayed afloat by making games for the personal computer, which was on its way up in terms of popular awareness and affordability. It wasn't just the videogame industry that suffered a severe contraction. Stagflation struck the entire country; the inflation in late 1982 was nearly 11 percent, and nine million people were looking for work. The most brutal recession since the Great Depression was a tough time all around, but the game companies were hit the hardest.

So Atari's time in the sun was over. And because of its gigantic failure, the whole videogame world crashed and burned. It was as though games had been a trend and nothing more. When Atari fell, no one wanted to take a chance on games—not investors, not retail chains, not consumers. In retrospect, the collapse does not diminish what Atari had done for popular culture. Videogames were now part of everyone's vocabulary and Pac-Man was even the subject of an irritating song called "Pac-Man Fever" that made the *Billboard* Top Ten. Nolan Bushnell's persona set the stage for other videogame entrepreneurs who learned it was OK to be full of Bushnell brag, bluster, and bull. The arcade scene, created by the release of Pong in the small Bay Area bar, would continue to be a force once the industry recovered. The cool hangout aspect of arcades, however, began to diminish in the mid 1990s. The VCS didn't die because of the crash, either. It survived because a small but passionate niche of gamers still bought Atari cartridges. Straightforward and utilitarian, the machine made games easy for everyone to use. You just popped in a cartridge, grabbed your joystick, and gritted your teeth for the roller coaster ride of your life. Actually, a very weakened Atari still made games for the VCS until 1992.

But with E.T., Atari was confronted with a tough lesson from which they really did not learn. Games are not about slapping a badly rendered movie poster on a piece of plastic in return for a slick licensing deal. While film can influence the artistic process, games are about intricately, lovingly designed computer code. Those in charge, whether it was Ross or Tramiel or any of the business-men who took the reins, knew nothing of how precisely to keep the business going, about how and when to release a new console, about when a new game could help to sell an older console, about when stodgy technology could be made to look as elating as new technol-ogy, or about how to market to the media the heroic individuals who invented games.

Yet a company in Japan knew. They seemed to know it instinc-tively, even though in the real life game of international business, they could be the worst kinds of bullies.

4.

OF MONKEYS, MARIO, AND MIYAMOTO

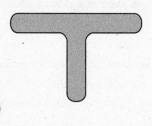

As a boy, he was not yet considered a genius. He was simply a curious, round-faced kid with an artistic bent, one of millions in Japan. He loved exploring, once finding himself in a cave within Flour Mountain, not far from his home. Inside, the kid with the wide, open smile was as nervous and gunned up as Tom Sawyer, as he wandered alone in the half darkness, among the stalactites and drops of water that echoed eerily on the limestone floor. On treks with the Boy Scouts, he loved watching the flora and fauna high on Mount Rokko, as the thick forest gave way to a shimmering lake. Awestruck, he took it all in, bending down to examine mushrooms and squirrels and flowers. At the time, he knew nothing of videogames, for videogames had not yet been invented. Nor did his family own a TV set. But he did love to invent his own toys, like his own driving game based on an electronic one he had seen at an entertainment center. He re-created the game at home with a belt and a steering wheel. And he was obsessed by making model airplanes, sometimes blowing them up with firecrackers.

If he knew of Nintendo at all, it was through the company's most popular item at the time, an old-school deck of cards used to play hanafuda. They were flower cards representing each of the year's twelve months. Sometimes they were used for gambling, but also for a variety of card matching games. More than cards, young Shigeru Miyamoto was fascinated by the outdoors, by every nook and cranny in his small town of Sonobe, a suburb of fifteen thousand people in the Funai District of Kyoto. Near him for inspiration were the caves and waterfalls of Ruri Canyon and the ruins of a sprawling 350-year-old castle.

As with Ralph Baer, the showman in Miyamoto staged puppet shows. His father, a strict schoolteacher, didn't encourage this artistic side. Instead, he wanted Miyamoto to keep his nose to the grindstone in all his class work. But his mother encouraged drawings and paintings inspired by the outdoors and movies. He loved the movies of the day, like Disney's feature-length animated classics, everything from *Peter Pan* to *Snow White*, from *Fantasia* to *Alice in Wonderland*. He also went gaga over the famous monsters of filmland, like King Kong and Godzilla. Shigeru Miyamoto was Every Kid, the kind you watch in the Spielberg movies. And he kept that childlike sense of wonder close to his soul as he aged. As an adult, he was able to communicate that amazement, if not verbally, then through artwork and through story. Uncannily, he would be able to touch the souls of children of every race throughout the world. And he would do this over and over again.

Miyamoto was nothing like Hiroshi Yamauchi, the man whose family owned Nintendo and who would become Miyamoto's boss and mentor as the two revolutionized gaming. You would not want to cross Hiroshi Yamauchi. As a child, the young Yamauchi was aware that his family was well off and that his parents rubbed shoulders with the elite members of Japanese society. Nonetheless, he was made to work—hard. Too young to go to battle in World War II, Yamauchi worked in a military factory instead of accomplishing his goal of studying law. As was the case with most who endured the tragic events of 1945, the bombing of Japan seared his heart and mind. The few films and videos of him rarely show Yamauchi cracking a smile. Sometimes, he looks like he really wants to laugh. But he holds it back, as if laughter would give any competitor the upper hand against him. He would not achieve his destiny—becoming the richest man in Japan—by acting all open and naïve, like Tom Hanks in *Forrest Gump*. Even as a child in prep school, he was a serious fellow. When he took the reins of Nintendo, he did so only when he was promised that his cousin would be fired and that he, the great Hiroshi, would be the only family member working at the company. Early on, other executives saw him as just another product of nepotism. At the young age of twenty-one, he wasn't taken seriously as the company president. This lack of respect toughened his hide even more. Within a year or so of beginning his reign, Yamauchi was called merciless, imperious, and downright nasty, after he fired a slew of career men who held a long and difficult labor strike.

His first big success came with the 1959 licensing of Disney characters, which would be placed on the back of American-style playing cards. Later ventures lost huge amounts of money—like a line of instant rice and a love hotel, where rooms were rented by the hour. When the card business suffered a precipitous decline, Yamauchi became dedicated to diversifying, and he was more than willing to experiment. Because the Disney cards had done so well, children's entertainment wasn't far from his radar. In the mid-1960s, upon seeing his self-effacing inventor Gunpei Yokoi's extendable claw, which the engineer had made just for fun, Yamauchi decided to try the toy business.

When he saw the claw, Yamauchi became excited and pursed his lips—about as close to a truly open smile as he ever came. In a moment of synchronicity with his designers, Yamauchi greenlit the 1966 Ultra Hand, an extending arm that gripped the three colorful balls included in the package. It sold like Hula hoops—1.2 million units—putting Nintendo into the black with a brand-new business. In 1969, Nintendo branded and marketed the perfect-for-hippies Love Tester, a battery-operated device that, at first blush, looked like something a CIA agent would use for torture. Instead, it buzzed as it supposedly gauged compatibility between partners. Both of these products went along with the Yamauchi theory of manufacturing, which the handsome, impeccably dressed Yokoi espoused over and over again. Unabashedly, Yokoi said, "The Nintendo way of adapting technology is not to look for the state of the art but to utilize mature technology that can be mass-produced cheaply."

Yamauchi saw the potential in videogames as soon as he saw Baer's Magnavox Odyssey, which Nintendo licensed and distributed in Japan in 1974.* The dashing Yokoi created an ingenious portable line of games simply called Game & Watch, starting in 1980 and continuing until 1987. The first in a series of about sixty (which would include Mario, Popeye, and Snoopy models) was a portable alarm clock with a game called Ball that let you feel some of the extreme joys and defeats of being a juggler. Although the humorous character's schnoz is Jimmy Durante–sized and there's no sound whatsoever, the game let you imagine being in a fast-paced circus, the crowd yelling for more as you deftly kept the tossed balls in the air, even while you stood on one foot. The caffeinated announcer spewed somewhat suggestively in a commercial: "They're pocket power! They tell you the score! And even the time!" Seeing that

---

* In a few years, Magnavox would sue Nintendo for patent infringement. Nintendo would countersue, trying to invalidate Baer's patent. Nintendo lost and had to continue paying royalties to Magnavox.

advertisement on Saturday morning TV, you'd forget your Kellogg's to continue playing until your stomach groaned and gurgled from hunger. You didn't need no stinkin' sustenance: You had games. You could be anything or anyone.

But it would be an early Nintendo arcade offering that would put the card maker on the map as a serious, inventive entrant in the nascent videogame space. It was one that Miyamoto would revamp and reinvent. But it wouldn't have happened if Miyamoto had found a job in the industry he first loved, comic books. Although Shigeru was searching for a job as a manga comics artist, a friend of his father was acquainted with Yamauchi. An interview at Nintendo's headquarters was set up immediately.

"Why should I hire you?" asked the bespectacled boss. He looked imposing. Everything in the office did, even his big desk. While Yamauchi had agreed to the interview as a friendly gesture, he felt he needed more engineers, not the artist and cartoon maker that the young graduate from Kanazawa Munici College so obviously wanted to be.

From a bag, Miyamoto produced some wooden hangers with elephant heads on them. Then, he showed off a sketch for an alarm clock with an amusement park theme. Yamauchi saw some promise, especially because Miyamoto was honest and enthusiastic.

Yamauchi nodded, but he didn't crack a smile. "If I hire you," he said, "it's because you have the talent, not because someone I know recommended you. The things you made are quite good." Yamauchi asked if Miyamoto could come up with a revolutionary playing card game, something big, something no one had ever done. Miyamoto didn't say he could. But he didn't say he couldn't.

After making Miyamoto wait for one month, Yamauchi had an underling hire him over the phone with the words "We hear you have an idea for a revolutionary card game." Miyamoto began his working days as a lowly apprentice in Nintendo's planning department, toiling quietly as an artist at the company's Kyoto headquarters for three years. Without that revolutionary card game, he was assigned to spice up the artwork for three Disney-themed board games featuring Mickey, Donald, Chip 'n Dale, and Snow White, old games he had played as a child. He liked what he was doing, sort of. But there was no real challenge to it. Yet he didn't have the temerity to ask for more.

In mid-1980, Yamauchi approached Miyamoto. It was a short conversation. But it was one that would change Miyamoto's life forever.

"What do you think of videogames?"

"Well, sir. I like them a lot." Miyamoto began to speak sincerely and enthusiastically, telling Yamauchi more than he needed to know. At one point, the young artist said, "The games are good. I like Pong. I like Breakout. But they should be more like movies or books. They should tell a story. They—"

Yamauchi interrupted. A look of concern came over his face. He didn't have time for a long, one-sided conversation. "You may know we have Radar Scope games for the arcade. It has not done well." In fact, the game, released earlier in 1980, had done abysmally.*

Since Nintendo had made three thousand Radar Scope coin-op games, they wanted to salvage what they could of the failure. Yamauchi had one question. "Can you make Radar Scope better?"

Under the supervision of Yokoi, Miyamoto tried to improve the

---

* Nintendo's previous effort, a clone of Space Invaders called Space Fever, lacked ingenuity. It was as if Nintendo didn't have the smarts to work in videogames in any way, shape, or form. Only Sheriff, a Wild West game where one lone lawman had to fight against sixteen bandits, was better. While it was slow moving, it offered a sense of the Hollywood Western. After indulging, you wanted to swagger like John Wayne and quote lines from *True Grit*, like "Young fella, if you're looking for trouble, I'll accommodate ya."

military action game. He was unexcited about the project, to say the least. The young artist found the game lacked style and substance. Not only was the crosshatched grid daunting to him, the graphics seemed more like blips on a screen than ships. Plus, he didn't like the idea of war games. In his mind, the best movies were about humanity, where the hero saved the girl, where miraculous fantasies replaced the mundane routine, where players could fit in and rule their destinies—at least electronically, for twenty or thirty minutes at a time. With Radar Scope, Miyamoto felt there was little to engage players in the way of drama and, more important, soulfulness. So, with pen in hand, Miyamoto drew from both his daydreams and his love for Hollywood to create a new game that would eventually be called Donkey Kong. At first, he thought he could make the game work with Popeye, a license that Nintendo had used with success in the Game & Watch product. Miyamoto worked on it tirelessly, drawing sketches and thinking of a possible story to include Olive Oyl and Bluto. When the contract with Popeye's producer and syndicator, King Features, was delayed, Miyamoto began to invent his own characters based closely on Popeye and other pop culture classics he'd loved so much as a child. He worked with a mix of fear and joy and all the elation that comes with having something to prove. More than anything, he wanted to be a valued Nintendo employee, not just an artist slaving away in obscurity. Yamauchi quickly saw the potential in what Miyamoto had done. It didn't take much convincing for the boss to come on board—especially since that Popeye contract wasn't going to be signed for some time to come. Yamauchi greenlit Miyamoto's game, which would be placed into the cabinets that held Radar Scope.

In the North American territories where Nintendo had gambled and opened satellite offices, the arrival of Donkey Kong arcade machines befuddled everyone who had toiled night and day to make the subpar Radar Scope a success. No one knew what the name meant. The guys in charge of sales and distribution, Ron Judy and Al Stone, were nonplussed. In fact, when Al Stone saw how the game played, he literally walked out of the room. They all feared that Nintendo, especially in America, was doomed: Donkey Kong was too Japanese, too foreign, too strange, too wacky, to become a hit.

Even Minoru Arakawa, Yamauchi's MIT-educated son-in-law, didn't approve of Miyamoto's brainchild. Yamauchi had trusted Arakawa enough to bring him into the family, agreeing to let him marry his daughter Yoko. Then, he bullied Yamauchi until he agreed to start Nintendo's North American division. In the late 1970s, Yoko and Mino struggled at first, in Vancouver, but they never asked for money from their families. Arakawa, who bought into profitable Vancouver real estate ventures for Nintendo, eventually amassed twenty-seven acres in Redmond, Washington, to house the company's headquarters. Then he purchased thirty-three acres more. Nintendo of America would remain there for decades to come.

If Yamauchi wanted everyone in the United States to push Donkey Kong, Arakawa and his motley crew would indeed suck it up and do their best to make the machine a hit. Arakawa himself wasn't above getting his hands dirty. When he met with distributors, he felt certain that some of them were connected to the Mafia. He would sing the praises of a game like Donkey Kong even as he saw the barrel of a gun flashing in a holster beneath an unbuttoned Italian blazer. Rattled, he would find the gumption to soldier on, always striving to make a deal.

Even as Donkey Kong went to market, Arakawa was leery of the fact that a lowly apprentice was making the game that would fit into the Radar Scope shell. Despite the doubts at Nintendo in the United States, the elder Yamauchi was forceful and unyielding: He believed the game was stellar, that Miyamoto was creative, if not a genius, and that Donkey Kong would be a big hit.

Yamauchi was right. Everyone else was wrong.

Miyamoto, Donkey Kong, and Nintendo would be responsible for revitalizing the videogame industry and for making Japan the world's most revolutionary publisher of videogames. Donkey Kong, which was released in 1981, ushered in a new kind of frantic but precision-oriented gaming for which arcade heads seemed to be longing. In its first year, Donkey Kong made $180 million for Nintendo. While most coin-operated games had a short life span, of a few months, Donkey Kong earned another $100 million in year two. The videogame industry wasn't just burgeoning once again. It was coming back big-time, thanks to Donkey Kong (and another Japanese arcade game, Frogger). With 255 levels to play, Ms. Pac-Man certainly aided the resurgence too. More than 110,000 Ms. Pac-Man machines were distributed throughout the states.

Seemingly instantly, the self-effacing Miyamoto had become a star of sorts. In fact, Nintendo was one of the first game companies to see the wisdom in showcasing its lead designer as a media hero. Within a year, the young, childlike Miyamoto would be the face of Nintendo.

The instructions on many of the machines began with "Save the Lady from Donkey Kong." While the characters in later years would have more backstory than Spock and Kirk in the *Star Trek* series, they were fairly generic in the insanely difficult game, the first running and jumping game ever made. The powder blue and brown case coaxed players near, just as the graphics of the giant gorilla were detailed enough to show a toothy, satisfied ape who would often become dour, frowning, and angry as he tossed barrels and constantly grabbed the Lady from Jumpman, just as the sad little guy was about to rescue her.

Donkey Kong, which introduced the soon-to-be-ubiquitous Mario the plumber only as Jumpman, a carpenter, was Nintendo's bestselling game though the first half of 1983.*

For a gamer, the result was like a compelling TV show that continued from week to week. Each screen was the ultimate cliffhanger, and Jumpman was kind of like your own personal Jack Bauer, seemingly finishing the job, only to be daunted yet again. On-screen graphics showed his poor pink heart breaking in two tragically, over and over again. He might never get the girl. It was so like life, it hurt.

In real life, Miyamoto was still all about going off the beaten path in the quest for adventure. He would walk down a sidewalk and turn down an alley or head through a pitch-black tunnel and imagine it held ghosts or goblins and, at the end, a treasure. His Mario games were full of flights of fancy and, with those ever present mushrooms, perhaps odes to the magic of drugs in *Alice in Wonderland*. As the years passed, Mario would sprout wings and fly or swim into great murky depths or fly through space, boldly going where no Mario had gone before. Beyond appealing to kids, Miyamoto felt he was making games for the many adults like him who sometimes saw the world as children. Those same adults went to the Disney animated films and the swashbuckling adventures of Errol Flynn, or today still love everything from *Star Wars*, which features men fighting with swordlike light sabers, to *Scrubs*, which showcases grown men as doctors who act like children when they aren't treating patients.

After Donkey Kong's success, Miyamoto and the engineers at Nintendo continued to innovate throughout the 1980s, and much of what they put on the shelves seemed sparkling and new to gamers. No one could the stop the Nintendo revolution. Its Famicom console started slow. But soon doe-eyed kids lined up and camped out to buy

---

* During the design phase, Miyamoto originally called the character that would become Mario "Mr. Video." Like Alfred Hitchcock and the manga comic artists of the time who inspired him, Miyamoto hoped that his signature Mr. Video would appear in brief cameos in many games.

it in Japan—even though some units were flawed and broken and had to be recalled. Donkey Kong ruled the arcades, and when Universal Studios sued because the gorilla looked like King Kong, they lost because they no longer had the rights to the famous movie beast. And then came the Famicon makeover, the Nintendo Entertainment System, an agile juggernaut that could not be halted, not by Atari or by any other console maker.

In 1985 Nintendo mined a vein of gold with that console. During its design and manufacturing period, there had been some serious trepidation within the company due to the recent video-game crash that had decimated publishers and made retailers reluctant to stock games. Who would buy it? Was the $199 sticker price too much for consumers to pay? Perhaps, but what if Super Mario Bros., their new platform game, was added to the package? Would that be enough? Bolstered by the success of Donkey Kong in the arcades, Yamauchi was certain that the console would be successful the world over. He felt the crash, though deep and worrisome, was part of a cycle and that games would rise again, renewed and reinvigorated. In the United States, the Nintendo Entertainment System featured some of the best offerings ever created in the Golden Age of Videogames in the 1980s. Its blocky eight-bit graphics were splendid, especially considering the machine had a mere two kilobytes of RAM to show them off. Really, it was the games more than the system that pushed the envelope, so much so that the machine would sell nearly sixty-two million units over time.

The aptly but clumsily named Jumpman was renamed Mario and given the working class job of ace plumber. Super Mario Bros. had kids forking over tons of cash, so much so that more than forty million copies hit living rooms and bedrooms, making it the second biggest selling Nintendo game of all time.

There you were in Mario's Mushroom Kingdom in a psychedelic war against scaly, lizardy monsters like the grumpy Bowser.

And Miyamoto outdid Alice in one respect. The Mario mushrooms were stranger and wilder than the fungi that Alice consumed while being watched by the hookah-smoking caterpillar. Orange ones with green dots gave you an extra life. Super Mushrooms let you grow into a giant (a fine thing for a small guy). Fire Flowers let you pitch great balls of conflagration. The Starman, like an aboral-armed doctor on house call, gave you health when you were wounded. You'd creep into green pipes and castles, never quite knowing where you'd emerge—in a dank cave where enormous Venus flytraps nipped at your loins, or within the wet, navy depths where white-tentacled jellyfish tried to sting you. And you even saved the girl, something you might never have done in real life. What a trip it was—sheer, empowering fantasy, where dreams came true so lucidly, if only for a while. Paul McCartney was so enthralled by the game, he said he would rather meet Mr. Miyamoto than visit Mount Fuji.

Or take the story and action within another Miyamoto classic, the bucolic The Legend of Zelda. In this console series Miyamoto's particular kind of genius seemed to rival the mastery of a George Lucas or a John Huston. As Miyamoto sat down to make the game, he recalled with almost photographic accuracy the paths he had traversed as a Boy Scout, how the forest looked through the evergreen needles, how the vision of the crystal blue lake at the top of the mountain engulfed his senses. With the brilliant Takashi Tezuka, who came to Nintendo in 1984, Miyamoto created a mysterious world of caves, waterfalls, forests, and artifacts that was part Peter Pan, part Zorro, and part Robin Hood. Zelda, the stunningly pretty princess of the fictional Hyrule, was named after Zelda Fitzgerald, the wild, energetic flapper who so entranced literary icon F. Scott Fitzgerald that he became obsessed with her. With its many monsters and short, haiku-like instructions, The Legend of Zelda made you feel like a hero. Even when life in the real world was full of unemployment or chronic illness, you could always wield a sharp and wizardly sword as the strapping, green-suited Link, to save someone who needed your help. In Zelda, you really could feel strong and victorious—no matter your age. The experience in the Zelda series was so deep and enchanting for so many that it spawned a book of essays called *The Legend of Zelda and Philosophy: I Link, Therefore I Am.*

Because Miyamoto was very right brain oriented, he had to learn how to manage and organize his time. But, always anxious to please, he adapted quickly. Promoted to the rank of producer, Miyamoto worked on multiple games at once, some taking more than a year and a half to finish. As many as a score of people would work on each game. The teams preferred to work late into the night during the increasingly brutal crunch times. They would go home past midnight and fall exhausted into bed, only to get to Nintendo again by eleven a.m. and do it all over again.

Once Nintendo became the "it" console maker and developer, Yamauchi and Arakawa became insatiable. They charged outrageous licensing fees to companies seeking to produce games for the hit console. A Nintendo contract of the time stated that the company had to approve the game—with no hard deadline and in its own good time—before it was given a green light for distribution. And they had the right, if they saw fit, to insert their own promotional materials into each package. Then the game's publisher had to purchase at least ten thousand cartridges from Nintendo, which Nintendo or one of their manufacturing arms produced. From 1983 onward, independent game studios worldwide complained about Nintendo royalty fees, which could peak at an astronomical 20 percent—and eventually led to a congressional investigation led by the drawling Texas Democratic representative Bob Eckhardt. But Nintendo was of the mind, as executives would verbalize in closed door meetings with potential licensees, "If you want to play, you have to pay." Nintendo was sued constantly for unfair and monopolistic trade practices. The idea of going to court never bothered Yamauchi too much—as long as Nintendo won in the end. And Yamauchi really didn't need to worry. Nintendo had terrific lawyers in the United States, like Howard Lincoln, who was a bulldog in and out of the courtroom.

Inside the Japanese offices, Yamauchi ruled with an iron fist. He was not a gamer by any means. But he could smell a hit. At the end, it was up to Yamauchi whether a game would see the light of day. Game designers and engineers cowered when he was scheduled to look at one of their inventions. Everyone, including Miyamoto, worried about his approval to the point of hand wringing. When support came, it was better than sex with a dream partner. It validated the engineer. He felt worthy, accepted, a real man. It was something that money couldn't buy. A thumbs-up from Yamauchi was validation, and in validation there was strength to go on to the next project, to start the crazed design process all over again. And if Yamauchi shook his head with a no, it was devastating, belittling, a sickening belly blow from which it took weeks to recover.

In the United States, Nintendo launched a kind of fanzine that touted tips on how to play its games. Kids could also call a hotline for information about upcoming offerings. The enterprise was helmed not by a journalist but by a marketer, named Gail Tilden. Its purpose was not to report objective news, but to sell more games by saying nice things about Nintendo and Mr. Miyamoto. Because it was successful, this was the sad template for much of gaming "journalism" for many years to come. Videogame writers of the time were also dyed-in-the-wool fans who looked at the company with subjective eyes. Very few had hard news backgrounds; they didn't need any semblance of objectivity when press releases and tips about how to play were all kids who played seemed to want. Not many asked the tough questions, for fear of being cut off by Nintendo. The long and short of it was that Nintendo presented itself as the new Disney.

Anyone who wasn't completely on board was deemed to be an enemy of the company. There was little transparency. To the contrary, there was a concrete wall so thick even Superman's X-ray vision couldn't permeate its molecules.

Miyamoto was constantly lauded in *Nintendo Power* magazine as a hero, a star, a videogame character come to life, who could do no wrong. The well-kept secret of the time was that the shaggy-pated Miyamoto had as many as two dozen people working on games with him. But no matter. The not-so-subtle marketing word from Nintendo was clear: Mr. Miyamoto would save you, your very essence, if only you played his games. Miyamoto's plate was full, and it became fuller as his star rose and he was required to make personal appearances and do interviews. When Miyamoto couldn't take the pressure of helping to make so many games at one time, he began to haunt the pachinko gambling parlors of Kyoto. It was a way to blow off steam, to relax after a long day at work, "to escape the cycle of worries I had." It likely wasn't just one simple anxiety, which he had pushed aside in the name of game making. It was the confluence of many, not the least of which was Nintendo's constant demand to have supremely successful games, one after the other. Yet pachinko began to become a habit, probably one at which the game designer began to lose money. Gambling was no longer a sweet release. Just as Donkey Kong took quarter after quarter from the determined gamer, pachinko took coin after coin from Miyamoto. After some time and effort, he substituted exercise in order to eschew the vice.

Just as Miyamoto was lauded as the human face of Nintendo and the man who helped to save the videogame industry, Yamauchi was despised by many as the superpowerful puppeteer behind the scenes. His attitude served the company well, and his commandment that there should be space in the game universe for "one strong company and the rest weak" has been true throughout the history of videogame companies. But it alienated his family. And no one ever got the impression that Yamauchi was truly a happy man. He was too caught up in the constant hope and drive to be number one to have the time to enjoy life fully and completely . . . or even to save the girl. It happens in other industries, so much so that it's almost considered cliché. Chicken mogul Frank Perdue was so business-driven that he had no family life and his wife eventually divorced him. Henry Ford was a complete workaholic as chief engineer with Edison Illuminating Company long before he began his auto manufacturing business.

At least Miyamoto had his art and his family to save him. Once he got home in the evening, he would not think of videogames—most of the time. He could sit in his garden at night and still be transported to that world that tantalized him as a child.

In the end, the often sullen Yamauchi only had his company to comfort him—and his endless love for the next dollar. He brought Nintendo and all of its weight home with him. His stomach would tie up in knots at the smallest error, and his moods swung as wildly as the stock market. He had taken over the family business, and like a loyal soldier, when called to duty, he made Nintendo the best videogame company in the world. He made people of all languages and many nations happy. Sullen as he could be, he was responsible for entertaining the millions of children of the world. Yet the great Yamauchi was never really at ease. Yes, Nintendo controlled nearly 90 percent of the worldwide console game market. Consumers purchased sixty-two million units of the NES console, far outpacing other systems of the day and eclipsing sales of the Atari 2600, which sold half as much in its heyday. Yes, Nintendo's games were engineering feats that stoked many a gamer's imagination. But Yamauchi always wanted more and more.

Yet he could take solace in the fact that Miyamoto would always think the best of him for giving him his big break. For that reason alone, Miyamoto would always think of his boss as a good man.

Yamauchi and Miyamoto, the oddest of bedfellows, made video-games popular in a way they had never been before. Mario, with that bush of a mustache, was on his way to becoming more recogniz-able than Mickey Mouse, no small feat indeed. Certainly, creating a star character was something Atari had never done, perhaps because Bushnell considered himself the star. (To be fair, no one else has had success with mascots, with the exception of Namco's Pac-Man and Sega's Sonic.) The plumber was so beloved by kids that they would remember him as they grew into college students and adults. Bob Hoskins would play Mario in a live-action Super Mario Bros. movie, which didn't evoke a smidgeon of that essential sense of wonder. Better was *The Wizard*, a movie about an intense, joyful videogame competition featuring Super Mario Bros. 3—even be-fore the game was released to the public. Beyond film, Mario smiled in a "Got Milk?" ad, toiled as the star of a syndicated weekly TV series, and was the first videogame celebrity to be memorialized in wax at Madame Tussaud's museum. Adults, still wistful, would later buy Mario games for their kids; after all, they were brilliantly de-signed, and they were never lewd, crude, or demeaning. Not only were Mario games smart, trustworthy pieces of popular culture, they made Miyamoto the Walt Disney of games.

Yet there would always be a mystery surrounding Miyamoto; while he had a fine sense of humor and a love for so much US cul-ture, he could not speak English. So he spoke eloquently through games, which obsessed him. Nintendo mined this inscrutability to portray him, not as a mad scientist ever at work in his lab, but as more of a glad scientist who toiled so intensely, he didn't have time to learn another language or talk intimately with the press. He would speak, but only under tightly controlled conditions. The occasional long-form interview still bubbled up over the years—notably, Nick Paumgarten's 2010 *New Yorker* profile—but those occasions were very much exceptions to the Miyamoto rules. For the most part, writers got twenty minutes or half an hour with the legend, during which they might be able to submit a single tough question (if they dared even that). Fans would be left to muse upon a tiny crumb of fact, while everyone in the world awaited eagerly the next version of Mario or Zelda.

In 1986, even as it held court upon the highest hill in the most magnificent of fortified castles, the Nintendo empire needed more. As they looked down upon the videogame world, there was one game Nintendo needed, one game Yamauchi coveted, one game Arakawa secretly yearned to own. It was a simple game, an addicting game, one that would herald the biggest-selling videogame series of all time, one that is played to this day and probably will be for decades to come. Its story is also one of the saddest, most frustrating dramas in entertainment history.

5.

FALLING BLOCKS, RISING FORTUNES

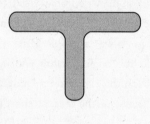

Nineteen eighty-six. In the United States, it was the year of the yuppies, of overspending everywhere and the heavy haze of Macanudos emanating from private cigar bars. Masters of the Universe, the moniker Tom Wolfe gave to CEOs in the pages of *Rolling Stone* magazine, described the new videogame honchos perfectly. Nolan Bushnell had flamed out and sold out, but he still had a swagger as he flew the first President Bush around in his Learjet. Nintendo's Yamauchi ruled the videogame roost with an iron fist. Coleco, which began as a maker of cheesy leather goods, hit it big with their Atari-inspired game consoles and then imploded when their Adam line of PCs didn't work when you got them home.

By 1986, the videogame world had recovered from its brief but grim recession, so much so that consoles and games accounted for a healthy $450 million in sales. The tally might have been much more, but Nintendo's innovative Disk System, released only in Japan, featured games that could be hacked and copied. The smirking, hacking pirates of videogames went *ho-ho-ho* as offerings like Miyamoto's The Legend of Zelda could be had for free if you had the right skills or the right connections.

Much like the early days of the music industry, when R&B stars and master bluesmen received a Cadillac in lieu of millions in royalties, the videogame world was still full of carpetbaggers and snake oil salesmen. These Bastards of the Universe were game developer manipulators extraordinaire. And young Alexey Pajitnov, the man responsible for the biggest game phenomenon since Miyamoto's Super Mario Bros., was about to be ripped off. If this had happened to a US developer like Nolan Bushnell, he would have yelled and moaned about unscrupulous business practices that were akin to torture.

But Alexey Pajitnov, born in Soviet era Moscow, to middle class parents who were writers, wasn't like that. Pajitnov was steeped in popular art from an early age, and he respected it. His mother, a well-regarded journalist whose focus was movies, took the child to many of the screenings she attended and the yearly Moscow Film Festival, as well. Pajitnov liked the action-oriented fare like James Bond as well as the intellectual on-screen machinations of the German cinema's auteurs. While he and his family enjoyed viewing American culture from a distance, he was throughout his young life immersed in the theories of communism and the constant political repercussions of the Cold War. He and his family were raised to believe in the Soviet idea of common ownership, not capitalism and the American dream. While he was leery and even cynical about communism, it was these Russian tenets that would help him deal more easily with what would happen when the most alluring game in the batch of ten games he was coding began to take off.

In school, Pajitnov gravitated to math because it offered a

constant stream of puzzles for him to solve. He loved riddles and puzzles in general, including math games like Moonlanding and board games like Dungeons & Dragons (although the Russian translation of the time was terrible). Computers held his interest, but he didn't exactly care for some of the drier, more technical aspects. He liked to muse upon the psychology of computing, what made people do certain things and why. Pajitnov considered himself a hacker, someone who took to coding for the pure, unadulterated art of it, like Steve "Slug" Russell and his pals had done so many years ago with Spacewar! The idea of money for art was not exactly an insult to the programmer, but he did not enter the world of coding with any thought of becoming rich. In his early twenties, he was already working in the area of artificial intelligence at the Dorodnitsyn Computing Centre, part of the Russian Academy of Sciences, which was created in 1724 after a decree from the warring reformist Peter the Great. As Pajitnov moved through its corridors daily, he admired the expanse of the sprawling building, its tall ceilings, even its drafty corridors. He did not care for the pretense of the academy as a place for the Russian elite to gather in order to preen themselves. Certainly, he did not think of himself as special.

Pajitnov had desk space in an echoing old hall, but he rarely used it. He spent most of his time at the computer table, where he placed his belongings and books, and smoked the strongest Russian cigarettes and drank the strongest tea he could find when evening approached. Sometimes, he'd spend sixty to seventy hours at the computer. He was that fascinated. But sometimes, he let loose, getting together with the team to drink hard. Those were the rare nights of debauchery, however. Pajitnov would often say to his cohorts, "Drinking is not compatible with working. For that you need fresh head."

With that clear mind, he kept going back to a game he played as a teenager, one that cost about 35 kopecks, or 40 cents. He had discovered the game back in the seventies, when he'd wandered into a toy store and begun looking at a dusty box of pentominoes. He pulled it off the shelf and opened it. Inside were seven plastic shapes that could be placed together to form a rectangle when he put them back in the box properly. The pentominoes game was likely based on the theories of polyominoes, first introduced as recreational mathematics dissection problems in *Fairy Chess* magazine in the 1930s, and later popularized by USC engineering professor and puzzle columnist Solomon Wolf Golomb in 1953. The game was always in the back of Pajitnov's mind, and with the dawn of PCs, it was in the forefront again. He had seen bootleg versions of arcade games on computers. He thought, "I'm quite disappointed with the banality of ideas. The graphics fascinate me, like the Mario games. But they don't keep me interested." As if he were under a spell, he kept thinking about those shapes in that box, daydreaming about them. His mind was turning into a jigsaw puzzle–making machine. The opened toy store box was like Pandora's, one that revealed little demons who would coax, nudge, and bully Pajitnov's thoughts.

In May 1984, he took a few long drags from his cigarette, bitched inwardly about the lack of tobacco in the wrapper, and coded at the old Elektronika 60 for so long that time seemed to stand still. He did this for two weeks, each night leaving the lab just before one a.m. to catch the last subway ride home. Sometimes, he was so stoked that the night got away from him and he couldn't doze off, let alone sleep deeply. In the game he conceived, a kind of tight minimalism reigned. There was no timer, no way to score, no way to level up, no sounds, no color. It was just the hypnotic beauty of shapes falling silently, which, through the computer keyboard, had to be put together in rows at the bottom. Soon, his colleagues gathered around, mystified yet curious. The game was more than compelling. Beyond the skill needed to organize the pieces in rows, playing was like watching a soft rain on the water. It was peaceful, relaxing.

"But what are the rules?" asked Dmitry Pavlovsky, a coworker who had made some games on his own as well, and who was interested in working with Pajitnov.

"There are no rules yet. You just fit the shapes together."

Everyone in the computer center who played became an admirer. Pajitnov quietly confided to Pavlovsky, "I really think I have something."

Through Pavlovsky, Pajitnov met with a Vadim Gerasimov, a young computer genius who was interning at the academy. Pajitnov asked the sixteen-year-old to make a PC version of his new creation.

"So what will you do with it then?" asked Gerasimov.

"Perhaps sell it," said Pavlovsky.

"Here? In the Soviet Union?" asked Gerasimov. The idea of individuals selling their own product was still highly irregular in the USSR. But he, too, loved the game, and made the personal computer version in less than three weeks. During the next month, the game was refined with sound, better graphics, and a way to keep score. They put some other games on a disk as well, including a clone of Xonix called Antic. Some say it was Gerasimov who copied the disk and passed it around. Others say Pajitnov made copies for colleagues, who made copies for friends, who made copies for their friends. Whatever the case, versions were being passed out all around Moscow. Tetris was the game people played far more than the others. The frenzy fed on itself. Copies were distributed and shared and then copied and shared again. They moved past the borders of Moscow to St. Petersburg and beyond the USSR itself. Not one was sold, not yet, not for even a ruble. Bootlegs of Tetris spread into Europe. For those in the know, it was the most alluring game they had ever played. And it cost them nothing. What a deal. "So much for selling it," ruminated Pavlovsky.

Pajitnov just shrugged his shoulders. "It would have been illegal to sell it anyway." He had done something good, he thought. He had made thousands of people who had computers happy. It was almost enough.

Word of the game's brilliance began to spread around the world, again among those in the know. To understand the full story of Tetris's decades-long success, you have to know one other player who was almost religiously enlightened when he saw the game: Henk Rogers. A young Dutch entrepreneur, and a game maker as well, Rogers had followed love from Hawaii to Japan. He was assertive and aggressive, but with his big smile that turned into easy laughter, he was eminently likeable all the same. In college in Hawaii, he and others had formed the ARRG, Alternative Realties Recreation Group, which was primarily devoted to playing lengthy games of Dungeons & Dragons, occasionally from Friday night right through Monday morning. With Black Onyx for the PC, Rogers made the first popular role playing game in Japan. Even though it was a mere 256 kilobytes in size, Black Onyx, named for a gem because Rogers's father was in the gem business, was packed with variety. It offered players fifty different monster heads and thirty bodies from which to choose.

Because Rogers had played Go with his father as a child, he had become something of an expert. Over the years, Rogers had become a Go fanatic, so much so that it extended to his game publishing venture. His company, Bullet-Proof Software, was the world's largest producer of Go games. Rogers tried to convince Nintendo to license Go with him, but he at first reached a brick wall in the form of one Hiroshi Imanishi, a trusted colleague of Yamauchi who was schooled as a lawyer.

Rogers shook his head and told his wife, Akemi, "It was the biggest blow-off ever."

"Wait. Hold on," replied Akemi. She rummaged through some newspapers and came up with a local magazine. "I read in this that Mr. Yamauchi plays Go!"

Indeed, Nintendo's Yamauchi was obsessed by Go. Rogers felt a fresh hope course through his veins. He began plotting, scheming. He looked at his Commodore 64 version of the strategy game, figuring that it could be moved to the Nintendo system fairly easily. The only drawback was creating a new algorithm for the Nintendo console. But the mathematics could be dealt with. Rogers sent a fax to the Nintendo boss. Brashly, he offered to play Go against Yamauchi, who was a master. Go was not merely a game for Yamauchi. It was something real men played, for within playing Go, there was the same kind of strategizing that proved one's acumen and mettle in the realm of business. On the next day, Rogers got a reply that read, "Mr. Yamauchi will see you tomorrow." He was so excited that he felt like dancing all day long.

Rogers quickly readied his pitch. He decided against bringing a translator, believing that much could be lost with other people attempting to decipher the language. Shortly after the meeting convened, the two made their moves in Go, and the tension in the room was high. Rogers was good, carefully thinking a step or two ahead. But he was not that good. Even though Yamauchi won, the standoffish Nintendo chief warmed to Rogers. Then they talked business. The hard-nosed businessman didn't mince words with Rogers.

"You want Go? I can't give you any programmers," said Yamauchi.

"I don't need programmers. I have them," said Rogers. "I need money to make the game."

Yamauchi arched his eyebrows. He had never before given money to an outside company to make a game.

"How much?"

Rogers, who was wound up and ready, let loose. "Mr. Yamauchi. This is going to be big. It can't fail. People love Go, especially in Japan." It was his nature to become excited and talk too much. He didn't want to do that with Yamauchi, who was an incredibly tough businessman with little time for bluster. Rogers had to think fast. Yamauchi was known not to give anyone a penny more than he believed a person deserved. So Rogers stopped talking.

"How much?" Yamauchi demanded again.

"Three hundred thousand dollars." He knew that if he asked for too much money, he would be out of Nintendo on his ass.

"What do we get?"

"One dollar for every game we sell."

Yamauchi thought for a long moment, which seemed like ages to Rogers. But then he reached out over the Go table, proffered his hand, and said, "Deal."

In nine months, Rogers returned to show his new baby to Yamauchi. After setting things up, Rogers noticed that the big boss had an underling use the joystick. Yamauchi still didn't know how to use the controls on the NES. But he knew what he didn't like.

"It's not strong enough," he said flatly.

Rogers protested, insisting that the game was very strong, the strongest Go game his company had ever made. He couldn't believe that Yamauchi couldn't see the beauty in it. Yamauchi was intractable. He didn't want the Nintendo name anywhere on Rogers's game.

Rogers was dejected, but undaunted. He went back to work to refine the game, polishing it so that Yamauchi could not reject it. Rogers, according to the terms of the deal, bought copies from Nintendo's manufacturing arm. Kyuroban Igo, the Go game, went on the market in 1986, and Go nerds bought 150,000 games. But Go didn't sell anywhere near the 300,000 Nintendo needed to make back its initial investment. To this day, Rogers owes the company

$150,000. Despite the setback, Rogers remained on good terms with Nintendo.

When he saw Tetris for the first time at the Consumer Electronics Show in Las Vegas in January 1988, it was as though Rogers had reached a kind of gaming rapture. It was beyond Go, beyond Black Onyx, beyond any game he'd every produced at Bullet-Proof Software. Just as Pajitnov couldn't stop thinking about making the game during its conception, Rogers couldn't stop thinking about marketing it.

But Tetris was already being distributed in Europe, a handful of companies throughout the world claiming they owned the licensing rights based on miscommunication with the Soviets and downright lies from sketchy middlemen seeking to make a buck. It was like B. Traven's *The Treasure of the Sierra Madre*, except in this case, the Soviet Union stood in for Mexico. Everyone, including the growing Microsoft, lusted after Tetris as though it were the south-of-the-border trove of gold and the game companies were the gringo prospectors. In the Soviet Union, Mikhail Gorbachev set forth new policy decrees that thawed the Cold War with glasnost and perestroika. But doing business within the layers of Soviet culture remained fraught with suspicion and never-ending enigmas, and those shadows of lingering distrust hung over the Computing Centre and Tetris as well.

Henk Rogers felt he could beat all the other companies with a trump card—Nintendo. He had honed his relationship with Nintendo to the point that his company was permitted to release a controller for the Nintendo system in the United States. The plastic piece of hardware had a rapid-fire turbo button and an ingenious slow-motion mode. It sold two million units.

After seeing and playing Tetris, Rogers met with Nintendo of America president Mino Arakawa in Kyoto in December 1988. "Can you keep a big secret?" asked Arakawa with a gleam in his eye.

"You can tell no one. We have the new game playing machine by Mr. Yokoi. It should be big." Arakawa used the word "big" when other English words failed him. But he didn't need a better descriptive. He had a prototype to show. Out came a plastic device that was about as large as a pocket calculator, but thicker. Rogers loved the look of the Game Boy. Arakawa continued, "Mr. Yokoi's last product [the Game & Watch] was a big failure in the United States. But this Game Boy will be big, very big."

Rogers saw an opportunity to pitch Tetris. He fired various volleys about the game's beauty, saying it would be one of the most significant games the industry had ever produced. It was as if he were a clone of a secret, more assertive side of Pajitnov, almost as though he were a partner in the very design of Tetris—even though he'd never met the game maker. Like Pajitnov, he lived Tetris. He looked Arakawa straight in the eye and said, "I think you should include Tetris inside the package of the Game Boy."

Arakawa did not hesitate. He shot back, "Why should we do that when we have Mario? All the boys already love Mario."

"If you want boys to play, include Mario. If you want everyone to play—mothers, fathers, brothers, sisters—include Tetris."

Arakawa paused for a moment to reflect. He looked outside the window to Kyoto below. "Whenever I see something new, I find Rogers's footprints. He finds new things faster than I can," he mused. Arakawa also thought about potential Game Boy sales and about the nature of Nintendo quality, the idea that innovation was always the key to success. Tetris sure seemed like the next step in creativity. But most of all, he thought about widening the already-vast Nintendo audience. He knew that Yokoi's Game & Watch had sold poorly stateside. He knew that he had to stay ahead of the other US game makers to please Yamauchi. He knew that Tetris was a gamble too: The lack of a Mario game bundled with the Game Boy could infuriate or befuddle young gamers. But the pros outweighed the cons.

In his quiet but assertive way he told Rogers, "Go get Tetris. Go to Moscow and get it." As Rogers readied to leave the Nintendo complex, Arakawa added, "You have ninety days to close. After that, we have no deal."

Rogers didn't waste time. Without an appointment with Pajitnov or with anyone at the Computing Centre, Rogers packed a few things, kissed his wife, and boarded a plane to Moscow. What Rogers didn't know as he traveled that February was that another Russian entity was about to become involved in the licensing discussions. Electronorgtechnica (Elorg), the Russian body of scientists and engineers that had the final say, had chided Pajitnov when it heard of the negotiations regarding Tetris. Pajitnov had been in contact with a handful of businesses in the West regarding licensing. He personally received no money, but his demeanor was such that greedy moneymen took his easygoing attitude as consent to market the game in Europe and beyond. But according to Soviet regulations, only Electronorgtechnica was allowed to deal with the import, export, and licensing of a game like Tetris.*

On the plane, Rogers hatched a plan to speak with Pajitnov not as a potential client, not as a businessman, but as a fellow game designer. He also felt that the Russians might not be as savvy as Western movers and shakers when it came to the ins and outs of the licensing business. He didn't want to take advantage of them. Rather, he wanted the Russians to understand what he had learned about the game business. But he didn't quite know how he would gain their trust.

Rogers walked into the enormous Computing Centre building and was awed by its vastness. It was nearly as cold inside as it was outside in the Russian winter. Rogers asked a receptionist for

---

* The complex and often sordid tale of the grab for Tetris rights is detailed in a truly great book about videogames, David Sheff's *Game Over* (Random House, 1993).

Pajitnov, who eventually came strolling down the stairs. Both Pajitnov and Rogers liked to take computer code apart to see how it worked and how it could be improved upon. On this, they bonded. The two couldn't understand each other very well. But they had dinner and then headed to Pajitnov's home to drink the Russian game maker's favorite, cognac. The Russian also showed Rogers other games on which he was working. But none of them intrigued Rogers as much as Tetris. As the evening turned past midnight, the two grew closer because Rogers didn't push too hard. He didn't promise anything to Pajitnov. All he said was that he liked the game and really wanted it for the Game Boy. He also said he wanted to help Pajitnov out with his other game ideas—eventually.

A number of frantic meetings with the Russians ensued in the days following. Rogers revealed that Nintendo had already made a version of Tetris for the NES in Japan, a version whose licensing rights he felt he had come by honestly. When the assembled powers at the Computing Centre saw the game cartridge, they nearly hit the snow-laden roof. They said that they had never authorized a deal for Tetris. There was yelling, even screaming. But Rogers calmed them down, saying he would find the perfect partner for the videogame console rights. A check was written by Rogers for the equivalent of nearly $41,000, a partial royalty payment for the 130,000 cartridges that Nintendo had sold in Japan.

"I want to do right by you," said Rogers to a group of still suspicious and confused Russians. He was doing everything he could to melt the ice that had threatened to freeze negotiations.

"You have three weeks. No more," to buy all the videogame console rights, said Nikolai Belikov, one of the Russian negotiators.

By the end of February, Rogers had negotiated the best Tetris deal of anyone: worldwide handheld rights not just for the Game Boy, but for any other handheld device. And there was a better than even chance that Nintendo would get the rights for Tetris on all home systems. If all went well, Rogers might make more than $10 million from Tetris.

Glowing, Rogers called Arakawa at Nintendo headquarters in the United States. Breathlessly, he said, "You'd better get over here to Moscow. You need to meet Alexey and the Russians in power need to meet you, too."

Arakawa brought Howard Lincoln, a strapping Seattle attorney who had become Nintendo's general counsel after helping to win the *King Kong* lawsuit against Universal Pictures. (Lincoln was, incidentally, the inspiration for one of two kids sleeping in pup tents under the stars in a Norman Rockwell painting called *The Scoutmaster*, crafted when Lincoln was a twelve-year-old Boy Scout.) After a sleepless journey to Moscow, Arakawa decided to get some money. But he was ripped off royally at the airport by an unscrupulous money seller. "Welcome to Russia," he thought to himself. After finding lodging, Arakawa and Lincoln walked the frozen streets to stock up on booze. They drank until they could drink no more, then went to bed to sleep the hard sleep of drunkenness.

On the next morning, the two met Rogers and Pajitnov at Elorg, along with the passel of Russians. They knew of Nintendo and of Mario and of the company's major successes. And they had outrageous demands before they signed off on Tetris. They hoped to manufacture all Nintendo cartridges, not just Tetris, in Moscow, and even to make Nintendo Entertainment Systems in Russia. Lincoln firmly said no to all these requests.

Pajitnov was ever the nice guy, trying to warm up to the Nintendo businessmen with small talk, moving to appease his bosses and lighten the atmosphere with a joke or two. It wasn't working. Pajitnov was discouraged. While he knew the Soviet Union owned the game, it was still his creation, his invention, his little baby. More, he was perplexed at the way the foreigners acted. They weren't as affable as Rogers; that was certain. He didn't realize that the mystified silence from Arakawa and the brusque commands from the bulldog Lincoln were simply their preferred business stances. It wasn't good cop, bad cop exactly. It was more talkative cop, quiet cop.

Pajitnov warmed up to Lincoln and Arakawa later that night at dinner. By the time they were at Pajitnov's apartment on Gersten Street, Arakawa was drinking cognac and opening up. Everyone was drinking, except for Pajitnov's young son, who was happily mind-melding with Tetris on the Game Boy prototype. It was an effervescent night full of laughter. These expensive-suited guys were A-OK with Pajitnov. He could even be friends with them someday, he hoped. It was like a scene out of *The Waltons,* Russian-style. That night, everyone was like family.

In the days and months that followed, all the bullshit drama and posturing was over and the contracts were signed. Tetris became *the* game to play for the Game Boy; it sold 33 million copies, and the game-playing device eventually sold nearly 120 million, and much of that had to do with Tetris. Both game heads and the mildly curious became aficionados. Even creaky President George Bush, diagnosed with an irregular heartbeat, played Tetris in his hospital room in early May 1991. A friendship between Pajitnov and Rogers remained vibrant throughout the years because they believed in Tetris with all their souls. After Rogers became richer than he had ever been, through licensing the game of falling blocks, he set Pajitnov up with money to develop more games in Russia. As Pajitnov headed to work each day via the cavernous Moscow subway, he seemed to stand taller than his sizable frame. He hired some of his friends and created an aquarium simulation that mimicked real-life DNA and made gods of those who clicked and tapped on their PC keyboards. Pajitnov wasn't rolling in dough, but he was well off. Occasionally, he would pinch himself, happy doing what he wanted to do. Forget the money. Pajitnov was simply satisfied that the game had affected so many millions of people in a positive way.

For the first time since Pong and Pac-Man, just as many women played the game as did men, perhaps because the game was more about organization than destruction. You'd see Tetris on TV, too, on everything from *Muppet Babies* to *The Simpsons*. There was even a Monty Python version called Drop Dead in which bodies blackened by the plague were substituted for the falling blocks. Later, Pajitnov himself was probably the inspiration for a character in Thomas Pynchon's 2006 novel, *Against the Day*. In that fiction, Captain Igor Padzhitnoff arranges bricks in a certain pattern before dropping them on his targets.

Pajitnov watched with fascination as scientists tested people who played Tetris. Research showed that it changed the brain for the better, that play made your real life choices quicker and more efficient. All along, Pajitnov believed that playing Tetris was like singing a song inside, kind of a visual earworm. Yet the finding that Tetris helped the brain was proof to Pajitnov that it was more than just a game. It didn't hype you up with adrenaline and make your heart beat hard. It didn't require you to hold your breath, grit your teeth, and aim and shoot like a marksman just to win. It calmed you, just as it stimulated your brain cells to match the shapes and clear the rows. Tetris proved that nonviolent games could sell as well as the early shooters, like Space Invaders. Playing Tetris was the most peaceful experience of the bestselling games, even more so than Pac-Man. Tetris presaged the casual game revolution by almost two decades. But back then, it demonstrated early in the industry's evolution that women would flock to gaming, stay with a game for long periods of time, and even get the same frozen fingers and knackered knuckles from indulging for far too long.

Even more than Miyamoto needed Yamauchi, Pajitnov needed

Rogers. Because of Nintendo's stringent privacy policies, no one could hornswaggle the company for long. But Pajitnov was ensconced in a Soviet Union where everyone outside of the country seemed like an angry wolf trying to rip him off—except for Rogers. As a close pal who was both a calculating businessman and a fellow game designer, Rogers empathized with Pajitnov's situation and stopped the stealing completely. Later, when the time was right, Rogers sold his cell phone game business for tens of millions and used that money as a partial payment to purchase all the rights from the Russians, partly in an effort to bring Tetris online for multiplayer contests. Pajitnov, who by then had emigrated to the United States, was brought on as a partner. He had finally become rich from Tetris.

Wealth didn't matter so much to Pajitnov. He had traveled the world because of his creation, and his fans were legion. Now there are fifty variants of the game, including one for the Apple iPad. It has been downloaded digitally more than one hundred million times. People flock to new versions of Tetris—*to this day*. Its soothing, addicting game mechanics always lure new fans, and every online game site of note has a version to play. And the money continues to roll in for Pajitnov. Now, when he goes to his window in Bellevue, Washington, and looks out upon a rainy day, his mind relaxes and he still sees those mesmerizing falling blocks in front of his eyes. They are part of his essence. At that moment when the blocks fall, there is nothing else present. He is not in Russia anymore. He is not in the United States. He is transported somewhere else. He is Tetris. And he is free.

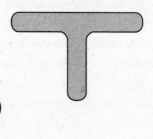

THE RISE OF
ELECTRONIC ARTS

William "Trip" Hawkins III hatched a plan for world domination through games very early in his life. From the age of ten onward, the son of a San Diego marketing executive wanted to overcome people with emotion so big, so overwhelming, so heart-stirring, that when they played a computer game they would cry. Just like the movies he loved, such as *Apocalypse Now;* just like the music he rocked out to, like the Rolling Stones and the Stooges. But it was more than that. Hawkins, nicknamed Trippy by his grandmother because he was the third William in the family, wanted to make games into a new kind of life experience. Even before he graduated from high school, the plan ballooned beyond a childish yearning. By the time he got to Harvard, it was a full-blown obsession. Hawkins wanted games to move, the way Steven Spielberg said movies should. He had the stuff to do it too, all the good looks and charm of a Golden Age movie star. And he possessed from his father the savvy saleman's instincts and work ethic of a young Willy Loman. From his mother, an Emmy award–winning producer who founded the San Diego chapter of the National Organization for Women, he got his assertive nature. Trip Hawkins had it all.

But it almost didn't happen. The idea for Electronic Arts, a company that would become the biggest and most influential of the computer game makers, was almost quashed. It was nearly killed at supposedly liberal-minded Harvard University in the 1970s.

On an autumn day in October 1973, when Trip Hawkins was walking past Wigglesworth Hall, he had his latest eureka moment about computer games. Hawkins realized he wanted to invent his own major. He wanted to major in strategy and applied videogame theory. He was so jolted by his concept that he began walking more quickly to an appointment with his faculty advisor. Despite his wit, his charm, and a prepared spiel he'd fashioned for the academic administrator, the professor said no. Not just no. As he showed Hawkins the door, he said, "You are wasting your time at Harvard by monkeying around with games." So Hawkins walked past University Hall in a fit of anger. He did not, as many have done, touch the shoe of the polished bronze statue of John Harvard for good luck—for the grudging gods of luck had evaded him. He felt that Harvard didn't want him. And if Harvard didn't want him, he was going to drop out. He would go somewhere that more fully comprehended his plan for the big picture, somewhere that would value him as the vision-ary he was so certain he was. But another, more beneficent Harvard counselor saw the passion in Hawkins's face and heard the sense Hawkins made when talking about his proposal. By the end of that meeting, Hawkins had his major, and he aced nearly every sociology and communications course and every independent study as well. For his thesis, he wrote a World War III computer simulation that was very interactive and, perhaps, equally annoying. Part of its development had Hawkins going into students' rooms to stir them at three a.m. to gauge how they would deal with futuristic war scenarios. In addition, he programmed his first computer game simulation on a PDP-11 computer at Harvard. It predicted that Miami would beat Minnesota 23–6 in the Super Bowl. The real score was 24–7.

Once he was out of college, however, Hawkins saw there were no takers for his particular form of passionate expertise. He felt ignored and unappreciated. But to those who would lend an ear, Hawkins would begin an oration: "There will be a revolution in computer games that will make games bigger than the movie industry. It's coming soon. You better get on board, or you'll be left behind." Even those who deigned to listen looked at Hawkins suspiciously. They often responded, "Man, what the hell are you smoking?" So Hawkins returned to California and went to Stanford for an MBA. When he finished, he still couldn't find the right job in the nascent world of games. So he took at job at Apple Computer. As employee number sixty-eight and the company's inaugural MBA, Hawkins was the first person at Apple to tackle the job of marketing.

Within a year, Hawkins had worked his way up to an executive position at Apple. He was in the right place at the right time. Apple was the "it" company. Like Apple today, with the iPod and iPhone, the company could do little wrong. The media hyped the Apple II personal computers, and business ("an elixir for U.S. industry," glowed the *New York Times*) and families loved the quality the technicians put into each piece of equipment. The computers, although fairly expensive, almost sold themselves, so much so that in his four years at Apple, Hawkins became a rich man with a niche he carefully carved for himself and his team: selling the computers to medium and large businesses. By 1981, the self-described computer nerd had developed the smoothest of swaggers and an indestructible yet affable egotism that would lead him to say with a wink that he was "smarter than Bill Gates and better looking than Steve Jobs."

When he wasn't selling computers, he was thinking about computer games. Late into the night, when his marketing work at Apple was done, he would loosen his tie and sit down at his Apple II to map out a business plan for a new company without a name. He already had his big idea: games about sports, ones that made you feel you were inside the game, whether you were coaching or playing. Games so intense that you could smell the sweat, the confidence, and the fear. To a select few, like his understanding pal Bing Gordon, he would posit, "You know those Strat-O-Matic baseball and football games from the sixties, the ones you would play with a pencil and paper? I want to make those for the personal computer. I want them to have good graphics and I want them to be endorsed by sports celebrities. Not just celebrities—superstars. I want the superstars to be in the game. The biggest. The biggest of the big." Each night, he continued to refine the idea, calculating a five-year plan with precise budgets and room for game designer creativity that had never before been seen in games.

In creating his own company, Hawkins was inspired by the popular nonfiction of the time, like Geoffrey Stokes's *Starmaking Machinery,* about the rise and fall of the star-crossed Southern rock band Commander Cody. He also devoured Steven Bach's *Final Cut: Art, Money, and Ego in the Making of* Heaven's Gate, *the Film That Sank United Artists,* about the disastrous making of director Michael Cimino's beautifully filmed western, during which the film's budget ballooned to $44 million, at that time the most expensive film in history. Hawkins vowed to avoid the mistakes of the music and movie industries. He told potential investors, "Not only will my company become the next big media company, videogames can be artistic and the people who make them should be treated like artists." Finally, the Masters of the Universe involved in those long-established media companies began to believe him. Cranky, straight-shooting venture capitalist Don Valentine gave the game maker $2 million through Capital Management, the company well known for its funding of technology start-ups like Bushnell's Atari. Hawkins had already reached into his bank account to pour $200,000 of his own savings into a company he called Amazin' Software. The company name was like a mirror image of Hawkins himself, down-to-earth with a g-dropped gerund and full of blustering hubris. Yet Hawkins's current reality was humble. He and the early hires were ensconced within a minuscule office given to him rent-free within the Capital Management complex.

Within six months, he had hired eleven people, including hire number seven, the brawny Bing Gordon, a failed actor who once waited tables at the New York City punk hangout Max's Kansas City. Gordon had tried many endeavors before games, including working on a shrimp boat and, according to Hawkins, acting in a porn film. He got into games after immersing himself in a business project about the Channel F game console while studying for an MBA at Stanford, and found that he thrived making computer entertainment. But he often disagreed with Hawkins's business decisions. Within six months, the company moved to larger digs. Office meetings, however, were invariably loud, and not merely because the employees were psyched about their endeavors. Just outside the window, roaring planes took off from a runway at the San Francisco International Airport. Yet it wouldn't have mattered if the office had faced a garbage dump. Hawkins had the touch.

Early on, Hawkins made decisions like an early movie mogul: He bet with his gut as much as his brain, choosing people he called artists based on not just their reputation as programmers, but whether or not he believed their ideas were a cut above the rest. His careful choice of words, the fact that he was calling kids who were fresh out of college "artists," had the salubrious effect of intriguing investors from the realms of movies and music. At the time, everything done at the company overflowed with originality. But no one really liked the name Amazin' Software. To name the baby, Hawkins took the group of eleven employees to the beach at Pajaro Dunes, California, for the weekend. The varied species of birds chirped, the Monterey Bay waves washed against the fan-shaped beach, and all day the game makers argued about the name. With a bonfire ablaze and booze flowing, the motley crew settled on Electronic Arts during an all-night brainstorming session. The name was a riff on United Artists, the movie company formed by Charlie Chaplin, Mary Pickford, and D. W. Griffith to give the artists more creative control in a Hollywood dominated by the often oppressive star system. But not everyone in the group of eleven had their say. A couple of them became too tired or too drunk and had gone to sleep by the time the name was finalized at two a.m. They had to live with the name even if they didn't like it.

If you saw Hawkins's crew at a convention, they looked like they were richer and smarter than anyone else. They all had MBAs, while all the other nerds were dressed in T-shirts and jeans. Sure, they were full of themselves, thinking they could perform miracles with software. But they could back it up too. The company's early offerings included an educational collaboration with Timothy Leary, a pun-filled role playing game called A Bard's Tale, and the exceptional Pinball Construction Set designed by Bill Budge, in which you could make your own pinball tables. But none of the games were runaway megahits. Then Hawkins remembered an old television ad for the unctuous hair product Vitalis. The hair care company aired a series of TV commercials that featured a one-on-one basketball matchup. It was kind of a basketball rendition of Home Run Derby, where the shooting of hoops was shown as short, one-minute vignettes. Hawkins told Gordon and the gang, "I want us to make a one-on-one basketball game. My hero in sports is Dr. J [Julius Erving], and he has a natural foil, Larry Byrd." Gordon, who was a sports fan himself, loved the concept.

Despite Hawkins's bluster, it was difficult to see the art within those early floppy disks. Dr. J and Larry Bird Go One on One was little more than two stick figures battling it out on an unadorned basketball court. But what you could see in the title was Hawkins's penchant for using superstars in his games to help sell them. Hawkins not only wanted to rub elbows with the greats, he wanted to be a superstar himself. But he could not be a superstar, a true superstar, until Electronic Arts made "The Football Game." Hawkins's real passion was football. He pored over plays and what made them work like a fanatical amateur coach. After Hawkins attended the NFC Championship football game in 1982, in which Joe Montana hurled a football to receiver Dwight Clark, a fantastic completion simply known as "The Catch," he approached the former Notre Dame star and asked him to work on his computer football game. Hawkins was discouraged to learn that the quarterback already had a long-term deal with Atari. Undaunted, he sought out a more minor subject, the tequila-loving Joe Kapp, who was a former football chucker for the Minnesota Vikings.

In a conversation on the UC Berkeley football field, where Kapp was football coach, Hawkins proposed, "I'll pay you a consulting fee if you give me some pointers on how to make an authentic game."

Kapp, who had a mammoth ego, perhaps because he was an actor in successful films like The Longest Yard and Semi-Tough, looked down the field as if he had seen his quarterback throw an interception in the end zone. He shot back, "I want my name on that game and I want royalties, too. And I want my picture on the cover." On the drive home, Hawkins thought, "If it's going to go that way, I'm going to go to the front of the parade and get the biggest I can get, John Madden." That wouldn't be easy. Hawkins needed

Madden—badly—but Madden didn't need Hawkins. Madden already had his share of fame as the Super Bowl–winning coach of the Oakland Raiders who had parlayed his success and personality into a likeable, folksy style of TV football announcing. He also had authored a few bestselling books and was the affable pitchman for Miller Lite beer's "Tastes Great, Less Filling" television campaign. (The *New York Times* judged that Madden made a "small fortune" for just the commercials.) Madden's celebrity was growing as fast as his waistline. Because of his rising star, the former coach wanted a greater cash advance than Hawkins had given Julius Erving for the basketball game. Madden received a whopping $100,000, a huge amount for the time. But Erving had had the foresight to accept Electronic Arts stock at a very cheap price as partial payment. Madden declined the offer. To this day, Madden still jokes that accepting stock in the new videogame company could have made him a richer man in the late 1980s and beyond. But Madden, a pragmatist to a fault, wanted his money up front because he didn't believe the newfangled technology would sell. In fact, he knew very little about computers and even less about computer games. The real reason he agreed to lend his name to the game was because he was teaching an extension class for football fans at the University of California and thought the game would be useful for his lectures and nothing else. (In the last twenty years, EA shares increased by 2,500 percent at their peak. Nonetheless, Madden is likely to have been paid between $75 and $100 million for lending his voice and name to the game during the last two decades.)

Even at the beginning of preproduction, it was not easy going, for Madden was a bit of a diva who didn't live up to his everyman image. In fact, he could be mean and demeaning. Every other word Hawkins heard from Madden was the "F" word. It was amazing to the young CEO that Madden could put up a front on television without ever dropping the F bomb. Yet the winning coach's input was invaluable. Hawkins traveled to meet Madden after a Broncos game in Denver and planned to take a two-day train ride with the airplane-phobic personality to Oakland. On the train, Hawkins asked Madden to create the playbook for the game, but Madden balked at a job of such immense proportion. Then, because of the data processing limitations of computers at the time, Hawkins, along with a game producer and game developer, suggested that the game be skeleton, a form of football that includes just seven players on each team. The blockers would be taken out, but all of the same plays would remain.

"Fuck that and fuck you people," blurted Madden. "Either we do it fuckin' right or we don't fuckin' do it at all."

Hawkins wanted to do it "fuckin' right" as well, but the road to release was filled with obstacles. Work on Madden took so long, and was so overbudget, that everyone at the burgeoning company became increasingly frustrated, even disheartened. Early investors began to worry that the Madden game could bankrupt the new company with the promising future. Most of EA's other games were on schedule, making it to stores on time. But the football game was so often postponed that whispering employees began calling it Trip's Folly. One day, as the planes growled from above the EA offices, Hawkins's first hire, Rich Melmon, called a Madden meeting in a cramped conference room. Rich Hilleman, the game's producer, and marketing whiz Bing Gordon began arguing about the seemingly endless production process. Soon, the volume of their words grew as loud as the din of the jets above. In a flash, the large men, who both played amateur hockey, were out of their chairs and in each other's face. Melmon leaped out of the way as Gordon threw Hilleman into the wall hard, the way a hockey player would check the opposition into the boards. Hawkins told people that "the force left this big indentation in the wall that was about three feet high and about a foot and a half wide. It just caved the whole wall in. And Bing wrote a note on it, commemorating the occasion. None of us is afraid to bang heads and fight for what we believe in. Literally."

After three years of game production and no end in sight, outside auditors trudged over to the Electronic Arts office and instructed Hawkins to expense and write off all the cash advances that the company had paid to John Madden. The auditors deemed them to be completely unrecoupable. They also wanted Hawkins to halt production on the game, then and there. Inside the new company, more staffers began laughing and joking about Trip's Folly. This time, they weren't just whispering. But to the young designers, there was one positive thing about Hawkins's football game obsession. As Ray Tobey put it, "At least it will keep him away from interfering with our other projects." Tobey was a boy genius, a brilliant but occasionally arrogant artistic phenomenon who was working on computer games while still in high school, toiling at babysitting jobs to pay for his $800 Commodore Pet 2001. Tobey spent most of his time at the computer trying to make a game that was as close to real life as a computer in the 1980s could make it. Through word of mouth, Tobey's flying and shooting game based on F-15 fighter jets came to the attention of Apple's Steve Wozniak when Tobey was just sixteen. Wozniak was wowed at the sound, graphics, and game play. He kept saying, "This can't be done on the Apple II. I can't believe it. This can't be done." He gave Tobey a calling card and added a note to Trip Hawkins, which read, "Please consider this flight simulator as the *finest* Apple game ever done."

Hawkins didn't waste any time. He wanted to make a deal right away. Tobey's parents came with him to EA's offices to oversee a lucrative royalty deal for Skyfox, a game that would eventually sell more than a million copies. While there, Hawkins took the teen under his wing, driving him around the Bay Area to see the sights. Tobey returned the favor by working extreme hours to put the finishing touches on Skyfox, sometimes for 110 hours a week. When the game became a hit, he bought with his first royalty check a fancy black JPS Lotus Esprit. He would speed through California's redwood forests like he was a young prince of the Silicon Valley, once with an Italian TV documentary crew frantically trying to keep up. Tobey wasn't exactly thrifty, and he liked the fame he tasted, likening himself to a rock star. If it weren't for his parents, he would have burned through all the royalty money he received.

Still a teenager, Tobey became part of a small, tightly knit group of twenty-five employees who met each Friday in a nondescript conference room to go over the week's events, everything from video-game schedules to marketing to office gossip. Always at the head of the table was Trip Hawkins, who constantly needed more money to expand the company's reach. Early on in his search for capital, the boss introduced his latest group of bankers, imploring his employees, "Be nice to them. They'll give us money." With the precision of a military maneuver, the jeans-and-T-shirts-clad staff lofted well-aimed Nerf balls at the suits, pummeling the financiers, who left the meeting in a tizzy. Hawkins was miffed, but he wouldn't take no for an answer. All evening long, he wined and dined and schmoozed them, telling them about his grand plans, telling them he wanted to make a game that would make people cry, just like the movies did. At the end, the moneymen gave Hawkins millions.

The graphics and play in the inaugural Madden effort that was finally released for the Apple II in June 1989 were like caveman drawings when measured by today's standards. The art looked like a cheap cartoon. Only sixteen of the NFL's twenty-eight teams were represented. While the real players were there, the teams' logos weren't. And while the stats for each player were carefully honed for realism's sake, every player looked the same. On the cover of the first game, the smiling Madden, holding a football running back–style, looks as much surprised as he is happy. It's as if he's about to say,

SHAF
KAY

xxxxxxx5251

10/14/2019

Item: 00100728807059 ((book)

"Gee, I know football, but what's this videogame thing all about?" Nonetheless, the gaming world went wild over the game. *Nibble,* an Apple II enthusiast magazine of the time, detailed the many functions of the game and highlighted the news that you could make your own plays "if you're really serious about football." Sports fans drooled. While television only permitted football fans to sit back and watch, Hawkins's computer game allowed fans to feel they were strategizing on the sidelines and on the field. They could call their own plays as coach, throw the ball as quarterback, and catch the ball as a receiver. They were inside football like they never had been allowed to be before.

A big part of Hawkins's videogame dream was making John Madden Football an even bigger success than Tobey's Skyfox. He considered this a given. But business deals kept him equally busy . . . and nerve-wracked. Electronic Arts was becoming a global player, but, according to its top executives, it still wasn't firing on all cylinders. Hawkins had been focusing on computer games, but he was very frustrated with what he saw as the shortcomings of the home computer platforms. He also encountered an extreme lack of interest on the part of the manufacturers of those platforms to grow the market from the standpoint of entertainment. Hawkins and his elite band of MBAs would make pilgrimages to companies like IBM to beg for the additions of joysticks or a sound chip that made more than an annoying beep. They wouldn't give up, the next time lobbying for sixteen colors to make the gaming experience even better than the supremely successful Nintendo Entertainment System. These pleas fell on deaf ears.

But consoles seemed little better to Hawkins, who didn't like the eight-by-ten-inch Nintendo console because the graphics weren't powerful enough and the machine had no storage capacity. To top it off, the Japanese company's licensing program was restrictive and expensive. Yet Nintendo was a behemoth, with an unbelievably tight lock on the vast majority of the home videogame market in North America. Hawkins's *Glückschmerz* grew by the day.

Then, two days before Halloween in the fall of 1988, Sega released the Mega Drive in Japan. Hawkins himself made the trek to Tokyo, stood in line to buy the machine, and brought it back to the United States, knowing that the console would be released within a year in North America as the Sega Genesis. Once Hawkins got it out of the box, he nearly jumped for joy. For inside was a sixteen-bit MC68000 Motorola processor, the same chip that was in the Amiga and the Mac, not to mention the Atari ST and all the arcade machines. EA employees, thought Hawkins, could make games based on that processor with their hands tied behind their backs. To his staff, Hawkins predicted that the Genesis would be a hit for $189 and that it would be available in the US market two years before the next generation Nintendo machines. The boastful CEO may have missed the boat on the first Nintendo boom, but he vowed that he wasn't going to be left behind with the Sega surge. Yet there were those in the company who believed that Nintendo would release its new, state-of-the-art system early—just to blow Sega out of the water.

So began a war with Sega over the Sega Genesis console during 1987 and 1988, a battle that Bing Gordon said included a "bet the company" decision. Hawkins had his technicians take the machine apart to see how it was made, just as he began thinking about how he could make money with Sega. Two separate teams worked feverishly on the project while Hawkins figured out a master plan. Hawkins knew that Sega's licensing policy was just as Draconian as Nintendo's. Then an idea coursed through his synapses. He decided to make games for the system without being part of the Japanese company's licensing program. Hawkins's aha moment, however, was his alone. Others disdained it. The arguments and anger Hawkins encountered came from everywhere. Middle management felt the concept was scurrilous. More important, the board of directors smelled an expensive lawsuit for copyright infringement, one that could put the company out of business. Don Valentine, the venture capitalist, told Hawkins tersely and in no uncertain terms that his scheme would risk the capital of all of his investors. Yet Hawkins stood his ground. It was a hard row to hoe, but there was one bright spot. Hawkins was thrilled when his engineers reverse engineered the Sega Mega System in a matter of weeks.

The directive went out throughout the company: Games, including Madden, would be built for the upcoming Genesis—with or without Sega's permission. The monumental risk took its toll on Hawkins: He couldn't sleep at night, worrying, plotting, then worrying some more. He told those closest to him, "Sega just wants to huff and puff and blow our house down. But you worry about a lot of things in a situation like that. You worry about having injunctions that prevent you from shipping your product, about losing and being liable for significant damages. You worry about them changing the platform so your games don't work anymore and you don't know why. There's just a lot of things you worry about."

The worry didn't slow him down. It energized his resolve. During the vitriolic war with Sega that followed, Hawkins played a combination of hardball and chicken. More quickly than expected, Sega caved and signed an astoundingly favorable agreement with Electronic Arts. That agreement brought the average cost paid to Sega per game down to about 35 cents. By contrast, other companies that joined the Sega licensing program had to pay the Japanese company an astronomical fee of about $8 to $10 per game.

In the coming years, Hawkins had everyone from racing ace Richard Petty to baseball coaching legend Earl Weaver appear in sports games. Yet Madden was the franchise that made history, earning more than $3 billion since it was first released. Much of that success was due to a new marketing plan for games, a kind

of preplanned obsolescence and keep-up-with-the-Joneses business ethic that would have given social economist Thorstein Veblen
pause: If you didn't have the new Madden, packed with this year's
players, this year's stats, and this year's plays, you weren't up to date.
You weren't as cool as your game-playing neighbor who procured the
newest version. Fans bought the hype of videogame-style conspicu-
ous consumption then, and they buy it to this day.

Still, Hawkins never achieved one of his goals: He never released
a game that had the emotion and drama to make people cry.

Ray Tobey and other early employees said that when Electronic
Arts went public and its stock began trading in September 1989,
things changed at the company. People weren't as friendly, and some
seemed to be out for themselves. The team spirit wasn't gone by any
means. Yet working there wasn't quite as much fun anymore. The
bonds were of employees working together, and of acquaintance, not
of friends having fun while making games that were like their babies.
Hawkins's ego became bigger, and he was harder to deal with as the
profits continued to roll in.

Then came the fall. In one of the most documented failures
in videogame history, Hawkins decided to move Electronic Arts
into the console making business. While he remained chairman of
EA, he left the company in 1991 to concentrate on a powerful new
machine. With two hundred employees in San Mateo, an EA spin-
off called the 3DO Company made a CD-based multimedia game
machine in 1993. Its partners, Time Warner, Sanyo, Matsushita,
and AT&T, were impressive, as were the 3DO's computing power
and graphics. Its licensing plan was more palatable and even-handed
than Nintendo's. The company would charge game companies $3
per game sold. Calling him a guru, the *New York Times* estimated
Hawkins's fortune at $200 million, and indicated he might be the
next Bill Gates, a visionary who "rejects the traditional symbols and
perks of corporate power." Hawkins had a car with sixty thousand

miles on it and a small-ish house. His only indulgence at the time was a $20,000 home entertainment system. The *Times* indicated that he was hell-bent on having Madden-like success with 3DO.

Unfortunately for Hawkins, the machine was long-delayed and far too expensive at $699. Within a couple of years, the company was out of the console business. By 2003, 3DO had ceased to exist. Hawkins boxed up its intellectual properties and sold them in the office, garage sale–style, for pennies on the dollar. His career in big games at big companies was over.

In February 2005, a group of journalists and many Electronic Arts employees crowded into a small restaurant in New York's Little Italy to rub elbows with Hollywood stars Robert Duvall and James Caan. As wine flowed and giant shrimp were consumed by the dozen, journalists wondered why EA was spending a rumored $20 million to make a version of Francis Ford Coppola's classic *The Godfather* and an equally jaw-dropping $300,000 to celebrate more than a year before the game even hit store shelves. Just before James Caan made a very brief speech, Electronic Arts vice president Jeff Brown sauntered over to a few of the assembled journalists. "I just don't know why people keep saying Trip Hawkins founded the company. He didn't." Having planted a seed of doubt, Brown faded into the crowd. Journalist Steven Kent wondered aloud why Brown was making an effort to change history. Then, twice in 2006, an anonymous user tried to excise Hawkins from Electronic Arts' Wikipedia page. Through the use of computer software, the changes were traced—to the offices of Electronic Arts. Today, Hawkins doesn't talk to anyone who works at Electronic Arts, nor do they speak to him.

Now, when Ray Tobey and a crew of the early staffers meet to eat Afghan cuisine for a weekly lunch at Kabul in San Carlos, they talk about the good old days, about how they changed the nature of videogames with their hard work ethic and pioneering spirit. But they don't talk about Hawkins much. At the company headquarters in Redwood City, Trip Hawkins's legacy is almost forgotten by those younger game makers who toil among the thousands of designers, marketers, and producers. When queried, the people who recently joined the large company (which at the peak had 8,500 employees) barely remember Hawkins's name. They know very little of the swagger, the toil, or the ingenuity. One man even called him Trip *Hopkins*. A current Electronic Arts worker bee said, "He's just a picture who hangs on the wall. The older people here said he was totally difficult to work for. Isn't he reduced to making cell phone games now?"

Football superstars have forgotten as well. On the twentieth anniversary of Madden Football's first release, five football players, all with Super Bowl rings, gathered at a trendy Manhattan club to appear before the press and discuss the game. All the players had been Madden cover stars, die-hard players who'd slip the game in a console after practice and occasionally gamble on Madden when they played together or on the road. Marshall Faulk, the Super Bowl champion running back, admitted, "Yeah, some of us have lost some cars or some mortgage payments playing the game." Ray Lewis, the fast-talking middle linebacker from the Baltimore Ravens, added, "The game's not like real life playing at all, especially the angles the players hit other players." But, he said, it's as close as anyone's ever going to get. When the name of the founder of Electronic Arts was brought up, none of the players recognized it. "Don't know him at all. Does he play?" asked quarterback Daunte Culpepper.

Trip Hawkins, who now innovates on a smaller level with mobile and Facebook applications through a company called Digital Chocolate, continues to think highly of himself—with good reason.

For without Hawkins's work in the 1980s, the oblivious workers from the sprawling Redwood City campus might not have jobs at all, certainly not at Electronic Arts. The big-time superstar football players wouldn't have the honor of being on the cover of a game, the appearance on which begets nearly the same respect and admiration as winning the Super Bowl. And for us gamers, it's unfathomable to imagine a world without Electronic Arts, without landmark games like The Sims, The Need for Speed, Dead Space, and, especially, intensely immersive sports games for FIFA, NASCAR, the NHL, and the NBA. EA is especially important for broadening games' appeal to include a new class of gamer: beer-guzzling armchair quarterbacks and towel-snapping jocks. With EA, videogames weren't just for the arcade crowds anymore; nor were they confined to those who liked those wonderfully cute (but difficult) Nintendo games. Games were now targeted at the booze-bellied Strat-O-Matic addict. These rabid fans goaded their friends, "C'mon. You gotta get this thing; just play it and see. Just throw the long ball and when Jerry Rice catches it, you'll understand." Games did not yet appeal to everyman. But they were inching closer by capturing legions of sports mavens and average fans. Because of Madden, Hawkins, and Electronic Arts, the industry had moved one step closer to taking over the living room.

7.

GAMES, MYST, AND
THE 7TH GUEST

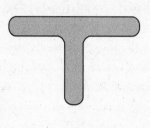

But what if you wanted to play games that had more heft, had more than action and more than puzzles? What if you wanted a story that could be as thorough and thrilling as a popular novel? Trip Hawkins's games couldn't make people cry. Could anyone else's?

While coin-operated games and console games were having their heyday, the adventure game was quietly becoming a mainstay on another platform—the PC. It was a slow, stealthy rise, flanked by science fiction cultists, sword and sorcery devotees, and code-appreciating tech nerds. Here was a thinking person's game genre, one for the Dungeons & Dragons role playing crowd, one that was more literate and arguably more profound than any arcade or Nintendo offering.

The niche began in earnest in early 1980 with an interactive text adventure series called Zork, which every adventure game maker onward cited as influential. Because it had no graphics, the game required you to imagine, almost in the same way you would read a novel and fill in the details in your mind's eye. As the game began, you entered a house, found a dungeon, and dealt with devious grues, batlike monsters. Described in Zork's fiction, the grue was:

```
[a] sinister, lurking presence in the dark places of
the earth. Its favorite diet is adventurers (you, the
player), but its insatiable appetite is tempered by
its fear of light. No grue has ever been seen by the
light of day, and few have survived its fearsome jaws
to tell the tale.
```

If you read that description in the middle of the night in the glow of your old computer screen, it chilled you right to the marrow.

Zork eventually was picked up by a million fans and inspired six traditional paperback novels, and its success marked an auspicious beginning for the new niche. But it was Myst and The 7th Guest, games of the nineties made around the same time, that were responsible not only for a tidal wave in videogame sales, but for a meteoric rise in the sales of personal computers with CD-ROM drives. Myst was cryptic, unique, and full of a graphical splendor that was part Salvador Dalí and part Jules Verne's *The Mysterious Island*—with a bit of the myths of C. S. Lewis and J. R. R. Tolkien thrown in for good measure. There was nothing to shoot. There were few words spoken by the characters. There was no linear story. The gamer wasn't asked to be the hero. Initially, players had no idea what *the hell* was going on, what *the hell* to do, or how *the hell* to progress in Myst.

To help, there were enigmatic books in the game written by a shadowy scribe called Atrus. As you read these tomes of science fiction mystery called *The Ages*, your skin crawled. You anticipated the adventure to come, and the game play. But you were creeped out by the unknown; these books were strange portals that let you travel to beckoning virtual worlds and solve the many puzzles.

But these books weren't enough. Myst was generally inscrutable unless you bought a step-by-step instruction book for an extra $10 or $20. Part of the addiction to the game had to do with the human need to win and to finish things. Myst, with its 2,500 images that were like paintings and its sixty-six minutes of video, kept you coming back with its hyper-realistic and moving paintings and puzzles. Many of its twenty-six musical compositions were lulling and ambient, not blaring like the amusement park sideshow that was Super Mario Bros. Part of your mind was frantic and frustrated, trying to figure out the solutions (without the hint book), while another part prevented teeth gnashing and mouse throwing because it was being soothed by the kind of music you hear in a yoga class.

In the game, you assumed the role of The Stranger, trapped on an island, trying to solve a mystery of mammoth proportions. Just that name—The Stranger—made the game cool beyond imagination. It was the same stranger toward which many gravitated in other media, the guys on *Route 66,* Spock on *Star Trek,* Brando and Dean in the movies, the mystical Phantom Stranger and the spell-conjuring Dr. Strange in comic books, and outsiders like Jack Kerouac and David Foster Wallace in literature. In life, you may have been the outsider/stranger in ways that weren't good. Maybe you were the nerd who was spat upon by the cool kids. Maybe you were passed over for promotions at work. But in Myst, you were the unfamiliar rambler who could be a hero even as you were isolated and alone. For once, you didn't simply read about the stranger or watch him passively. Since The Stranger was never seen on-screen, I imagined myself as a bald man wearing the blackest of leather jackets, scuffed Doc Martens with grungy skulls etched upon them, and a menacing owl tattoo on my chest. It was, after all, the era of Kurt Cobain and

Nirvana. No wonder Myst sold so many millions of copies. It had its own alt rock coolness.

The story behind Myst is the story of young guys in a garage, making a weird indie game on faith and hope—as cheaply as they could. Tirelessly for two years, Robyn and Rand Miller and five of their pals worked out of their garages in Spokane, Washington, on the game made originally for the Apple Macintosh computer. The Millers were frugal, buying everything from video equipment to dictionaries on sale or used at flea markets. For the sound of bubbles underwater, they placed a tube in a toilet bowl, hooked up a microphone, and blew through the tube. They paid excruciatingly precise attention to detail in the artwork, story, and puzzles, which were mapped out on legal pads. They weren't making a movie, but they referred to their computer graphics as virtual movie sets and to the software as a virtual camera.

Myst was one of the first decidedly nonviolent games for adults. The Miller brothers, who had previously made software for children, were sons of a pastor, ingrained with a moral sensibility and the commandments of the Bible. Myst itself was loosely based upon a kids' game they had made. They didn't want the character to die and they didn't want him to shoot anyone. When they talked about it, Rand said to Robyn, "Violence is a big tool in storytelling and one that should not be wielded lightly. If you use violence without any point, people just get immune to it. So let's do what we think is responsible." Long hours in a cramped room took their toll. They were almost insane from the constant game making. They made the game harder than most any other game just because they could. Obsessed by their own stories for Myst's mythology, they loved the idea that they were producing something unequivocally original. Both brothers felt they were creating a game for a niche audience, one that would appreciate their artistry. An old proposal for the game reveals that the Millers expected the game to sell, at most, a hundred thousand copies. Instead, it sold nearly eight million, all on an initial investment of $300,000.

Yet the Millers' travails paled in comparison to the pals who decided to make a game filled with live action video. Inspired by a board game and a television show, The 7th Guest and its sequel were so fraught with frights that they drove one of the game designers crazy, literally. Like Myst, The 7th Guest was responsible for selling millions of personal computers. Occasionally terrifying, always campy and over the top, The 7th Guest boldly led the way for the future of horror games. However, the making of The 7th Guest and its follow-up, The 11th Hour, showed in microcosm the rift that could develop when those who held strong ideas about movies worked side by side with those who cared more about game design.

The 7th Guest co-creator Graeme Devine was born in Glasgow, Scotland, and then moved to Crawley, a south-of-London town famous for its Stone and Bronze Age artifacts. Introduced to computers by his carpenter-turned-techie father, the super-smart nerd with the high-pitched laugh began making and disassembling computer code by the age of ten. He worked on a Commodore PET (Personal Electronic Transactor) and TRS-90, learning how graphics worked and where they were positioned in the computer's memory. He haunted video arcades and tried to remake on his home computer science fiction space games that he loved. The graphics were nothing but black-and-white blips. But for Devine, when a ship disappeared after being hit, it was blowing into a thousand pieces as in *Star Wars*, full of explosions and fireworks that only the speculative mind could conjure.

At sixteen, he shocked Atari's UK office with a demo for a PC version of the popular Pole Position racing game, which he created in one night. But the teen, who had made the demo just for fun, was biting off more than he could chew when he promised Atari to make a full game. With the videogame to code and high school assignments, the deadlines accumulated. Devine told his parents that "the pressure is terrible." It was the first instance in which he would make the mistake of putting far too much on his plate. While he loved to code, the seemingly harmless obsession would ultimately make his business dealings somewhat star-crossed.

Devine took a week off from school, and when the principal asked him where he'd gone off to, he told the truth. Rage flushed the principal's face red, and Devine was promptly expelled. Shortly thereafter, he received a note from the new Atari owner, Jack Tramiel, the Polish-born former taxi driver who'd come from Commodore International. In no uncertain terms, Tramiel said in one paragraph that he would not be paying the 3 percent royalty rate detailed in Devine's contract for Pole Position. Despite this experience, Devine still wanted to make games. After high school, he created his own company and found some shadowy investors and a cheap space to set up shop, only to find that his partner was on drugs. Freaked out, Devine hastily packed up his belongings and left the office to face a windy and bracing English afternoon. The investors rang him up the next day. A gravelly voice on the end of the phone threatened, "I'm gonna come down there and break your legs." For a moment, the frozen Devine could barely speak. He began shaking as he promised to meet two goons in the office. On the next day, he spied them from the window as they parked the car outside. He was only nervous now, less timorous—because his father hid behind the door with a golf club, ready to swing at the investors' heads.

The stairs creaked. The investors knocked on the door and stepped inside. Everyone was on edge. "Your son is a horrible person. He left us high and dry," said one goon.

"He's untrustworthy, a really bad person." He took a step toward the boy.

"You're the idiots," growled Devine's father. "I trust my son." He raised the golf club. "You get the hell out of here." He started swinging the club as a weapon, and the goons ducked to avoid the iron head. They grumbled weakly. Then they left. Devine, for some time, was still traumatized, believing they would return.

He had had his share of bad luck. But the young game maker was certain that it wouldn't continue. Devine plodded on, working for Martin Alper at Mastertronics, a UK maker of budget game offerings priced at a couple of pounds and under. It wasn't the most stimulating work; he was doing more porting of games to the PC. Devine headed to California after Mastertronics opened a US office in 1986. When Alper went on to work at Virgin Interactive (which in 1987 bought a 45 percent stake in Mastertronics), Devine followed. There, Devine became buddies with a young graphics wizard called Rob Landeros. Landeros had mucked around the Berkeley scene doing everything from bawdy underground comics to amazingly life-like scrimshaw with animals and American Indian motifs. He was a "drop in, drop out" kind of college student, who told Devine he tried successfully to keep from getting a regular job and doing hard work. But Landeros felt he'd found his calling when he began to make artwork on a Commodore 64 and an Amiga computer, pixel by pixel. He would say to others that "it was like taking your first hit of LSD or peyote. Life becomes different."

With a portfolio of artwork, a self-programmed card game, and a knack for networking, Landeros had made a name for himself in Southern California without much effort. He didn't want to work too hard. He found a cushy job at Cinemaware, which was making graphically detailed, story-oriented games like Defender of the Crown. When Landeros met Devine at Virgin, their mutual interest in graphics, story, and technology—along with free trips to tech conventions—forged a strong bond. But in New York City in 1989, a fascinating, odd idea for a game made them inseparable. Or so it seemed.

At the InterMedia Conference at the Jacob Javits Convention Center (the same place where Atari failed miserably during Toy Fair), the pair witnessed the dawn of the popularization of CD-ROM technology, CDs that could hold an encyclopedic amount of data and still have room for music and video as well. CD-ROMs were a revelation, holding six hundred times the data of floppy disks, the format to which PC game makers had previously been limited. At the show, companies like Compton's and Microsoft showed off the massive amount of text the disk could store. CD-ROMs were indeed amazing. There was just so much there—videotaped speeches of King and JFK, interactivity, reams of text—it was an educator's and researcher's dream. Both Devine and Landeros wanted to make it a gamer's dream. They began thinking about using the plastic disk to make a game movie-like in ways games had never before been.

At the Newark airport, the two brainstormed and outlined their plan, with Devine writing a few notes on a paper napkin.

"We don't want to do Nintendo games with those blocky little pixely characters jumping around," said Landeros.

"I agree. They're for kids. It's important to tell a good story. Everyone can play, but it's more mature," said Devine.

Landeros had been an avid board game fan for years. He suggested that the game be a version of Clue, the strategy-oriented murder solving game by Parker Brothers, first created in 1949. Landeros was also a puzzle aficionado, with a subscription to *Games* magazine and a love for Fool's Errand, the difficult but award-winning 1987 adventure for Mac computers. Based on foreboding tarot cards, the game featured a hopeful, affable Silly Willy wandering around the countryside in medieval times. Each time he solved a puzzle, he got a piece of map leading to fourteen treasures of the Land of Tarot.

The two wanted to meld that idea somehow with their favorite TV show of the time, David Lynch's creepy, somewhat absurdist mystery *Twin Peaks*. They spoke excitedly about the dark intelligence of *Twin Peaks* for a while. Devine wrote the show's title down on a napkin. Then he circled it.

Said Devine, "From what we've seen at Intermedia, we can add little bits of video to the game."

Landeros became excited. "But we can't have people driving all over the place. By virtue of the technology, which is cool but still limited, we have to keep them confined to one place." That "one place" would be a creepy old mansion. The appearance would be menacing and ominous, a look that conjured the feeling of pure evil.

The two friends made an odd pair. Devine had the long hair of an eighties heavy metal guitarist and big black-framed glasses like those that perch on Joyce Carol Oates's nose. He was often seen wearing a bomber jacket with a smiling Mickey Mouse embroidered on the back. Landeros had a Hollywood slickness about him and often kept his cards close to his vest. He habitually wore a baseball cap and one of those silk stadium jackets so popular in the 1990s. It made him look just a little like a Hollywood director. Together, they were like a Lennon and McCartney of videogames, or at least they could have been.

At Virgin Interactive, an invigorated Devine worked like a man possessed. He cranked out a twenty-page pitch and game design document and quickly sent it over to Martin Alper, the company president. Alper responded within an hour, asking the pair to lunch at the Farmer's Market and driving them there in his Rolls-Royce. As they all sipped grossly sweet yogurt shakes, Alper, still a little cagey, said, "I read the pitch. You really want to do this?"

Devine and Landeros eagerly nodded and said, "Yes." Devine took a sip of his shake.

"If this is what you want to do," Alper said, "I'm afraid I have to fire you."

Devine nearly spewed the thick shake onto his boss. He and Landeros were completely shocked. They were director-level middle managers who liked their jobs and salaries. What had they done to deserve dismissal? Alper leaned forward and laid down the law. "It comes with some good news, too. I'm going to give you a contract to make this game." Yet he cautioned that there was no way in the world that their horror game was going to be profitable. He said it was valuable merely as a proof of concept, as a trophy game that would display what CD-ROMs could do. Then he pounded the table with his fist and said only four people would ever buy it. Alper had some other demands, too, including a request for the two to produce a floppy disk version of The 7th Guest, a next-to-impossible task that the duo immediately pushed to the side. In addition, the pair could not establish offices beyond sixty miles from the Virgin Interactive offices. Alper felt that Devine and Landeros were too unseasoned to leave the fold completely, and he didn't completely trust them with company money. Having said that, he agreed to provide a healthy budget for the CD-ROM, twice the $200,000 to $300,000 that Virgin usually paid for cartridge games.

Devine and Landeros broke the rules immediately. They set up shop that November in an office above a tavern more than sixty miles away—far out of state, in the small town of Jacksonville, Oregon, an old gold mining community that perhaps was best known as the home of the original Bozo the Clown. Devine had to be convinced about Oregon after stopping in rainy Ashland, which looked like a dreary logging town. But when their car pulled into Jacksonville, the rain turned to wet snow, with big, fat flakes, and the townspeople gathered around their car to sing Christmas carols. A waving Santa Claus even rode past in a sleigh. Devine saw this popular-culture onslaught as a fortuitous sign. The two found what they saw as the perfect office as well, one with thirty-foot ceilings and a $1,000-a-month rent.

As Devine packed his boxes, the phone rang. Ken Williams, the persuasive head of Sierra On-Line, which made the King's Quest adventure games, among others, tried to hire Devine. While his offer of royalties was less then the spoils of the first years of Sierra, when a freelance designer's cut amounted to an astonishing 30 percent, it still neared 10 percent for games Devine would make for Williams. Devine casually took a bite of cold pizza and said, "Sorry, Ken. I've got my own company now."

Trilobyte, named by Landeros after a cheeky character in an old underground comic, had only four core employees. The staff was lean, the hours long, and the camaraderie close as could be. Landeros oversaw the script writing. He also kept tabs on the director, who budgeted $25,000 for the two-day video shoot, one that included a cardboard blue screen purchased at a local flea market. During the shoot, done in the Super VHS format, one of the actors fell through the blue screen, which was then taped up. The blue screen was still ruined, and wasn't even the right shade of blue; the marring showed up in the editing room after the shoot. Trilobyte had to hire expensive video editors to take out the frames where the tear showed. Within six months, which was the budgeted development cycle, they were running out of money—fast. The 7th Guest was becoming a microcosm of the haphazard nature of the videogame industry, still in its teething phase. Deadlines passed. Milestones were not met. And the game was not finished. Devine and Landeros were suddenly faced with a difficult reality: They had to use their own money to fund Trilobyte.

Devine began working on creating software within the CD-ROM disk that would play full-motion video. Within days he had a robust but small ninety-kilobyte player called Play that was so good, it was licensed by Autodesk, the makers of the best 3-D animation program of the time. Then Devine figured out a way to compress the huge video files so that they would easily fit on two CD-ROMs. Video had never before been used in a game, nor had video compression. It was genius work, fueled by coffee strong enough to bore holes in a cast iron stomach. Days would pass in the blink of an eye. Surprising to Devine was Landeros's stamina; he was no longer in his twenties or thirties, but he kept going like an old Timex watch. The royalty money from Autodesk helped everyone tread water. From the shareware version of Play, cash came in via drips and trickles; about ten copies a day on a good day meant an extra $200 for the company. During the rare moments that the duo wasn't working together, they were watching laser discs together. When UPS delivered Stanley Kubrick's *The Shining*, they drove to Devine's home to watch it. When it was over, they watched it again.

Some of the furniture and house wasn't finished, and there was some blue space where objects like paintings with moving eyes would be, but by January 1992, they had pieced together a rough demo of the game to take to the Consumer Electronics Show in Chicago. Once there, they asked the Virgin Interactive representative to remove a videogame version of the Monopoly board game from one of the computers so they could show their game off on a large monitor. As they put The 7th Guest through its paces, word spread throughout the show floor that full-motion video was being shown off in a game, and people swarmed to the booth. Within minutes, it was standing room only, with people peering from the outside in to view the invention. The 7th Guest was the biggest hit of the convention, and the two were treated like emerging Hollywood stars, recognized everywhere on the show floor.

On the plane back to Oregon, Devine and Landeros had mixed feelings. They were proud and elated. They felt they might have a game that would sell exponentially more than Alper's prediction of four copies. They were also so terrifed that they felt sick to their stomachs. Now they would have to deliver a game that was even better than the demo.

"Shit," said Devine.

"Shit," added Landeros.

Back in Oregon, the company couldn't afford a proper tech department, and their computer network, which only stored five hundred megabytes, kept crashing from the weight of the sizable video editing projects. They had to make the game look like it had full-motion video; that was their hook. But the opening scene alone, in which the camera moved up an old staircase, had to be tweaked for a month before it looked like a smooth scene shot by a movie camera. The whole problem seems ludicrous today. Today, nearly everyone has QuickTime or Flash to run videos on YouTube, MySpace, or Facebook; you download trailers in seconds with three-megabytes-per-second broadband, and even waiting those seconds can seem like an eternity. But back in 1990, playing video was a novelty. Placing video into game code was a monumental hurdle to overcome, even with the help of Devine's magic video player. Handling and compressing the data was a complex puzzle, more brain-busting than anything in The 7th Guest itself, and more horrifying, too. An hour's worth of video took months to organize.

One day during crunch time, Alper and a few business executives flew up to Medford and drove over to the Trilobyte offices in Jacksonville. Alper was still forcing Trilobyte to create a floppy disk version of the product. Equally pressing, since the game was delayed by four months, was Alper's need to make certain that hard work was being done. As the meeting began, Landeros suddenly excused himself. Minutes went by. At the ten-minute mark, Alper was getting more and more annoyed. Devine had no idea where his partner had gone.

"What the hell is this, some kind of negotiating tool?" complained Alper.

The minutes passed too slowly for Devine, who was now sweating. At the fifteen-minute point, Landeros returned and calmly sat down. "Where were you?" asked Devine, who had anxiously tried calming the executives to no avail.

"I'm sorry. I just got married." Landeros explained that the only block of time he could find to get hitched was during the hours when Virgin Interactive was in town. He had gone down to City Hall to meet his betrothed, place a ring on her finger, stand for a brief ceremony, and kiss the bride. Then he got back in his car and headed back to the meeting. Alper was impressed with the work ethic, and Virgin Interactive never again demanded a floppy disk version of the scary mystery.

Once Alper departed, one of the employees got up, opened the window, and screamed to the world in vitriolic Peter Finch/*Network* fashion, "I screwed up! I screwed up!" He had made an error writing code to a CD-ROM and had to dispose of it. CD-ROMs for testing on Trilobyte's prized $5,000 CD-ROM copier were priced at $100 each in the early nineties, and they weren't rewritable. Making a mistake with one disk was an expensive proposition, but one that was difficult to avoid because Trilobyte needed to experiment in order to break new ground. The neighbors and passersby on Jacksonville's streets heard the plaintive and pissed off cries all too often.

Yet there were saviors swooping down from the heavens, the first in the form of one of the more forward-thinking game companies, the second in the form of the world's most paranoid game company. The Consumer Electronics Show buzz caught on throughout the industry, and Sega now yearned to have The 7th Guest for the CD-ROM-based Sega CD attachment to its Genesis console. The Genesis, which started slow in Japan, was on its way to becoming the bestselling game player in Europe. Sega was also releasing the first in a series of games featuring its speedy, cheeky mascot, the very blue-colored Sonic the Hedgehog. Sega approached Trilobyte with a lucrative offer. But Nintendo, which would soon begin to lose market share to Sega, got wind of the company's interest and preempted the deal, licensing The 7th Guest for the Nintendo Entertainment System for a staggering $500,000. However, they never planned to publish the game. Nintendo had made a Go-like strategic move to stop Sega from gaining any more ground. Trilobyte received half of those monies and Virgin the other half. Better for the ego than money was the fact that Nintendo sent superstar Shigeru Miyamoto to the little town in Oregon to see what all the fuss was about. Devine planned a grand barbecue for the Legend of Zelda maker. On a hot August day, as steaks sizzled on the grill, Miyamoto seemed happy to hang out with Devine, although the Japanese game maker was somewhat confused about where he was in the world. Through the two translators who arrived with him, Miyamoto told Devine, "I don't think this CD-ROM technology will ever become popular. At Nintendo, we have cartridges. Cartridges cannot be broken by children. Kids will scratch and smudge these disks, making them unusable. That's why Nintendo is sticking to cartridges." Devine knew that CD-ROMs were the future, but he didn't dare challenge the great Miyamoto.

The finished game was nothing like Mario or Zelda. It had moments that scared you to the point of shivering. The game opened by showing players a Victorian house on a hill, a lone bright light in one second-floor window. Below, a barren, moonlit path snaked its way to the door. Above, the midnight clouds looked like the gnarly fingers of Nosferatu, ready to grab, hold on, and choke until death came. Wind ravaged, thunder pillaged your ears, and tentacled lightning blinded. In the distance, a lone wolf cried out in pain. There was the unsettling sound of a door creaking, somewhere. And that was just the first seven seconds.

Instead of The Stranger, you meet the The Drifter Stauf, sleeping in a trench coat under a craggy hundred-year-old oak tree. An echoing, disembodied voice tells you The Drifter was "moving from town to town, robbing a gas station here, a grocery store there—until one night . . ." As he steals her purse, Stauf kills a young girl coming home from choir practice because "he had nothing, no life, no possessions, no dreams." Stauf has visions of toy making, and the toys he carves make him rich. But they might also kill children. The scene is shot in front of a blue screen, a wide shot with a static camera shooting the actors straight on, somewhat like the films of the silent movie era—crude, but effective. In a few moments, you realize that the name Stauf is an anagram for Faust. You shiver, thinking your goose bumps will pop like acne. Once inside the dark old mansion, a bony skeleton's hand beckons, suggesting where to go for clues. Upstairs goes the shaky camera, Steadicam fashion. At the top, a ghost with long tresses floats across the wide floor planks and through the walls. It's often written that scary games are best played with the lights off. However, even if your sixty-watt gooseneck lamp was right next to your PC, you were utterly spooked by The 7th Guest. Even better than the frights (which featured a passel of eerie toys) were the peculiar puzzles that Devine and Landeros invented for the game. Moving the blue cells in the old microscope around so that they outnumbered the green cells, which Stauf controlled, was an enigma solvable only by genius math gurus with a major in algorithms. You would curse aloud and throw your trackball mouse against the wall and then go out to the corner bar for a stiff drink.

Back in California, the honchos at Virgin Interactive were well aware of the heat around The 7th Guest. And they were ready to take advantage of it. Keith Greer, the company's chief financial officer, led the charge to put a $99 sticker price on the game, which would be a collector's package that would include a video documentary, a small book, the soundtrack, and a bizarre box that looked as though red-eyed demons would crawl out of it, Pandora style, when it was opened. Both Devine and Landeros protested, thinking $99 was an outlandish price to pay. But they had no say in the matter. Virgin Interactive had what it felt was a genius plan, and Virgin Interactive was going to stick by it. They also were asking for a sequel, which Landeros was already working on. Just as Devine was finishing the technology for The 7th Guest, Landeros was involved in shooting the script for The 11th Hour. Without Devine's input, filming commenced in the spring of 1993, partially at a sprawling National Guard armory in Medford, Orgeon. Even during preproduction, there was trouble. Matt Costello's script was too long and was severely rewritten by director David Wheeler. The story, which took place sixty years after the horrific events of The 7th Guest, was steeped in sex and was much more violent. Heads exploded to reveal a gross mass of brain, eyes, and gore. Fingers were smashed. Throats were slit. Flailing, alien insects emerged from toothpaste tubes. When Devine walked onto the set, he fumed when he saw the filming of a woman in S&M gear, including a spiky leather collar. She was bare breasted as well. But Devine could do little beyond worry; filming had already commenced.

Ultimately, The 7th Guest was only about five months late, and when it was released, it became an overnight hit. The modest pressing of sixty thousand copies was gone from store shelves within days. The retailer Software, Etc. wasn't content merely to sell the game; in a sign of sheer greed, the chain began bundling The 7th Guest with a CD-ROM drive. Virgin Interactive struggled to keep up with the demand for a game that was played by every member of the family. Along with Myst, industry analysts claimed that The 7th Guest was responsible for selling hundreds of thousands of PCs equipped with CD-ROM drives. By the time it stopped selling, more than two million copies of The 7th Guest had been sold. For its break-through in technology, Trilobyte received eleven awards from multimedia organizations and magazines between 1993 and 1995. Devine and Landeros had become millionaires on paper. For a project that cost at most $750,000, the financial return for Virgin Interactive was in the stratosphere. For the time being, Trilobyte was hotter than Nintendo, which was seen by pundits to be losing its steam. Devine and Landeros were the new stars of an industry in which adventure games were the Next Big Deal. Overnight success, however, was the worst thing that could have happened to Trilobyte.

Venture capitalists began to swarm and pick at the company like turkey vultures on fresh carrion. An advisory board full of hotshots and moneymen was created. A bigger office, featuring tens of thousands of square feet and bulletproof glass, was leased and sixty employees were hired. Devine and Landeros were forced to spend a lot of time looking at financial projections and spreadsheets. Trilobyte was being groomed by Wall Street to be the next gold-mine initial public offering. Microsoft, Disney, and Fox representatives pulled up in fancy cars, thinking seriously about investing in the company or offering Devine and Landeros lucrative gigs. They proposed a Clive Barker horror game, a *Blade Runner* game, and an *X-Files* game. Trilobyte passed every time. Some analysts, who valued the company at more than $50 million, said Trilobyte was on its way to becoming a company more massive than Sega, with more reach than Nintendo. Two million sold? That was nothing, they said. The next game would do Super Mario Bros. numbers. Microsoft cofounder Paul Allen became a believer, adding $5 million to Trilobyte coffers. How utterly wrong they all were.

The new video movie for The 11th Hour was the bugaboo. The director was drunk with adding camera angles he perceived to be crucial to the plot. There were long pans, close-ups, and outdoor shooting in the miserably rainy Oregon spring at a rushing dam. There

was running through the forest with a Steadicam. By the end, there
were two and a half hours of video in the game. An overwhelming amount of compression work for Devine awaited. As he dug in,
the pressure began to take its hold. A making-of video shows an exhausted, halfhearted Devine almost whispering his answers. In the
same video, Landeros, who had gained weight from the stress, talks
about how big the game will be. Yet both appear somehow sad. They
don't seem to believe their own words. At least no one fell through
the blue screen this time.

The two were no longer in sync. Devine disliked the gore in
The 11th Hour and became freaked out by the massive amount of
work before him. The company was working on six projects at once,
including a game that would take place in Antarctica and which
dealt with an archaeological dig and dinosaurs. Landeros's direction
changed too; he wanted to do an interactive movie for the theaters.

Then Devine locked himself in his office. He was alone with his
thoughts, too alone, trying to figure out how to compress the video,
all the time knowing that technology was changing, month by month.
He fretted that by the time The 11th Hour was released, it would
seem old to consumers. Day after day, he kept the door to his office
shut. By his own admission, he was hell to work with because to find
better solutions, he would literally turn the game technology upside
down every week. Charged up on caffeine, he sent e-mail missives
at four a.m. He would go home, drop into bed, only to return a few
hours later. The amount of change that he expected and demanded
was very hard on the creative team. But he felt he constantly had to
do something, to say something. He kept thinking, "Trilobyte can't
fuck up. I can't fuck up. There's too much at stake."

By the end of the development cycle, Devine and Landeros
were no longer speaking. For the making-of documentary, they
were shot separately, not together as in The 7th Guest promotional
video. Somewhere in Devine's brain, in a deep place he could not

consciously get to, he knew he was screwing up, that Landeros was screwing up, that the whole project was doomed. By 1994, they had earned $5 million from The 7th Guest. But they were not happy or fulfilled. As The 11th Hour's budget added up to $2 million and then some, Devine was enduring terribly painful migraine headaches.

When the game was released one year and eight months late, in 1995, it was beset by technological issues that made it difficult to install on computers; half of those who purchased the game had problems getting it to run. There were one million copies of The 11th Hour on the market, and this time, the buzz was not good. Landeros was off with director Wheeler making his sex-drenched $800,000 interactive movie called *Tender Loving Care,* a film in which the audience would answer multiple choice questions to move the story along. It was the wrong direction in which to take the already bloated company.

With The 11th Hour underperforming, Devine dreaded going to work. As he drove through the town's pretty streets, he felt ugly and sick. He no longer wanted any part of Trilobyte. But they wouldn't let him go. The board elected to fire Landeros and to let him keep the rights to *Tender Loving Care.* They decided to keep Devine, who was working on an online tank combat game called Assault, which could accommodate as many as twenty-four players at one time. Even though Paul Allen put more than a million dollars into the game (later renamed Extreme Warfare), it was, like the others, deadline plagued. It would never be released.

Devine lamented, "The friendship is over. I sided with the board. I didn't side with my partner. I didn't side with my friend. And now I feel lost." He would be lost for many years after that. Eventually, Devine tried to sell the company to Midway, but Midway backed out at the last minute. There was nothing left to do but close the shop down. Admitted Devine, "I'm mentally exhausted, mentally ill, poor, have no money, and am literally living on money from my parents and my wife's parents." For his part, Landeros felt that the real horror story was not in the game, but in real life. The company became a monster, the two friends mere puppets in the quest for financial reward. Everyone was pushing them to build a gleaming publishing empire so they could take Trilobyte public. Worse, Landeros had seen the writing on the wall: Interactive storytelling was becoming a thing of the past.

While it wouldn't happen immediately, he was right. Games themselves were changing. While adventure games hadn't yet peaked, gamers would soon turn away from them in favor of first-person shooters full of Nazis and monsters and bloody action. Yet Devine and Landeros (along with the Miller brothers) were responsible for making games begin to look as good as the movies. They had set the bar high. And they had made their mark, just as Myst did; games now had to look so real, you could almost smell the reeking, rotting corpse in Stauf's mansion. Without The 7th Guest, games like BioShock and Heavy Rain, both of which rely on lifelike graphics and expertly written tales of horror, would likely not have been so frightening. Because of The 7th Guest and Myst, the future would be all about graphics that looked hyperreal, so much so that the moving pictures and artwork would tell the story better than words. The efforts of these men—and the power of the CD-ROM—also helped make the PC into a viable gaming platform in the 1990s. So now games were in the arcades and bars and bowling alleys, in the consoles in the living room and bedroom, and in the PCs in the den. And with the ubiquity of laptops, you could take your game on the road with you and see it in more glorious detail than with a Game Boy. Weirdly, the platforms did not cannibalize one another. They all thrived. Games were available on just about every cool tech device a nerd—and the quickly growing companies—could imagine.

But beyond its essential role in the horror genre and beyond turning families into PC gamers, the tragic, friend-ending story of Trilobyte became a cautionary tale for all videogame changers. Once close friends whom some called the Lennon and McCartney of videogames, Devine and Landeros would not speak to each other for well over a decade. Some developers wouldn't pay attention to Trilobyte's fate. Many, full of haughtiness and swagger that led them to cut corners and drop deadlines, would follow a path down into the musty greed cave, just like the devilish Mammon in Book II of Spenser's *The Faerie Queene*. But a few would listen as they raised their fingers to test the winds. They could predict the trends and, through diligence and just a little bit of dumb luck, would become millionaires many times over.

8.

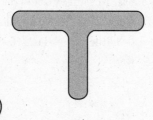

THE PLAYSTATION'S CRASH

There were cornfields, cattle, and blue sky as far as the eye could see, but all the two guys in a silver Honda Accord could think of was Sonic's Ass.

Unlike movies, which often start with a detailed story treatment, games often begin only with genre, in this case a running and jumping game called a platformer. The design on the two road-trippers' minds that day would be heavily influenced by Sega's existing Sonic the Hedgehog character and by a sneak preview they had seen of a game that updated the classic Miyamoto gorilla—Donkey Kong Country. As the two young designers hatched their plan, it became clear that their platformer would appear to gamers to have a huge depth of field. But there was a big challenge. Since games didn't yet have the capacity to be 3-D, the only way they could pull this off technologically was to have the gamer control the character from behind and fake the gamer out to give the illusion of moving down paths, roads, and rivers.

"Sonic's Ass!" cried Andy Gavin, referring to the from-behind-the-butt perspective the gamer would have. They were somewhere deep in the plains-filled farmlands of Iowa. The crack made his co-conspirator Jason Rubin, who was driving, laugh his butt off.

For their three-day cross-country drive to Los Angeles, Andy Gavin and Jason Rubin had packed up the car in Boston with as much stuff as it could carry—along with Rubin's barking black Lab and ridgeback mix. Unlike most guys in their twenties, Gavin and Rubin had already made it, kind of. They had some industry clout from their handful of game deals, thanks primarily to their relationship with Trip Hawkins at Electronic Arts, who published their games and acted somewhat like a mentor to them. But they had also been living in an apartment with little heat to save money. They were frantically waiting for payment for the Way of the Warrior game they had made for Hawkins's 3DO machine. They were told the check was in the mail.

Now they were heading to Universal Pictures to work for the studio's new videogames unit. They'd been lured by a three-game deal and a cushy space on the Universal lot, right near Steven Spielberg's office. Life was going to be good for the hardworking pair.

Rubin and Gavin had met as tweens in 1982, at a weekend Hebrew school in Virginia, near Washington, DC. Once they discovered they both were fascinated by computers and games, they congregated in the back of class and discussed computer programming manuals and how to hack games so they could get them for free. The friendship continued. The two loved talking about making games, their small piracies, and how they subverted the system. They made a good team, so much so that their mothers couldn't get them off the phone even after six-hour-long bull sessions. Rubin had a knack for drawing and a gift of gab; Gavin was a magician when it came to programming. With a pal, Mike Goyet, who had amassed $130, they began a teenage enterprise they called Jam (for Jason, Andy, and Mike) Software. Since Mike didn't do anything much to help out, they booted him from the company within months. But Gavin and Rubin kept on going. They were so obsessed that they headed to a local video arcade with a cheesy camera and photographed dozens of Punch Out!! screens so they could program their own version of the wacky boxing game on their home computers.

Between 1984 and 1987, Gavin and Rubin made three games together, an educational title called Math Jam, a sports title called Ski Crazed, and an adventure called Dream Zone. None really pushed the envelope, but they worked. All were sold to a somewhat shady Midwestern outfit that Rubin felt was created as a tax writeoff for, well, someone.

But this venture with Universal—it wasn't CBGB's anymore; as the Talking Heads sang in "Life During Wartime," they ain't got time for that now. The road trip to the big time was thrilling in the way that many places can be when you're just passing through. But it was nothing compared to the excitement of the game they had in mind. The two couldn't stop talking about the first thing they would pitch to the movie company's game division. "Hey, maybe it could be a movie, too," enthused Rubin. If the pitch worked, they surmised, the game would probably be perfect for Trip Hawkins's 3DO machine or for a new system that Sony was about to release in Japan called the PlayStation (the US debut would come about a year later). Publishing on the ill-fated 3DO system, which wasn't selling well, was then considered nearly akin to everyone in a video-game studio committing hara-kiri. The pair would counter that the 3DO might be flopping, but that was because it was way ahead of its time. It was still a pretty cool machine. While they didn't drink all of the Trip Hawkins Kool-Aid, they saw Hawkins as a visionary. That's what Gavin and Rubin told people when they asked. After all,

Hawkins had given the two their first real shot at gaming stardom, in the late 1980s. Both kids could see that Hawkins was up-front and candid, and one of the more honest businessmen they had met in the videogame industry. Their relationship with Hawkins began when they cold-called EA as the principals of a new company called Naughty Dog and talked their way into a $15,000 advance. The two then developed an Apple IIGS game called Keef the Thief, about a blond-maned kid who was a master thief and who met richly imagined characters, like a musician called The Cross-Eyed Demon of Death, who played for your dark satisfaction a tune dubbed "The Demon's Dirge."

At the time, the two knew that Hawkins had a team hard at work reverse engineering the Sega Genesis. Gavin actually saw the process in action, in a big, sterile-looking room at Electronic Arts. Thick cables came out of a Sega Genesis and into a computer. Shocked, Gavin said to Hawkins, "There's no way you're not reverse engineering here."

When Gavin told the company founder that he and Rubin had a perfect role playing game for the Genesis, the usually loquacious Hawkins took time to listen. It was a big game, one of the biggest RPGs ever, explained Gavin. He called the game "Ultima on steroids," a bold statement considering that Richard Garriott's Ultima II was so sprawling, it came on two computer disks. But Gavin continued, "You would have seven magicians to work with, not just one, and over one hundred spells to wield. You can control tornadoes and ride dinosaurs, too." As Gavin outlined the hundred or so characters and quests, Hawkins warmed to the idea. Gavin also felt Hawkins might give Naughty Dog a contract in exchange for their silence about EA's highly illegal process of reverse engineering. Gavin was right. He and Rubin guaranteed their silence, and Rings of Power went full steam ahead. In the end it was so big that the cartridge needed a battery inside to make it work. Ultimately, it sold a respectable sixty thousand copies, but it could have done much more business, at least according to Rubin. Rubin sometimes lamented to Gavin that Madden was taking up all the time at the factory with which EA contracted to make its games. Because of the football game's popularity, scheduling the manufacturing of Rings of Power cartridges was placed on the back burner, so far back that many would never be made.

Once they were ensconced in Los Angeles and developing games for the movie company, the two Naughty Dogs moved forward with the game project they dubbed "Sonic's Ass." In September 1994, at the Cafe Del Sol near the Universal lot, Gavin riffed on what the antagonist would be even before they had a main character. As he downed lobster ravioli, he changed his voice to that of an evil mad scientist and said, "I am Dr. Cortex, Dr. Neo Cortex." Rubin loved the idea. Gavin told the others present that there was a kind of secret sauce to game making, a tight combination of game play, graphics, and technology. The art sells it, he said, and the technology makes it happen. Without game play that's new, it's not fun. But it can't be so difficult that it becomes daunting. In the game, the plan was for you to run and jump through a jungle world full of artwork so lush, you could smell the exotic flora. But who would their funny animal protagonist be and of which species? More important, could they pull it off for Sony, the company that offered the best deal for the game? After all, the forthcoming PlayStation was rife with hardware challenges, to put it subtly.

Inspired by the Looney Tunes of their youth, Naughty Dog hired two experienced animators who had worked on Hanna-Barbera cartoons and Disney's DuckTales series to draw pen-and-ink prototypes for their character. Rubin, with his male model good looks, turned out to be a genius at communicating with the people who wrote the checks, while Gavin refined his MIT-schooled tech chops so that few other game designers could touch him. Both were armed with an almost enyclopedic knowledge of games. At first, their character was going to be a wombat called Willy. But when they came across the word "bandicoot" in a travel guide to the South Pacific, they became enamored of the marsupial's exotic-sounding name. In a meeting with the animators, Rubin announced, "We're going to own that name, bandicoot. When people think of that word, we want them to think of the character in the game, not the animal."

Gavin added, "Think of him as bold, clever, willful, good-natured, and gung-ho, but not the brightest bulb on the planet." Yet Gavin and Rubin knew that the way the bandicoot looked would have to be informed by the limitations of the PlayStation. The machine's graphics chip did not produce enough resolution for the detail Rubin wanted in the marsupial body. Crash's bottom-heavy frame had to be orange because all of the other available colors were being used for backgrounds on the island in which the animal dwelled. He would wear brown gloves, too, because the digits in Crash's orange hands would get lost when they moved in front of his orange body. The early tool kit Sony sent to Naughty Dog was easy to work with. However, the software was barely usable for the technologically forward-thinking game that Gavin had in mind—especially because it contained a graphics bug. In addition, the unrefundable rental fee that Sony charged for the tool kit was an astounding $70,000, for a package that included a blue console and game making software. Although it was expressly forbidden, Gavin took the PlayStation apart and reverse engineered it so that he didn't have to use Sony's software.

"Oh my God," said Rubin, stunned when he saw the results.

"Mind-bogglingly better, right?"

Due to the nature of their deal with Universal Studios, the movie company tried to keep Naughty Dog away from the powers at Sony, perhaps because of a fear that the duo would jump ship. But they did eventually meet. When Kelly Flock, a Sony executive who had done a stint at LucasArts, saw a demonstration of the game, he was floored.

"How the hell did you do that?" Flock wondered aloud. Gavin confessed that he had gone into the PlayStation to make it work to his specifications.

"Hold on," said Flock. "How are you getting all that data into the system? How many times will the game access the CD-ROM drive?"

Gavin got out a pen and paper to make some calculations. "About one hundred and forty thousand times."

Flock was not amused. "That's not good. The life expectancy of the PlayStation is eighty thousand hits. It's a guarantee that this game will break the PlayStation." Nonetheless, Flock knew the game could be huge, even a Mario Killer. At the time, few, if any, games being made for the PlayStation in the United States could do graphics the way Crash Bandicoot did. Flock did nothing to daunt the game makers. Instead, he encouraged them to finish quickly. As with the dozens of other companies Sony was signing up to make games, Sony offered Universal a royalty rate of at least 10 percent. Meanwhile, engineers in Japan were working on increasing the life span of the all-important CD-ROM drive. They did their job well, and Crash was deemed safe for the system.

What Naughty Dog did not fully realize at the time was the intense power struggle going on within Sony Computer Entertainment in the United States. Of the three executives in the running to head the US division, none seemed to know precisely how to deal with the cultural and business machinations of those who were in charge in Tokyo. When a US executive pitched an idea for the PlayStation hardware, it didn't fly. He was told flatly, "No." The Japanese executives had already given their stamp of approval to even the smallest detail. Suggestions were not appreciated. Sony sorely needed an American executive who could understand Japanese culture and who could foster an essential company-wide trust and comity. Finally, Bernie Stolar, a gregarious entrepreneur with wide and varied management skills—including a stint as president of Atari—was brought in to run the American division. Stolar had thrived in the game milieu beyond Atari, beginning in 1980 with an arcade game called Deep Death (later renamed Shark Attack). Stolar hired a diminutive, quick-thinking Brit from Wales called Andrew House, who was tapped to lead the marketing charge. The race to release the PlayStation in the United States—and to try to beat Nintendo into submission—was on.

Sales of the Japanese version of the PlayStation, which was released in early December 1994, were brisk; 300,000 machines were purchased in its first thirty days on the market. Yet the initial slate of games was not of the jaw-dropping variety. The driving game Ridge Racer was creditable with its integration of a Galaxian arcade game, which, if you won, let you unlock and drive any of twelve souped-up cars. But it was nothing completely new. Sony still needed a game to differentiate itself in North America when the PlayStation hit those shores within a year. Even when the PlayStation was unveiled at the first E3 convention in Los Angeles in May 1995, with a $4 million booth and an appearance by Michael Jackson, Sony showed off games from Japan and England like the fighting game Tekken and the anti-gravity, vertigo-inducing racing game WipEout. To truly rule the videogame world, Sony needed to present the US market with a compelling, American-made product.

Yet there was resistance from Japan regarding how precisely to raise the awareness of potential PlayStation buyers in America, especially on the part of the father of the PlayStation, Ken Kutaragi. Kutaragi's mandate was to have games made by Sony itself become the bestsellers. To that end, Sony in the United States made Twisted Metal, a freewheeling demolition derby game featuring a grinning clown character called Calypso, who was as insanely creepy as a serial killer. But games that came in from the outside, like Universal's Crash Bandicoot, were secondary in his mind. And he hated the idea that Crash Bandicoot might be a mascot for the PlayStation. To Kutaragi, the PlayStation wasn't a toy like Nintendo's products. And it wasn't just for kids like Nintendo was, either. The PlayStation didn't just play games. It played music CDs as well. Therefore, in Kutaragi's mind, the PlayStation was more versatile than the other consoles ever were. When Kutaragi looked at Sony, he saw the Walkman. The Walkman didn't attach its essence to any one artist, not even to superstar Michael Jackson, Sony's biggest artist at the time. Such a folly would have been disastrous to the Walkman's continuing success with every other artist and record company in the world. So there was no way that Crash Bandicoot would be the face of the PlayStation. It wasn't that Kutaragi hated the strange-looking marsupial from Naughty Dog completely. But perhaps because it reminded him of a nasty Nintendo debacle, he seemed to have a special place of disdain for the game in his heart.

Kutaragi's work with the maker of Mario games showed him to be an unbridled maverick who was concerned with creativity that would push videogame technology forward. Still, the problem with Nintendo presented itself in the late eighties, after Kutaragi had worked with Sony making early digital cameras. Kutaragi, an über-smart engineer with a high-pitched voice, who spoke English well, was a force of nature within a company that played everything by the book. In 1988, when Kutaragi discovered that Nintendo needed a sound chip for the next Nintendo game system, he surreptitiously began work on the project—without the knowledge of Sony's higher level executives. Yet he wasn't fired. Because his work was considered so valuable to Sony, he was let off with a stern warning. Through sheer, commandant-like persistence, he convinced Sony CEO Noria Ohga to fund a collaboration with Nintendo called the Super NES CD-ROM drive. The machine would be able to play both cartridges and CD-ROMs. Sony struck a sweet deal with Nintendo to be the only maker of the latter media. Nintendo, which at first loved the idea, started to sour on it when Hiroshi Yamauchi began to believe Nintendo would lose a share of the market to the electronics behemoth if they were in bed together. Kutaragi as well would create the sound chip that the Nintendo machine would use—also to be manufactured by Sony. When Sony announced the PlayStation at the Consumer Electronics Show in June of 1991, word of a landmark agreement between the two companies was greeted with shock and amazement. Within twenty-four hours, Nintendo issued a press release that stated it would partner with Philips, a serious Sony foe, for its CD-ROM drive. In essence, it had broken its contract with Sony. Kutaragi was at his wit's end; he not only had lost a lucrative contract for his employer, he had lost face as well. Sony never made that particular version of the PlayStation, and Nintendo didn't make a CD-ROM drive for the SNES, either. Ultimately, the partnership was a failure, probably because the two companies were too competitive to work together in anything that resembled harmony.

But Kutaragi soldiered on. He had a dream to make videogames look as good as one of his favorite movies, *Blade Runner*. Through a combination of yelling, screaming, and nose-to-the-grindstone hard work, Ken Kutaragi had fought tooth and nail to get his PlayStation up and running in Japan. Though early on Sony as a corporation did not really see the potential for a game machine, Kutaragi continued to evangelize. And none of the operating companies within Sony wanted to look after the PlayStation. Electronics didn't really want it. Nor did any other division. But Kutaragi kept on fighting. He knew that if the PlayStation failed in the territories beyond Japan, he would be out of a job.

Understandably, Kutaragi made it one of his life's goals to beat Nintendo at its own game. At the very least, he made it clear to the US operation that he wasn't going to put all his eggs in one basket and make Crash Bandicoot the face of the PlayStation. To that end, Kelly Flock, a savvy businessman who was very calculating and could hold a grudge, had another mascotlike game made by Sony itself. It was called Harry Jalapeno, and was so inferior to Crash Bandicoot that it never saw the light of day.

Yet not long before Crash Bandicoot's release, Kutaragi still didn't believe in the game's potential. And he was about to make it known. At the first E3 convention, Kutaragi was approached by Mark Cerny, a former teenage Atari game maker turned Universal Interactive vice president, who was desperately searching for a hit and thought he had found it with Crash. Cerny, a soft-spoken, erudite sort, was very proud of his association with Naughty Dog and the possibilities for the marsupial, especially since he hadn't had a million seller in decades. Since Atari, Cerny had been involved with dozens of games. His history in the industry didn't matter to Kutaragi. For more than forty-five minutes, the Japanese inventor railed at him. Kutaragi's words became more and more roiled. "This Crash—" He spewed the words from his mouth like he was spitting out spoiled food. "This Crash is never going to sell. It has no heart at all. The only thing to make it passable is if every plant would dance to the beat of the hearts of the animals in the game. But it does not. So this game is crap. This game is crap!" By the end of the conversation, Cerny was shaking, almost in tears.

Kutaragi and his minions in Japan may have disliked Crash, but the Americans felt it was the perfect fit for the US audience. Stolar, Cerny, and the small Universal Interactive marketing department were ready to stake their jobs on Crash. Finally, Japan caved. Even if Crash was for kids, and kids weren't the intended audience for the PlayStation, the US executives convinced Japan that maybe, just maybe, Crash could take a substantial amount of money away from the Mario franchise.

Before Crash was placed on store shelves on August 31, 1996, advertising agency Chiat\Day, along with Andrew House and the Sony marketing department, carefully crafted an advertising campaign based on the daffy marsupial. It included a brash television commercial that would cement the bandicoot as a mascot in the minds of the American public. In the thirty-second spot, a man in a Crash Bandicoot outfit traveled to a spot outside the US offices of Nintendo in Redmond, Washington. With a bullhorn, he called out, "Hey, plumber boy, mustache man: Your worst nightmare has arrived." As he removed a tarp from his rusty flatbed truck and revealed six monitors, all playing video of some portion of the Crash game, he bragged, "We got real time, 3-D, lush organic environments. How does that make you feel? Feel like your days are numbered?" As he was unceremoniously escorted from the property, a security guard asked if his name was Italian. "No," said Crash. "Bandicoot. It's an Australian name." After the spot aired constantly on prime time TV and during football games, Sonic's Ass was known to millions of Americans. Game magazines pitted Crash against Mario and Sonic. "Who will win the console wars?" was the question every games journalist began to ask.

While the 3DO was dying, Sega had released the CD-ROM-based Saturn console, which did not set American hearts afire due to its higher price of $399, although it did well in Japan. Nintendo's N64, which still used cartridge games, was a fine machine but with old technology. Cartridge games cost so much more than CDs to produce that the N64 was doomed from the start. With the PlayStation's price at a more reasonable $299, it had a fighting chance in the United States. But, wondered every Sony executive, could Crash Bandicoot raise PlayStation awareness enough so that it would help sell the console? To make Crash popular in Japan, as well, Naughty Dog made changes for Asian culture, including six hundred in-game hints done by a Tokyo comedian, which would pop up in the game. The changes added what Gavin told Rubin was a "hideous amount of work at no small personal cost."

If you were a music fan, the first thing that lured you to Crash was the bouncy Afro-Caribbean-influenced soundtrack by Mark Mothersbaugh, the prank-playing cofounder of eighties new wave band Devo. If the rhythm-filled music didn't get you, the game play, inspired by Nintendo's landmark Donkey Kong Country, did. There were boxes full of power-ups that the spinning rodent would crash into, along with jungle beasts like wild boars to ride and giant enemies to beat, including the laughing Dr. Neo Cortex, who shot death rays at you from a hovercraft. And then there was Crash himself, madcap and stalwart, almost as speedy as Sonic the Hedgehog, certainly as lovable as Mario. Nerds yearned for Crash action figures, which would eventually be produced by a company called Resaurus and become collector's items.

Within a month of Crash's debut, Nintendo released Super Mario 64 for its new system. The game was full of imaginative environs in which gamers could roam freely and explore the plumber's world like never before. Nintendo would always be successful with Mario. Yet Crash was helping to sell PlayStations the world over, even in Japan, where Mario was considered a kind of miracle-making saint by gamers. What that success demonstrated was the rising power of Sony's US PlayStation unit. It was their innovation, their marketing prowess, and their games that were responsible for the incredible success of the PlayStation, at least as much as the mother company. Though Sony had been a company that was full of warring fiefdoms, Kutaragi would be forced to see the United States as an equal partner in crime, perhaps one that would be even more powerful than the Japanese PlayStation division. Within three years, fifty million PlayStations had been sold the world over. At a Las Vegas event for Spyro the Dragon, another funny animal game à la

Crash Bandicoot, Sony Computer Entertainment COO Kaz Hirai announced that a PlayStation had been sold once every eight seconds since its debut. Sony's little gray box would be top dog in the videogame industry for years to come. Crash Bandicoot, a silly but powerful soldier in the console wars, had helped to bloody and bow the great Nintendo.

For Sony, Gavin and Rubin would make four Crash Bandicoot games, and the series would eventually sell forty million copies worldwide. But it did not come without a cost. Rubin felt he did not really see his twenties because he had no social life. In fact, he rarely saw the light of day. By the end of the production cycle for those four Crash games, Rubin was losing his hair, not just a little, but in tufts. He was gaining weight from eating junk food. He had developed a strange rash and during his nightly five hours of sleep kept waking up with game ideas. Then he couldn't get back to sleep. Gavin, too, had his problems—with his back and with serious carpal tunnel syndrome. The industry had aged them before their time. At one point, Gavin told Rubin that he had had only one date for the whole year because he had no time beyond coding games. And in the office, he also was tired of holding the hands of game designers who would freak out and lose it during crunch time. Gavin understood that the tight schedule could lead to breakdowns. In videogames, breakdown was the new black. But Naughty Dog was a team; there were millions of dollars at stake. *Millions.* "How dare anyone we brought in to work try to break up the team at deadline time?" he thought. "Look at Jason." Jason would fall asleep under his desk or next to the latest Naughty Dog on its dog bed. He didn't bitch. *That's just how it was.* Long hours were what you signed up for.

One night during a drunken binge at a sake bar in Japan, Kelly Flock suggested that Rubin and Gavin sell the company to Sony. Not long after, Rubin took a month off to go to the mountains to muse and meditate. When he came down from the mountains, he talked with Gavin. They had been together since childhood. They knew each other's proclivities almost as well as twins who could sense each other's emotions. Rubin didn't have to say much, except to discuss other offers from Microsoft and Electronic Arts. Both agreed they had done almost all they could with Naughty Dog. Both knew that if they sold the company to Sony, it would be in the able hands of game designers the pair had mentored. They had become millionaires many times over, and selling the company would just add to their massive coffers. Sure, they would work again. But, as with the many game changers before them who cashed in their chips, it was great to know they didn't have to.

What they had done with Crash, in spite of the early resistance from Japan, not only created a series of bestsellers. Gavin and Rubin had launched a series of bestsellers that kids liked so much that they had their parents, who often played the game with their kids, buy the Crash action figures. Kids flocked to McDonald's for the Crash Bandicoot Happy Meal toys. Most important, though, those kids remained loyal to the PlayStation as they grew into teens. And when those Crash fans grew into young adults, they descended upon the next generation, the PlayStation 2, like vultures. In that sense, Crash Bandicoot was more central than Gran Turismo to Sony's rise as the preeminent videogame platform in the middle nineties and on into the early twenty-first century.

9.

WHEN THE ADVENTURE ENDS

They were killing it. They were sucking the life out of the most important series she had created, something millions of fans had loved for a decade and a half. Outside, it was a beautiful late day in the spring of 1998 in the Pacific Northwest, and the sun peeked out from the clouds. But it didn't matter. In the car, it was black. This was more than just difficult; it was a nightmare. And there was very little Roberta Williams could do about it.

She drove home to Ken, her husband, the man with whom she had started it all. Then she got under the covers and she cried. Usually, she was not like this. She knew her own mind. She knew what worked. She knew how to make games, intelligent games. For God's sake, she was a videogame pioneer. Roberta Williams had helped to turn Sierra On-Line into a billion-dollar business, a player among players. Through the many ups and downs of their business, she had learned how to be tough.

But not this tough.

That night, she wished she could go back from 1998 to 1980, when she and Ken had first met. They were teenagers who met on a double date, just after graduating from Garey High School in Pomona, California. They both dumped their dates and fell in love. Roberta was shy, kind of a post-hippie girl who was more Emily Dickinson than Dorothy Parker. As a child, she loved to stay at home, quietly reading fairy tales and adventure novels, like Defoe's *Robinson Crusoe*. She would lie awake at night, thinking of those stories, inserting herself as a character, whisking herself away to faraway fantasy lands. She hung out in the library, too, taking home as many books as she could carry.

Roberta thought Ken, who was taller than she and a man's man, was shy as well. But he made up for it by trying hard to be outgoing. He told Roberta he wanted to study physics. "I want to be somebody and I want to be rich," he would say. They had deep, exciting conversations and shared the same Midwestern values. The two would marry before they were twenty.

Ken tried to study physics at Cal Poly in Pomona, but switched to computer science in his second year. Roberta yearned for a career, too. She started college. She had some jobs in which she dabbled with computers. But nothing really inspired her. She felt bad about the fits and starts. It was the height of the women's movement, and she felt she was letting feminism down by not having a career. Then Roberta became pregnant with their first son. Those damn Midwestern values crept in; if you got married, you stayed home and raised the kids. The pair retreated to the Midwest for a while, but that experience was stifling. Back in Southern California, Ken taught himself all about computers, and when he didn't know about a programming language for a job, he said he did anyway. If he got the job, he'd pull all-nighters reading the technical manuals to get up to speed. And he always got up to speed.

From time to time, Ken would bring a computer terminal home so he could access the mainframe for one of his clients. There was no monitor, just a printer with a roll of paper, a keyboard, and a modem. To impress her, Ken introduced Roberta to games, including Colossal Cave, a very early adventure game by Will Crowther and Don Woods, with no graphics, just text. Made in the seventies, it was based on the world's longest cave system, near Brownsville, Kentucky.

For Roberta, typing in her Cave commands and waiting for the computer to answer was not unlike lying awake at night and starring in her own adventures. In her mind, she would wander around underground caverns and meet a little dwarf who would shoot arrows at her. She might get stuck in some interminable maze. Gigantic snakes might block the way. Gruesome trolls would ask for money. Sometimes she typed in the word "Xxzzy," to teleport magically to another location. Roberta died a lot while playing the game. But she always came back. Sometimes she could not stop thinking about Colossal Cave. She couldn't stop playing, even to change the kids' (she now had two) diapers. She couldn't sleep, staying up all night, thinking about how to move past a dragon. What words would she type in? What was the proper logic to use to move forward?

All the while, she thought about two things. "If I'm addicted to this game, other people must be, too. And I always fancied myself as a writer. I can make a game that's as good as Colossal Cave. Maybe I can even make it better." While Ken was away working during the day, she mapped out a game on paper based loosely on Agatha Christie's *And Then There Were None*, the bestselling mystery novel of all time.

She called it Mystery House, and when the writing was completed two weeks later, she was proud of herself, full of a new self-esteem. Roberta was so psyched that she wanted Ken to program it. But he wanted nothing to do with it. So she did what every spouse does when there's an abiding need to make the other partner see your point of view. She decided to get Ken drunk. At the Plank House Restaurant, the fanciest place in town, she said, "Just give me five minutes."

Ken made a face like he didn't want to hear about it, like the idea was silly and stupid. Really, he was interested in creating a word processing program in Fortran. He thought that was the fastest way to success. But he saw the look in Roberta's eyes. She really meant it. And then there was the booze. He gave her the five minutes.

"Look, I don't get obsessed over, well, anything. But if a housewife like me likes games like this, there are others, too. I have it all figured out." She showed him everything—the design, even some rudimentary graphics she had done. The look in his eyes changed from steely and bored to mildly interested and then to raptly enthusiastic. Soon he was talking about how to program the game, even how to add her pictures to it.

Ken was on a roll, thinking he could do all the programming on the brand-new Apple II for which they had scrimped and saved $2,000. "I can write the algorithm that includes graphics," he told her. "It hasn't been done before, but I can do it." He forgot all about his Fortran program.

For the next three months, they rarely got any appreciable amount of sleep. Roberta was making more drawings in black-and-white while Ken worked well into the night to code the software engine, the way the game would understand what you typed in. In a eureka moment, he was even able to add a few colors, a first for an Apple II game. Roberta felt they were really on to something big; she told friends that every pore in her body was gushing with creativity. When they were done, they had the first adventure game in the world that included graphics.

Roberta put several Mystery House disks into Ziploc bags with a Xeroxed flyer that showed the price, $24.95. Ken took their small inventory to the computer stores that were springing up around Los Angeles, doing his own distribution with some help from Roberta's father. He would drop five games at one store, maybe ten at another. The proprietors were often dumbfounded that the game included pictures. When they saw colors, they were delighted. The Williamses' print marketing effort included one ad. Roberta cut the words out of a magazine and pasted them together for a quarter page, $120 ad in *MICRO* magazine.

Mystery House's artwork today seems undeveloped, almost as if the drawings were made with an Etch A Sketch. An evergreen outside the Victorian manse looks as much like a housedress on a pole as it did a tree. But the words remain alluring: "You are in the front yard of a large, abandoned Victorian house. Stone steps lead up to a wide porch." What else could you do but go inside and discover the gruesome murders within as you played amateur detective? But it was more than that. If Ken could use colored lines to gussy up Roberta's pictures in a computer game, maybe all you needed was just a little more RAM to make a full-color game. Or how about a graphics card that would deal with all the art and all the colors, shades, tones, and hues? Technologically, Ken and Roberta had opened the door to a new world of graphics, one that would in the coming years be as emotionally thrilling as seeing the Northern Lights for the first time.

Then the torrent of orders began. All Roberta did all day long was copy disks, which took about a minute each, put them in plastic bags (which Ken bought in bulk), and place them in packages for the UPS man to pick up. By August 1980, after just three months, the game had brought in $51,000. This was their wildest dream come true; they were on their way to becoming millionaires. As Roberta conceived of a new game, the two were thinking about moving to a house near the California mountains, a place near Roberta's parents' house, surrounded by nature for the kids to grow up around. They chose an A-frame house in Coarsegold, California, an obscure former mining town best known for its proximity to the Sierra National Forest and for its abundance of tarantulas.

From the mountains the mom-and-pop company they named On-Line Systems grew by leaps and bounds. While Mystery House sold about ten thousand copies, Roberta's new fantasy adventure, Wizard and the Princess, sold sixty thousand at $32.95 each. At night, when the kids were asleep, she and Ken would sit outside and clink their wineglasses as they looked up at the stars, wondering aloud at their luck. By 1981, their office down the road in Oakhurst bustled with activity as Ken proselytized to potential young programmers: "This is like the gold rush. You better come up and join us. You could be a millionaire too."

Ken lured teen hacker geniuses like John Harris to the mountains with a 30 percent royalty rate and a rent-free house in which to live. Harris, still pimply and working all through the nights like a kid possessed, would come up with a Pac-Man knockoff for the Atari 800 in just a couple of months. Ken was psyched. But when Atari sent out an industry-wide cautionary note stating it would prosecute pirates, the name was changed to JawBreaker. Pac-Man was replaced by evil-looking chomping teeth that bit into candy inspired by Life Savers. Atari still sued. Not only that, their lawyers threatened Ken with such gusto, the young entrepreneur literally vibrated from fear. Before the case went to court, Ken and Roberta settled the suit with Atari. Harris, a smart, trusting kid with groundbreaking coding chops, also made a version of Frogger for the Atari 800. But he took his code—and all of his software tools—to the Software Expo in San Diego, and while Harris casually spoke with a fan, someone ripped off the whole kit and caboodle. And he didn't have a backup copy. It took the depressed kid a long time to recover, but he rewrote the code

and Frogger succeeded. His royalties for the first month of sales were
more than $35,000.

Ken's biggest problem was dealing with the constant expansion of On-Line Systems. The crowded offices, packed to the gills
with employees, were not neat, and neither was Ken. Sometimes he
couldn't find contracts amid the piles of papers and boxes on the
floor. Sometimes he couldn't find disks that had essential computer
code on them. Music blared to the point of cacophony. There was
drinking to drunkenness on Fridays, and on Tuesdays there was
Men's Night, which included more boozing. Pot smoke filled the air
too, and sometimes employees howled like banshees in the company
bathroom, screwing with abandon. Nevertheless, the money was still
coming in, a ton of it. It was then that Roberta and Ken had a serious
discussion. If they wanted to keep growing, they knew they needed a
manager who had business school experience. That didn't mean they
still couldn't have fun making games. They just needed to tighten
and streamline the process.

In early September 1982, Ken hired Don Sutherland, his boss
from his software programming days. Sutherland tried his best to
tighten things up, but both Ken and Roberta were resistant. After
all, they had created this multimillion-dollar company and they
wanted to have their say. It all nearly fell apart when the Atari-induced
videogame crash came. Sierra On-Line, the new name of the company (sporting a logo that featured a mountain peak reaching for the
sky) nearly became a victim. Roberta blamed Sierra's venture capitalists, who, after putting $10 million into the company, had pres-
sured them into making cheesy Atari games for naught; after all,
Atari's greed was the cause of the crash. Roberta told Ken that taking
the money was the worst mistake they ever made. Both of them felt
they were being treated like hicks by the money people from New
York and Boston. At a meeting in San Francisco, those money people

said the only way out was to sell the company to Spinnaker Software, an edutainment software firm with dubious titles like Fraction Fever.

In a kind of fuck-you voice, Roberta, knowing she and Ken controlled 60 percent of the company, said, "We're not selling anything. This is our lives."

"Then you'll go down. You'll die with the company," said a bespectacled man in an expensive suit.

At that point, the Williamses walked out of the meeting and got the hell out of Dodge. Back in the mountains, they eliminated nearly three quarters of the staff, which took its toll on Ken, who rarely relished firings of any sort. After the carnage, Sierra was down from 129 employees to 29. Ken and Roberta leveraged their house and maxed out their credit cards to keep the other employees. Through all this, Roberta was plotting a comeback with a new adventure game. To save money, she wore many hats, including heading up Sierra's purchasing department. Sutherland was gone, and Ken was both CEO and COO of a company that people began to think of as a mere fad. The smartest money analysts and Wall Streeters in the country felt that Sierra On-Line was on life support.

"We have to get back to our core," Roberta told Ken as they walked together in the woods near their home. "Let's do what we do best."

"Forget all that Atari crap," agreed Ken. "That's over. That's water under the bridge."

Their critical center was in adventure games, in particular an ambitious project Roberta called King's Quest: Quest for the Crown. It would be the first adventure game to feature an animated world to explore. Ken had wangled a deal with IBM, which would be producing a computer it hoped would be as popular as the Apple IIc. The PCjr, which would be available in March 1984, had so much marketing muscle behind it, you couldn't avoid seeing it on TV or in magazines. To help launch the machine, which sported two ports for joysticks, IBM asked the Williamses for an adventure game. The fantasy game, which took place in the fanciful kingdom of Daventry, was a $700,000 gamble for Sierra. It took six full-time programmers eighteen months to create. But Big Blue didn't even ask for exclusivity, so Ken sold a version of King's Quest to Tandy for their home PC, the Tandy 1000, which was distributed through RadioShack stores across the nation.

Confident that the code was clean, polished, and well tested, the Williamses unleashed King's Quest in May, to much acclaim. Even though the PCjr was a failure, due to its high price and badly designed wireless keyboard, King's Quest was a critical hit on that machine and very popular on the better made Tandy 1000. It did so well that Sega, Apple, and Atari came knocking to license it.

"We're back, baby," Ken would say to his creditors as if it were his own version of the Bronx cheer. Not much more than a year after the tempestuous meeting with venture capitalists in San Francisco, Sierra had paid all of its outstanding bills. It was a remarkable rise from the ashes, one that led the money people to trust the Williamses again.

From that point on, Sierra seemed to be unable to do any wrong. At an Apple Fest, Ken signed up Richard Garriott, the son of a Spacelab astronaut who was so far ahead of his time that his Ultima II: The Revenge of the Enchantress fantasy role playing game had thousands of orders before it was released. Ken and Roberta also brought in Al Lowe, who worked on the pun-filled and slightly naughty Leisure Suit Larry, featuring a protagonist whose one goal in life was a simple one: to get laid. There was a deal with NASCAR for racing games and a deal with Hoyle, the one-hundred-year-old United States playing card manufacturer, to make poker games. Soon Sierra became so flush, Roberta and Ken moved north to swanky offices in Bellevue, Washington. From Washington, they acquired a dozen smaller companies. Ken knew precisely what he wanted in games, and he could tell if they were right for Sierra in a matter of minutes. Partially, Roberta and Ken's success came because Sierra fans were forgiving. If there were minor errors in a game, the fans of a popular series would still buy it, as long as it stayed true to its roots. By the time Roberta's King's Quest V: Absence Makes the Heart Go Younger was unleashed in late 1990, the frenzy for Roberta's games showed no boundaries. With its hint-giving, bespectacled owl, Cedric, King's Quest V sold more than 500,000 copies, making it the bestselling computer game of its time. By then, Ken and Roberta ruled their kingdom with elegance and strength, just as the royalty of her fictional kingdom of Daventry ruled theirs. Ken and Roberta weren't like JFK and Jackie. But within their milieu, they lived in a sort of Camelot—if only because there were no other husband-and-wife game company moguls in the industry.

At the time, Roberta was becoming bored with the King's Quest series. She wanted to do something that was a bigger, better version of Mystery House. In 1991, she began voluminous research into the horror genre that extended beyond games. She read horror classics. She watched so many scary movies that she'd wake up in the middle of the night feeling that she'd been bitten by a vampire or haunted by a ghost. She asked everyone she met what their favorite eerie campfire story was. She had notebooks full of stories, outlines, and general thoughts on horror. The Seattle area itself was the perfect place to go deep into what makes up the essence of fear. You could see strange beings in the misty rain if you tried, and the mystery of the Green River Killer, a man who was murdering dozens of women, was often in the news. For a year before she started writing the game, it was all horror, all the time for Roberta.

The time for Ziploc bags had long since ended. Budgeted at $4 million, Phantasmagoria would be Sierra's costliest game, one that would take four years to make. If you were a reporter at the time, you might dine with Roberta in Seattle, and she would expound upon the making of the game. It was like making a real movie, she would say. There were eight hundred scenes and a 550-page script, which she had written. There were Screen Actors Guild performers cast in the roles and a top-notch casting director, too. The Gregorian choir that sang in Latin included 135 people. There was so much video, it would take up seven CD-ROM computer disks. Myst and The 7th Guest had moved PC computer games into new territory by adding snippets of video and by helping to make CD-ROM drives de rigueur. But Phantasmagoria came at the very peak of the adventure game's popularity. So Roberta stuffed in two hours of video, as much as a Hollywood movie. "Turn out the lights when you play it," Roberta would say, "and light some candles. This game is going to scare the bejesus out of you."

When it was released in July 1995, the horror game was criticized for being derivative. The movie-like introduction appeared to have been cribbed from The Twilight Zone. Horror fans could see elements of The Shining here and bits of A Nightmare on Elm Street there. There was even a grimace-filled nod to serial killer Ed Gein (the inspiration for Hitchcock's Psycho) when the crazed protagonist's husband dons a human scalp and hair. Roberta had felt that art director Andy Hoyos, who collaborated on script ideas, wanted to add things that were too violent, so she'd put the kibosh on some of the bloodier suggestions. Beyond that, the adventure tale itself moved too slowly before you encountered the scares. And, in a bid to lure the new game player, Sierra had made the game's puzzles too easy.

Yet it could induce terror. During its monstrous rape scene, Phantasmagoria creeped you out. And the tension was palpable when a giant horned demon chased the stalwart though panicked heroine through the Victorian manse. The creepiness came to a head when the creature, sharp talons at the ready, ripped her face in two. But it was the portrayal of sexual violation in the game that led chains like CompUSA to ban it.*

The controversy and the mixed reviews didn't hurt sales of Phantasmagoria very much; priced at $70, it went on to sell more than a million copies in its first six months. If you added together the sales of all the other Sierra games in 1995, they wouldn't have matched those of Roberta's adult horror offering. She had reached the highest of videogame heights, and so had Ken, whose days were filled with managing the various companies Sierra now owned. Even as Sierra was adding early Internet multiplayer abilities to some of their games, Ken and Roberta were getting tired. It was especially evident with Ken, who had always liked the technology that made games run more than the games themselves.

In 1996, they sold Sierra On-Line for a mammoth $1.5 billion in stock to CUC International, a company known primarily for its shopping service. CUC became Cendant. Ken and Roberta, who still owned 60 percent of Sierra when it was sold, became filthy rich on paper.

Then, in April 1998, Cendant became embroiled in the biggest accounting scandal of the time; during 1996 and 1997, it had inflated income by $500 million. Cendant stock plummeted to about 15 percent of its market high, and both the CEO and vice chairman were sentenced to a decade in jail. Cendant's game division began pumping out really horrible games. Ken left the company, feeling completely disenchanted. He couldn't believe he hadn't seen that CUC was run by such scurrilous individuals.

Roberta, on the other hand, was still obliged contractually to finish

---

* CBS television came over to interview me about the rape scene. I mentioned to them that parents or the faint of heart could turn off the offending portion of the game. "There's no story in that," announced the annoyed reporter. In a huff, the CBS team packed up their equipment and left.

King's Quest: Mask of Eternity, the eighth in the landmark adventure
series. There were problems from the get-go. Sierra was now overseen
by another Cendant acquisition, a conservative Christian edutainment
software company called Davidson & Associates. The Davidsons, especially former schoolteacher Jan, looked down on the Williamses in
the way a wary parent might look down on the punky teenager who
comes to date the pure-as-snow daughter. Roberta told people that
the Davidsons believed Phantasmagoria was immoral, something that
would ruin the nation's youth, who might go on rampages of violence
in imitation of what they'd witnessed. If the Davidsons had been fully
behind Phantasmagoria—which had still been on shelves and selling steadily at the time of the CUC acquisition—Roberta believed it
would have sold far more during its retail life span.

Roberta tried to hold back her feelings, but she felt sick inside.
At times she was livid; she no longer had true control over her work,
in particular the next installment of the King's Quest series. As
Roberta worked on her script and puzzle ideas, another team worked
on theirs. When it came down to it, she felt like she wasn't being
listened to. When it was crunch time, Roberta saw that the graphics were subpar. Worse, Mask of Eternity hadn't been aggressively
tested for bugs. In the end, the last King's Quest was a mishmash
of styles. Critics gave it the worst reviews of any game in the series.

That was why she was in bed, crying, that afternoon in 1998.

Deep down, she realized that times had changed. It was now a
console world, one Sony controlled with the PlayStation, with racing
games like Gran Turismo and with Crash Bandicoot. PC games like
Roberta's had had their time in the sun, but now they were becoming
old-fashioned.

Friends in the business had cautioned her, "Once you sell the
company, get out. And don't look back." Finally, in late 1998, she
heeded the wise suggestions of her peers. Now that King's Quest:
Mask of Eternity was on the shelves, she could leave. Soon she would

sail the world with Ken in a twin engine Nordhavn 68 yacht called
Sans Souci. She would begin writing an Alex Haley–like novel about
her Irish roots. Roberta Williams would have a new life, sans souci,
and she would try not to look back.

She would never make another game.

Sierra certainly grew big, but it also grew bloated. It had a computer game in every genre imaginable, and even had its hands in releasing productivity software for the home office. Even so, Sierra did
not change with the times. So freaked out were Ken and Roberta by
the fall of Atari that they never worked with consoles again, even
when the PC was no longer a go-to platform for gamers. That was
a mistake because videogame companies need to be agile enough to
stay ahead of the trends. Still, their core games were a cut above the
rest when it came to writing, and that was key. It would be nearly
another decade before writing in games would deepen again. But
Roberta was also the *only* woman game company founder who consistently made creditable, bestselling series. The fact that she has
not made another game is troubling. Women certainly have made
strides in game making over the years. For instance, Jade Raymond
produced the Assassin's Creed series for Ubisoft, and Amy Hennig
directed and wrote the Uncharted series, influenced by the old penny
dreadful novels and Indiana Jones, for Sony. Both have been massive
bestsellers that consistently receive stellar review scores. But sadly,
no woman since Roberta has had such a long-running impact on
games and on game companies. Decades later, Sierra still represents
the high point for women in videogames.

10.

EVERQUEST: ORCS, ELVES, AND A CAST OF THOUSANDS

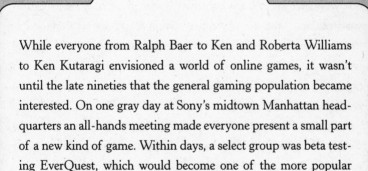

While everyone from Ralph Baer to Ken and Roberta Williams to Ken Kutaragi envisioned a world of online games, it wasn't until the late nineties that the general gaming population became interested. On one gray day at Sony's midtown Manhattan headquarters an all-hands meeting made everyone present a small part of a new kind of game. Within days, a select group was beta testing EverQuest, which would become one of the more popular massively multiplayer online role playing games.*

MMOs (massively multiplayer online games) feature the

---

* Unlike the bulk of this book, this chapter comes from personal experience as well as reporting. I played early versions of EverQuest while working as editor in chief of Sony Online Entertainment, where, in addition to writing and editing, I helped to beta test MMOs and casual online games before they were released to the public. In addition, I helped to create Sony's Web portal to EverQuest, so I had a firsthand look at the game's genesis.

most communicative, expansive game play ever devised. Thousands of happy, rabid nerds can play online at once. The idea was revolutionary. You hustle over to your favorite game store, buy the game, and install it on your PC. Then with your modem you connect online with throngs of people who are of the same mind. All these people want to level up and become powerful wielders of magic or they want to be healers, peaceful helpers. But more, each one has an impact on the way the game evolves. As a social group, you all create a sprawling, somewhat chaotic city of fantasy, full of paladins, rogues, wizards, trolls, and shamans. The choices are like riches to a nerd, and they include a wide array of customized powers and physical features for your avatar. With friends, you set forth on dramatic adventures to kill dragons and other beasts, and then you bore everyone who isn't playing the game with what you firmly believe to be vast accomplishments. As you play, you suspend disbelief and ignore the occasional errors, like the egregiously bad grammar and spelling in the text, knowing that it's a work in progress. The problems will always be fixed over time. And then there will be new problems. It really is like a city online.

But Sony had needed to be pulled kicking and screaming into the world of PC gaming. The germ of the idea came from John Smedley, a longtime Dungeons & Dragons fan whose childhood dream was to make that game into a computer role playing game. At nineteen, the San Diegan son of a naval officer was a college dropout, already making great money in the videogame industry. The optimistic, nerdy Smedley had toiled away at Sony Imagesoft, learning the rosters and minutiae of all things puck-related for the ESPN National Hockey Night game. While he did the job well, he hated it, spending his free time instead on a proposal for a game that included orcs and elves and dragons. In January 1994, he gave the proposal to Rich Robinson, the head of Sony Imagesoft development. Robinson, who was more interested in collaborating with established properties like

Mickey Mouse, Dracula, Frankenstein, and the awful Last Action Hero, didn't get it and passed on the idea quickly. In the meantime, Smedley continued to be an enthusiastic gamer who spent way too many of his dollars playing online role playing games at home. During just one month in 1993 he spent $600 playing CyberStrike, a graphically low-tech combat game in which up to sixteen giant walking robots blasted one another to smithereens via General Electric's early online service, GEnie. (Back then in the early nineties, you were charged an hourly rate for time online.) He would not give up on his dungeons or his dragons, pushing on various occasions to get the powers at Sony to move forward with an online game for the PC, somewhat à la Ultima Online, but with more distinct, more human-looking graphics. But with the success of the PlayStation all over the world, no one would listen. Finally he met with Kelly Flock, now head of the PlayStation sports division called 989 Studios. After the slew of meetings for which Sony is famous before it moves forward, Smedley convinced Flock to go ahead with a *Lord of the Rings*–style online game. To that end, in early 1996, Smedley hired two young game designers who had already worked on their own online sword and sorcery game in 1993. War Wizard, which was released as shareware, was invented by Brad McQuaid and Steve Clover for their small company, MicroGenesis. Graphically, it was no *Mona Lisa,* but the online game did offer its cult following the ability to aim and shoot at portions of an opponent's body, giving the enemy a mortal wound that would hinder him from retaliating.

Smedley briefed McQuaid and Clover on what was generically called Online Adventure Game. At the same time, Flock had secured the assent of Terry Tokunaka, the CEO for the PlayStation business in the United States. His primary mandate was "Don't spend a lot of money."

Making Online Adventure Game would be a colossal, multifarious undertaking. Even though Smedley's team had the auspices of

Sony as a kind of all-seeing, all-knowing Yoda, there were reasons for all to be daunted. Not the least of their worries was finding a way to program what was essentially an online country, miles long and wide, in a way that seemed like a 3-D experience, light-years beyond CyberStrike. Moving through this world would feel fresh and real, like walking through actual pastures, bogs, forests, giant lakes, and mountains. If they did it right, Dungeons & Dragons–type characters would come to life and gleam with the varied personalities of the people who controlled them.

While Smedley and Flock continued to get flack from those above about doing a PC game and not a PlayStation game, McQuaid and Clover spent a month working on an eighty-page game concept document that was so detailed, it had computer-generated maps and artwork within. Clover came up with the game's name in a flash. After a few godawful suggestions, the name EverQuest flowed out during a morning drive to the Sony offices in San Diego. The name was a stroke of genius. Not only did it flow off the tongue, it said simply and precisely what the game would be: a series of quests that, due to planned game expansion packs, would never really end. If it worked, it would be a gold mine for Sony. If EverQuest failed, Sony calculated that it would probably fire the twelve-man team Smedley had hired, and lose $800,000, which translated to thousands of man hours that could have been used making a PlayStation game. Development took much longer than was projected, in part because Sony decided to make their own proprietary software to create the orcs' and elves' world online. In addition, the infrastructure needed servers and customer service representatives on the phone to answer questions—requiring a nightmare of organization and research.

After three years, seemingly endless testing in San Diego and in New York, and $5 million spent, EverQuest was nearly ready to go. But since the budget had ballooned, John Smedley and Kelly Flock would likely be fired at the first hint of failure. None of the suits on the Sony food chain beyond Flock believed EverQuest would be a success, including Flock's boss, Howard Stringer. As the head of Sony Pictures, Stringer, though he knew little about games, also oversaw Sony Online Entertainment. Although they had their hopes, many on the EverQuest team, including primary artist Bill Trost, didn't believe it would recoup its investment either. Sony's best prognosticators felt that EverQuest might garner thirty thousand players and eventually pay for itself if the expansion packs, smaller versions of the game, were compelling enough. Success for EverQuest would be a Las Vegas–style gamble—a long shot at best.

Even after its initial release, in April 1999, EverQuest was buggy. "EverQuest is down" seemed like a daily warning, as server problems crossed SOE desks via e-mail. The graphics could be choppy, even with a speedy T3 broadband connection. And even seasoned developers felt the game was brutally challenging and often unforgiving. But despite the initial glitches, EverQuest was an immediate success, an all-around victory for those involved, selling one hundred thousand copies in the first day alone. The core team was ecstatic because their royalty rate would be above 10 percent. But more, they were gamers who were proud of the niche they had popularized.

EverQuest succeeded not only because it filled a void at the right time. People were flush with disposable income in the late nineties, so they did not mind paying EverQuest's monthly fee along with a hefty retail price for the game disk. But it was more than the money. In New York, half of Sony's Madison Avenue office was still entranced by the game that would make *Time* magazine's "best of" list in 1999. At night if you looked over the various cubicles, you saw that people in the office were utterly under its spell, staying in midtown until all hours of the night just to play and, on many occasions, to flirt with each other in-game. It wasn't simply a game in which you played the role of a mage or elf and leveled up. EverQuest was an early social networking experience in which one of the snooty directors of some Sony media company could fall in love with one of Sony's equally snooty consultants as they hacked and slayed flying insects together in the early levels of the game. It was love at first fight.

Massively multiplayer online role playing games were considered the next big thing in the 1990s, but they'd been present in some form for decades. As early as 1974, Steve Colley created a game called MazeWar that would work with as many as thirty players on the feeble Apple network. MazeWar's graphics looked like a black-and-white pen-and-ink drawing come to life. It was, though rudimentary, a 3-D-ish game where you played as a *Chien Andalou*–style eyeball. The goal was straightforward: shoot from your eyeball to hit other eyeballs. MazeWar's inventiveness helped Colley land a job at NASA, where he worked for a while on the Mars rover. Then, in 1997, Richard Garriott made an admirable foray into the MMO genre with Ultima Online. Within months of its debut, Ultima Online had 100,000 subscribers who paid monthly fees to play in a world that, except for more primitive artwork, was not unlike EverQuest. The financial success of Ultima Online allowed Garriott, whose father was a NASA astronaut, to take a $30 million ride to the Russian space station and to create a remarkable collection of space-related memorabilia—including a Lunokhod 2 lunar rover from the USSR that still is parked on the moon.

To the number crunchers at Sony, the beauty of MMOs was akin to the beauty of cell phone services in which subscribers pay for outgoing and incoming calls. In other words, they get you to pay twice. In the world of MMOs, users bought the retail disk in their local game store. Then, after a thirty-day trial period, they paid a monthly fee of $10 to $15 for unlimited play time online. Most of the online games in the 1990s had merely acceptable graphics because the modems at the time could only handle fifty-six kbps of data—if you were lucky. The computer servers (not just Sony's) seemed to go down with a steady constancy. But you didn't moan all that much, because you were experiencing something that let you dream communally in worlds you before could only experience in solo play. In EverQuest, what amounted to the population of large towns were online at once, cooperating in little groups. They were loving it, exploring a vast world that seemed to have no end—and occasionally becoming so addicted that players nicknamed the game EverCrack. When a couple got married in EverQuest, everyone at Sony's Manhattan office was elated, marveling over the minor miracle of modern technology. When a guy had a heart attack after playing incessantly, everyone tried to hush it up. The party line on the sixth floor was "It couldn't be the game that jump-started the heart attack. It was the guy's own fault if he played for days on end without a break, certainly not ours."

Thanks to EverQuest, PC gaming felt new again, reinvigorated, magical. You could listen to a song for a few minutes. You could watch a movie for a couple of hours. You could read a book for maybe thirty hours. But EverQuest was the epic's epic; once you were in it, you didn't want to leave. It was essential to your existence.

If you were an EverQuest gamer, you were a faithful, committed gamer, one who had to purchase a graphics acceleration card, an attachment with its own memory that juiced the animation quality for your computer, just to get the game to work. You played because the world was so vast, so much so you felt as if your life span would have to be extended by a decade to finish all the quests within. For all intents and purposes, you were living within another world. EverQuest dared you to become addicted by making you sink perhaps forty hours to get to only the tenth level of experience. You would think, "Maybe if I just spend another hour, I'll level up and be stronger. OK, maybe two hours. And then maybe I can cast that spell and defeat that——." And then when you looked up to the real world clock, it was three in the morning. At that thirty- or forty-hour point, you would gingerly set foot in a land called Crescent Reach and proceed

cautiously into the ghostly Blightfire Moor. There you would per-
ish if you chose to engage creeping, dragonlike Hedge Devils or the
dreaded Southern Moorwalker, kind of an overfed Komodo dragon.
What EverQuest was trying to get you to do was to start a gang,
a group of six friends who would do more than pillage and fight.
Your friends from hither and yon would help one another out, save
one another from dying at the hands of others, and try to kill that
generally unkillable Sleeper, a dragon the size of the Empire State
Building, who, once awakened, would pounce upon all those near
and far on the server, killing hundreds of characters unlucky enough
to be online in its evil wake. More generally, if you were slashed by a
monster, the designated healer in your group would fix you up with
alacrity. And if your soul cried out for peace and musing, you could
get a pole and fish, or sit and darn clothing instead.

Each month the number of EverQuest fans grew by leaps and
bounds, often by the thousands. It was like the stock market at the
time: Nothing could stop its rise into the millions of players. If
EverQuest only sold three million copies at retail stores, it would
have been a talked about hit. But that crazy monthly subscription
revenue added to Sony's coffers in an off-the-charts way.

In this new world, Sony was unprepared for the cheaters and
snake oil salesmen, those players who would hawk items on the auc-
tion site eBay that would make your warrior become stronger, like
spinach to Popeye. Sony was forced to assume the role of politicians
and policy wonks who needed to police a city and keep people safe
from harm. When a member wrote fan fiction that included the rape
of an underage girl, that player was banned forever. Customer service phone lines were often jammed, leading the company to create
an army of part-timers at phone banks in San Diego, who would
eventually number more than the full-timers.

Yet EverQuest's days on top of the MMO heap were numbered.
The first blow came when Shawn Woolley, a clinically depressed

twenty-one-year-old player from Wisconsin, shot himself in front of the computer on Thanksgiving morning, 2001. It happened either after a friend known online as "iluvyou" stole his achievements in the game or after he decided to no longer be friends with Shawn. His family firmly believed the MMO was the tipping point in Woolley's demise.

Woolley's tragic death was an aberration. The vast majority of those who played felt they were made better by the social experience that led to a collegiality among gamers, gamers who would actually meet one another face-to-face at the EverQuest Fan Faire convention. In this new world of PC gaming, CD-ROMs were the old thing. The new killer hardware was the graphics card and the modem, for with that online connection, social gaming exploded. In the process of leveling up, you made virtual friends in addition to the friends you hung with every day. You felt worldly when you talked online with a pal in Vancouver or Los Angeles, and you had a stake in his or her life, too. If you were shy in a crowd, you could let loose online, where no one could see you. In other words, you could reinvent yourself and become the character you always wanted to be. And you could cosplay, dress up like your character at conventions or meet-ups, playing the role you had online in real life. It was nerds together and nerds as one, up all night and having the time of their lives. Once EverQuest hit, every publisher had to think about making an MMO. No one wanted to be left behind. It was that powerful a force.

But even as EverQuest's popularity skyrocketed, someone was building a better nerdtrap. By 2005, there would be a new behemoth in the shire, one that would make many forget about the joys of Norrath. Three college kids, generally unassuming but very aware of the state of games, knew in their Orcan souls that EverQuest was too difficult for many gamers to play, something that Smedley, McQuaid, and the team hadn't realized when they made their first version.

11.

THE EVERQUEST KILLER

Chris Metzen was finishing a wry but passionate set in some dump of a coffeehouse off the Imperial Highway. He was not singing about games, for games really were not his true passion; rock and drawing ruled his life. The comic book lover and speed metal musician had named his metal band Ouroboros, for the serpent that constantly devours its tail in Greek myth. In *Timaeus,* Plato describes Ouroboros as "a being that was self-sufficient," and that was part of Chris's reason for giving that name to the band: They would take things into their own hands to be successful. That night in Brea, Metzen was playing under his own name with a bandmate, and the crowd wasn't large, to be charitable. But they liked his songs and they liked Metzen's banter. Metzen was blessed with a brilliant gift of gab, and he exuded enthusiasm, kind of like Handsome

Dick Manitoba, the philosophizing front man of punk rock's the Dictators.

Metzen was a natural when it came to comic book art. So he performed his set for a few people, sat down at a table, and started doodling an intricate dragon on a napkin to pass the time before heading back to the stage. He drew constantly, sometimes just to take himself out of a situation, sometimes just to calm down. He gravitated toward rendering superhero teams, like the X-Men or Fantastic Four, where family structure had been broken down by often acerbic personalities who were broken themselves. But in the end the freaks with superpowers always seemed to come together and bring out the best in one another as they endured severe adversity. As a kid, Metzen would pedal his bike to the local liquor store to plunk down 60 cents for, say, Walt Simonson's magnificent version of Marvel's *The Mighty Thor*. Once at the liquor store, he couldn't stop buying, stocking up on as many comics as he could afford.

But neither the artwork nor the band gigs were going anywhere as far as money went. He hated school, and school hated him back. He was a teen stuck working on the loading dock at the local JC Penney, breaking his back and making about $8 an hour.

Later that night, a friend of a friend stopped by the table to shoot the shit and noticed the drawing with the winged dragon. "Geez, that rocks, man," he said before passing on a business card for a new company called Chaos Studios (soon to be renamed Silicon & Synapse). The guy told Metzen that they really needed artists there. Metzen put the card in the back pocket of his jeans and didn't give it much thought. Two days later, he set up a meeting. If the interview in Costa Mesa went badly or if the boss dissed his portfolio, it wouldn't matter too much. He would forget any failure by heading to Arizona for some wild days of off-road racing—right after the meeting.

Just prior to the job interview, Metzen stopped at the local

Kinko's to photocopy his work. In the line, comic book artist Rob Liefeld, who was so famous that he had done a TV commercial, smirked as he glanced at Metzen's art. Chris was crestfallen. "Why'd he have to do crap like that?" he thought. "I didn't do anything to him."

As he walked through the doors of Chaos, Metzen believed he was heading into the belly of a fledgling comic book company. But around the office of the game company, he saw what could only be described as a kind of nerd heaven. The walls were filled with nerdily demonic posters for Iron Maiden alongside action-filled posters of Superman and Wonder Woman. An adult sat on the floor, playing with a remote controlled car. Metzen's heart swelled and he became emotional. It all felt like home. He told those who interviewed him that he would do anything to work there, including washing the floors. Metzen was hired on the spot as an artist—for the same $8 an hour he got at the loading dock.

It didn't matter. Chris was going to be part of a small community that was full of people like him. He was going to do it right. He was going to make a difference there. Videogames? He didn't know much about them and never had a SNES or an Atari. But he could learn, right?

That is precisely what the founders of Chaos Studios themselves had done. Allen Adham was a true videogame nerd who could be heard talking in his soft-spoken but enthusiastic way about making videogames pretty much throughout his college days at UCLA's Irvine campus. Adham got his start in the industry testing games for his friend Brian Fargo, who worked at a tiny game company called Boone. When Boone went belly-up, Fargo invited Adham to code games during summer vacations at his new company, Interplay. It was at Interplay that Adham really got the videogame creation bug. Because of Fargo's just-do-it work ethic, Adham felt he could start his own company. It wasn't magic. It just took balls.

Then Adham met Mike Morhaime, a smart electrical engineering student with a nasal voice, who had been playing games since childhood when his father got him a $299 Bally Professional Arcade System, the console with the wacky thumb controls that looked like one of those *Jeopardy!* game-show buzzers. Morhaime also subscribed to a newsletter that sent him code through the mail, even one for pinball, which he loved typing into his computer to make a real game. In college, Adham and Morhaime would often ditch class and head to the video arcade to play games. After graduation, Adham kept trying to get Morhaime on board for his new company. He didn't have venture capital. He didn't have any backers. But he met with Morhaime and his father to try to convince both of them.

"What do we know about games?" asked Morhaime.

"We don't," admitted Adham, undaunted. "But we can learn by doing. What do we have to lose? We're young."

Morhaime's father warned him against the foray, saying, "Be very cautious. It sounds risky." Actually, Morhaime wasn't the kind of nerd who would jump into anything willy-nilly. He needed to know about every detail, in addition to Adham's constant urging. But by early 1991, Morhaime had gotten a $15,000 loan from his grandmother and put $10,000 of it into the company. The same went for Adham, who, through sheer determination and a promise to sign over 10 percent of the company, had gotten a contract from Fargo at Interplay to do videogame ports for the SNES. By February, Morhaime, Adham, and Frank Pearce, another pal from college, were building desks in a small office space on Jamboree Road in Irvine. Pearce was completely gung ho, having had a gadget geek father who worked in computer sales. His dad even had one of the first cell phones, the ones that came in an unwieldy suitcase. As a child, Pearce was a fan of Mattel's Intellivision and played Astrosmash, the combination of Space Invaders and Asteroids, constantly as a kid. Even though he didn't get very far, he tried his hand at coding a text-based adventure game on his Apple. Pearce's father urged him to take the job with Adham and Morhaime, not that Frank really needed a push.

The money for their SNES games with Interplay never came in fast enough. Cash flow problems were common—even though Adham and Morhaime didn't pay themselves for the first couple of years. Their dating lives suffered due to seemingly endless hours in the office. At the time, they probably didn't have money for even a cheap date; their Discover cards were maxed out with office items and payroll.

But the excitement was still there. They were making *games*. Adham did much of the programming on RPM Racing (Radical Psycho Machine Racing) for the SNES, and Interplay supplied much of the graphics. There were also some boring ports to the Amiga, and Interplay contracts for chess and typing products. By the time Interplay released Silicon & Synapse's The Lost Vikings, the dozen S&S employees had bonded on the long hours. They often sat on the floor, a frat house atmosphere abounding, eating fries and burgers, talking about games and comics and the pressures of young life, maybe shooting a Nerf gun when someone said something stupid. When Metzen joined this tightly knit crew, he thought he had found a new family, so much so that he didn't want to go back to his house at night.

Metzen tried to create artwork on a computer, but it was like drudgery, so precise and time-consuming that it took the fun out of drawing. His challenges with computer graphics didn't stop the team's first big game, Warcraft: Orcs and Humans, from becoming a success when it sold more than 300,000 copies after its release in November 1994. Warcraft was probably the second big real time strategy game, a fantasy genre that mimicked the careful plotting and decision making during the fog of real-life war. It was inspired by the game Dune II, in which, à la Frank Herbert's novels, you became an intrepid sci-fi commander who enforced a micromanaging control over your troops. You could build strong military installations and marvel at marauding giant sand worms—before you figured out how to trash them. In Warcraft, you were given quests in godforsaken fictional places like the Swamps of Sorrow, colored in green sludge like that in the Toxic Avenger movies. But you couldn't get to the evil Orcish outpost of Kygross and its burnable huts unless you built lumber mills and fortified your Grand Hamlet. Each time you commanded an archer, one would exclaim, "Yes, my lord!" in a laughable British accent. Yet the words never failed to give you an ego boost. You trained bearded clerics to heal your wounded archers and you forged on to burn down the Orcs' stronghold. If you failed, you would hear this sadistic chiding, "You pitiful worm, your defeat could mean our loss in the war against the humans." If you and your troops died more than a few times, you'd grimace and yell at the screen, "Forget you, Warcraft. Forget you and your stupid war. Damn your oafish, overpowering Orcs. I won't be back for your insults. I have better things to do. I have a life." And the next day, there you were, trying to win again.

It wasn't until Warcraft II: Tides of Darkness that Chris Metzen's impact was felt in a game. Until that time, Morhaime, Adham, and Pearce didn't feel the need for anything more than a cursory story. In fact, Morhaime would sometimes comment, "You don't think about the backstory of Sonic the Hedgehog or why he collects gold rings. You just want to speed through the game." Though story had become more complex in adventure games like The 7th Guest and King's Quest and in some role playing games, in other genres it was still given short shrift. That lack of story was one of the reasons that much of the mainstream press had stayed away from reviewing videogames with any regularity.

Despite the long hours of game making, Metzen stayed around the office later than usual one night. Sitting at his computer, he typed up a couple of pages of backstory for the Warcraft universe. He didn't have the guts to send it on up the chain; a colleague did it for him. Everyone at the small company seemed to appreciate the fact that Metzen could write fairly well. His short backstory document, which he thought was full of terrible prose, was a harbinger of an extraordinary change in the company culture, one that would lead his colleagues to value an immersive narrative for each game the company would publish in the future. Metzen himself was thrilled at the opportunity for more creativity. Deep inside he had wondered, "I don't know if doing tile sets like I'm doing is the right thing for me. I like to draw with a pencil, and I think I might crash if I continue to be a computer animator. It's just too much about the left brain." Tile sets made up the backgrounds in the humorous side scroller Lost Vikings 2, which sported funny characters like Erik the Stout. There was no shame in doing backgrounds, but Metzen's ideas were far beyond the kind of art that few really take the time to appreciate while jumping, stabbing, and luring monsters to their eye-popping electrocutions.

During this time, change was coming for the young executives. Adham and Morhaime decided that their cash flow problems were just too monumental. They sold Silicon & Synapse to Davidson & Associates, the same educational software company with which the Williamses would have so much trouble during the release of Phantasmagoria and during the making of Roberta's last King's Quest game. Unlike the founders of Sierra, Adham and Morhaime's experience with Davidson was a positive one. After a $10 million deal that was settled with stock and no cash, the Davidsons gave the company complete creative control—with one exception. Jan Davidson hated the name Silicon & Synapse and demanded that they change it to something more understandable. All titles in the future would be published under the more accessible, decidedly un-geeky name of Blizzard Entertainment.

In the ensuing years, Warcraft II was a success and so was its painstakingly detailed science fiction counterpart, StarCraft. But just as StarCraft was being released, Davidson's parent company, Cendant, had its dirty troubles with the SEC. The financial security of every employee at Blizzard was thrown into serious jeopardy. Adham, Morhaime, and Pearce were left to consider the woes of their treasured staff when the conglomerate's stock tumbled down, down, down, like one of those Vikings who missed the ledge of a cliff. With the shares trading at $6 after plunging from a high of $42, Pearce and Morhaime felt discouraged, angered, and betrayed. Their employees had lost hundreds of thousands of dollars in stock options, almost everything, literally overnight. Financial futures had been destroyed.

The three founders talked about the blood, sweat, and tears, the sacrifice of time, family, and even health. Adham himself was becoming both mentally and physically weary of putting on a brave face in front of employees when times had gotten tough. He would leave Blizzard for a long sabbatical. (In the long run, however, Blizzard was able to take care of its employees—those who stuck it out and remained—with a profit sharing program that had nothing to do with the vagaries of the stock market.)

Shortly after Blizzard was sold once again—this time to the French-based Vivendi/Universal—EverQuest began demanding hours upon hours from the lives of hard-core gamers everywhere. The staff at Blizzard in Irvine was not immune to its many enticements, and Adham, now back in the fold, was completely fascinated. So was one of his newer hires, Rob Pardo. Pardo originally had dreams of becoming a movie director, but he ended up managing a local Software Etc. store. After becoming a game tester, he worked his way up to producer at Interplay and was slowly moving into game design. Pardo looked at the smart but soft-spoken Adham as a game design mentor. They began to have intense, constructive discussions; but the two really began to bond when playing EverQuest together. Pardo was so fascinated by EverQuest that he became the Guild Master of Legacy of Steel, one of the gangs of guys who became über-experts at the vagaries of the game.

Meanwhile, Blizzard was bogged down in creating a role playing game called Nomad, which had a post-apocalyptic theme and dinosaurlike monsters that were outfitted with tanklike weapons. The wow element would be that you controlled not just one person, but a complete squad of characters. Yet few were satisfied with the direction of Nomad, because none of the Nomad team was able to explain satisfactorily to the top dogs why people would want to play the game and what was special about it. It also had a new game engine, the software that made the game work, which wasn't quite perfected.

In mid-1999 Adham began to consider making an MMO at Blizzard. With the team, he tossed around the idea of using one of their established series as a springboard into the worlds of massively multiplayer games instead of creating a new universe from scratch. Adham and Pardo began retreating to the food court of the Fashion Island Mall in Irvine to have intense discussions.

"Should we do StarCraft, Warcraft, or Diablo?" wondered Adham. The latter, a game based on epic throw-downs between the forces of heaven and hell, was being made at a separate office entirely, in northern California. Whatever the game would be, it would be centered in the Irvine headquarters, where it could be easily overseen. Diablo, while alluring and popular, didn't seem to have the great depth of a StarCraft or Warcraft. And as they looked at EverQuest, which they admired to the point of drooling, they saw that that world could be improved upon.

"There are a lot of questions to answer," said Pardo. "What

would the classes be comprised of? What about the healers; how powerful should they be? When a player dies, what is the penalty; how much of his experience does he lose? Or shouldn't he lose any?"

The challenges Blizzard needed to deal with seemed endless. In addition, Metzen thought the non-playable fantasy characters could be fashioned to have short but appealing tales to tell when a player engaged them. For story, he gravitated toward the mythology of Warcraft, which was not completely unlike that of his favorite comic books, like Simonson's *Thor*.

In meetings, Metzen noted that while EverQuest was really cool, its pantheon of gods wasn't in the foreground. He felt that Blizzard could better weave the fabric of story in this world of sword and sorcery. Tales would be the lure that would lead the gamer through this endless world full of social engagement. It was story that would constantly intrigue the gamer during the otherwise often banal game process of leveling up to make your avatar stronger.

Pearce, gruff on the outside but a sweet guy on the inside, didn't object to a rich story by any means. But he wondered aloud if building such a massive world was the right path on which to tread. "I know everyone here likes EverQuest. But the gaming experience I'm accustomed to and have enjoyed is playing something that has a beginning and an end. I like to play something and have a goal to finish the game. An MMO doesn't have an end. Why do I want to play this game in perpetuity?"

But the passion for EverQuest won out quickly, and even Pearce came on board after getting sucked into playing SOE's game. Within a month, Morhaime was on the first of a muckle of trips to Havas Interactive, the videogames arm of Vivendi, at the Universal lot. During lunch, he tried to convince members of the board to sign on to an expensive MMO based on the Warcraft franchise. While Vivendi had questions about the budget of $10 million, Morhaime came armed with projections showing that a million players would subscribe in the United States within the first year. During the presentation, he also made a good case for four million players around the world, including Europe, South Korea, and China. The Frenchmen were supportive, but dubious of those numbers. There were logical questions: Why would a company that was so successful with its strategy games move into a completely new genre? Morhaime said that MMOs were the way of the future, and the future was now. It didn't hurt Morhaime's cause that EverQuest had been a runaway success. And other megacorporations wanted to get on the bandwagon. Warner Bros. was spending a small fortune to publish The Matrix Online, an MMO version of the Wachowski brothers' cryptic films. So was Sony with its LucasArts collaboration for Star Wars Galaxies. No one wanted to get left behind, including Vivendi.

Blizzard's goal with World of Warcraft had been the grail of game makers since the beginning of the videogame revolution. They wanted to make a game that was a challenge to master but also easy to play. Pulling that off was like the ultimate leveling up for a videogame executive. The task they faced, if they looked at it in the long run, was terrifying. A mountain of work had to be done beyond game design. The only way to go about it was to put in long hours every day and do it bit by bit.

Metzen, art director Sam Didier, and the development team went full steam ahead with a design that included a much creepier and more sinister kingdom of Azeroth than the one seen in previous Warcraft games, one that took place in the future, during a time in which Orcs and Humans had nearly been annihilated.

"The artwork is epic," said Didier. "But it's dark. . . ."

"There's something not really right," added Metzen. Everyone agreed that the realistic future fantasy was going too far to change the treasured and familiar franchise. If fans felt there was too much change, there might be a backlash that would affect not only the MMO, but Blizzard's sterling reputation as a whole. Instead, they decided to go with a style that was close to that of Warcraft III, with comic book–inspired artwork featuring characters that looked larger than life, godlike and epic. After Blizzard hired some MMO veterans and went into early game testing, it became clear that the quest portions of the game were what gamers enjoyed most. Once the quests were completed, the testers became uninterested. So there were more and more quests and mythic tales included as the game progressed, a veritable tsunami of work to do to keep the already-engaged nerd coming back for more—and to attract the more general gaming audience. Individual quests were varied and quick to complete, as opposed to many of the tasks in EverQuest, which were repetitive and time-consuming, especially in the early stages of the game.

With a year to go before release, the amount of work to be finished was still enormous. Adham himself had had enough. Not only did he have to deal with the pressures of crunch time, the roller coaster ride of business dealings was getting to him. He left his day-to-day role at Blizzard to become a less-harried consultant for the company. Pardo took over the role of lead designer. While Adham's departure was a blow, there was no time to mourn; the game itself needed nurturing. As the deadlines mounted, Pardo began to grow as a person. Blizzard staff noticed that where he used to try to play devil's advocate to keep out ideas he didn't think would work, he now began to look for the gem within, say, a programmer's idea and try to keep it in.

Still, much of the work for World of Warcraft wasn't finished. In MMOs, customization is one of the keys to gaming paradise. But the way the various classes and races would interact wasn't yet certain. The classes still needed personalities and features that the gamer could tailor so one character could be distinguished from another. And the way characters would fight, one against the other, had to be completely revamped. Finally, the concept of having up to one hundred players ganging up and raiding dungeons, in a larger-than-life battle you could engage in near the end of the game, was debated constantly. Blizzard settled on a gang of forty as the maximum size.

When World of Warcraft hit the market on the night before Thanksgiving 2005, everyone from Blizzard drove from their Irvine offices to a launch event at a Fry's Electronics store in the nearby middle class enclave of Fountain Valley. Everyone was nervous, tense. Metzen, his heart pounding, wondered if more than a handful of people would show up. Though people had shown up for their other games, and though they all believed they had made a feature-filled entertainment, the anxiety was palpable. As Pearce drove up to the discount store, he saw a traffic jam before him. Cars were honking, backed up on the ramp all the way from the store's entrance. There was some smoke as well.

"Did someone have an accident?" wondered Pearce. In reality, the smoke was from a barbecue in a tailgate party. Thousands of game fans had turned out, partying while waiting for their stars to show up. Some of the team had to park as far as a mile away from the festivities. The 2,500 copies of the game they'd brought weren't enough to go around. So they went back to the Irvine office to get some more.

In the coming months, small bugs were found and fixed each day. Worse, just as with EverQuest, customer service was an immediate issue, with upward of 150,000 questions being asked online every day. And just as with EverQuest, servers crashed constantly.

Fans complained a blue streak, but they still kept on gaming. Within a year, Blizzard had ballooned to 750 employees and Warcraft had amassed $250 million in sales. Two hundred million dollars was earned from subscription sales alone.

WoW wasn't just a hit. It was becoming a lifestyle. The reason for gamer loyalty was in the game. World of Warcraft was all about the white-water rush of adrenaline that flowed when you entered a magical land that matched your own personality. You could be as outgoing as a TV reality show host or as introspective as a literary-minded poet. You could be as casual as a bingo player or as rah-rah hard core as someone who'd finished tough games, like Zelda II or Battletoads, that hack your brain cells like a Slap Chop. The loner would gravitate toward becoming a rogue and creeping around stealthily in the shadows of trees or bridges, then attacking to steal, maim, or kill. You could be more magnanimous, a cleric who heals the fellow fallen. Whoever you were, whatever your background, you were struck by the looming Gothic architecture of the Scarlet Monastery, alluring in its size yet foreboding. You could find and collect peculiar, rare pets. You might find the Darkmoon Faire, a traveling carnival that could feel as quirky, ironic, and strange as any David Lynch movie. There, you would find a beer-drinking frog. There, perhaps inspired by the remote control cars in the Blizzard offices, were Steam Tonks, tiny vehicles equipped with bombs to blast at other Tonks. Even at the carnival, you might not be in the safest surroundings. Someone still could come up and try to kill you. You might meet Chronos, a necktie-wearing, blue-green-faced ghoul who looks like Lurch in the old *Addams Family* television show. Chronos might give you a quest to help him complete his zoo by searching for a boy who was raised by crocolisks, a scaly, hungry combination of crocodile and basilisk lizard. Chronos would also like you to find a murloc, one of a strange amphibious group of beings who looked somewhat like the Creature from the Black Lagoon. The murloc's peacock-rainbow coloring belied his cunning, nastier demeanor. But if you killed a murloc, his fins supposedly made a tasty broth.

Eventually, even the darkest solitary soul with an antisocial bent would find other such nerds and join together in a guild to battle the weirdest of foes. Yes, there were dragons. But one baddie looked like an ever-growing fleshy serial killer who wielded a massive butcher knife like something out of Clive Barker's "The Midnight Meat Train." In the major battles, forty of you would come upon a vitriolic, drooling monster. And surely after the first few minutes, it would lay waste to all of you. Forty would lie dead, bloody, and torn on the virtual battlefield. But you kept coming back. For a while, it felt like abuse. Everyone would die, again and again. But then—the miracle. The boss would shake, quiver, and fall, giving up the ghost. "Crap. Crap. Crap. Three in the damn morning? I really need some sleep," you would complain. Instead, you and your raiders, like thousands of others who were playing at the same time, would move on to consume a new monolith, fighting on right through until dawn. You did so because WoW wasn't just a house of gaming. It was a welcoming home for nerds. It was in this way that World of Warcraft would sustain itself. This mystical continent of Azeroth, with its Horde and its Alliance, with its monsters and humans, with its evil and its good, had become Chris Metzen's Ouroboros on steroids, no speed metal required.

EverQuest popularized MMOs for the serious PC gamer. But World of Warcraft brought MMOs to EveryNerd, even to people who rarely played other games. They flocked to it to let their bad selves loose, to go wild without committing a crime, to escape from the constant boredom of suburbia, and to meet people who were like-minded, fantasy mavens who might become their real life friends. It moved into the pop culture mainstream, was featured in its own DC comic book and in a Toyota Super Bowl commercial. In an Emmy award–winning *South Park* episode viewed by 3.4 million people, Cartman, Lyle, Stan, and Kenny vow to defeat a griefer, a powerful, irritating player, by doing nothing but playing WoW day in and day out. Beyond the pop culture paeans, WoW became a pre–Second Life Second Life. It was where you wanted to live. It was idyllic, too, unlike Second Life. No marketing, no ads, no friends incessantly hyping their local gigs muscled in on your fantasy. Because some games now had in-game advertising, nerd purists were giving up their consoles in favor of WoW. It was such a phenomenon that Blizzard merged with Activision to form the biggest company in videogame history. Blizzard now has 12 million WoW players around the world, including China. And as of this writing, its popularity shows no signs of slowing down.

12.

BIOSHOCK:
ART FOR GAME'S SAKE

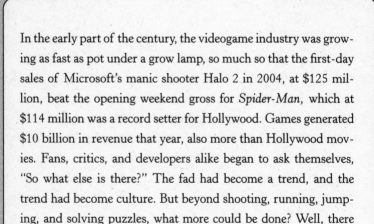

In the early part of the century, the videogame industry was growing as fast as pot under a grow lamp, so much so that the first-day sales of Microsoft's manic shooter Halo 2 in 2004, at $125 million, beat the opening weekend gross for *Spider-Man*, which at $114 million was a record setter for Hollywood. Games generated $10 billion in revenue that year, also more than Hollywood movies. Fans, critics, and developers alike began to ask themselves, "So what else is there?" The fad had become a trend, and the trend had become culture. But beyond shooting, running, jumping, and solving puzzles, what more could be done? Well, there was popular art.

Could videogames be considered seriously as art? Most "serious" publications didn't think so, so much so that they wouldn't even review games with any regularity. Games were seen the way rock 'n' roll was in the fifties; they were dirty, sex-stinking, over-the-top with no redeeming social value, despicably lowbrow. Developers, from Mario Bros.' Shigeru Miyamoto to Metal Gear's Hideo Kojima, would say throughout the 2000s that the medium was still developing and should never be considered art. Others believed that the art was in the technology. And perhaps it is. According to institutions like New York's MoMA, artifacts like Wagenfeld lamps and Gropius teapots are high art. So why can't we say the same for the bits and bytes and the words and drawings of videogames? Some mainstream writers are coming around to the idea that games are more than just diversions. *New York Times* writer Seth Schiesel wrote that the height of videogame art could be seen in Ratchet and Clank Future. In fact, it was a buddy game so homoerotic, it would have driven Leslie Fiedler to amend his brilliant essay "Come Back to the Raft Ag'in, Huck Honey!" to include the relationship of a lionlike, five-fingered cat and a creaky robot. Made for the Sony PlayStation 3, it cost nearly $30 million to make and was brimming with artwork as keen and clever as that in any Pixar movie. But games that are artful from start to finish are few and far between because, as in the mainstream comics world, game makers are often mired in arrested development. It's difficult to find an M-rated game (for those over seventeen only) without giant-titted, Frank Frazetta–like women drawn by artists who spend months working on applications to make breasts wiggle as they do in real life. Bloggers and even G4 TV's witty "X-Play" have compiled long stories on the history of breast physics in videogames.

A handful of underground artists have indeed used games to espouse their popular art on a higher plane. Artist Mary Flanagan reprogrammed the software from Unreal Tournament 2003 to make Domestic, a memoirlike tale of her father being trapped in the family's house during a fire. Anne-Marie Schleiner and her band of rebel artists invaded the violent Counter-Strike online shooter with a Velvet-Strike application, adding peace symbols and the phrase "Make Love, Not War" to the virtual walls in the game (she often was shot and killed before completing a graffito). And in early 2010, New York's Museum of Modern Art featured *Long March: Restart,* an effulgent eighty-by-twenty-foot video installation by Chinese artist Feng Mengbo, which mixed a frenetic Mario-style side scroller with the history of China's Red Army.

But could art in games go beyond such personal ventures? Could a game that sold millions of copies be art as well? To that end, in 2007, art, technology, and literature came together to forge a horror story that became one of the decade's bigger selling videogames. The charge was led by Ken Levine, a former writer of screen and stage plays who, in addition to games, had a passion for literature. Levine used the novels of Ayn Rand as inspiration for writing and rewriting the game's script, which was more than sixty thousand words in length.

I first saw BioShock at an evening event on April 20, 2007, in a crowded party room on Manhattan's West Side. Paranoid to a fault, I didn't want to wear the scummy headphones that every other writer was using to hear the sounds of the game, but even without audio, my first ten minutes with the game startled me with its dark underwater beauty, and terrified me with its gripping horror plot. When the event was over, I trudged home, wishing I could have played all night long. That night, I couldn't sleep. I kept dreaming about the disturbing characters, the watery environment with its art deco building, and the brand-new videogame history to which I was privy.

When the game finally arrived in the mail, it was a gorgeous, psychologically enthralling experience from the moment the opening sequence played. Your plane crashes. You find yourself underwater, drowning, gasping. A purse drifts by, then a locket, floating upward in waters that are cold and black. Like the character on-screen, you feel you can't breathe. When you swim toward the surface, you see brilliant orange. It isn't the joy of daylight, but the burning wreckage of the airplane. The ocean is full of oily water, somehow angry that fire has disturbed this blackest of nights. Further on is a tower and slippery, fog-smoked black steps illuminated by six lanterns. Under a grim-faced brass statue, a sign reads NO GODS OR KINGS. ONLY MAN. As you walk down a corkscrew of seemingly endless steps, a plaintive, instrumental version—a saxophone's riff—of "Beyond the Sea" begins to play, for just forty-five seconds. "Haunting" is the wrong word; fear strikes you like love at first sight. It is as chemical as seeing the girl of your dreams; you know you can't get enough. If you took an MRI of your brain's mush at that exact moment, it might well show that the caudate section, which is responsible for cravings, had lit up. So would have the ventral tegmental, which makes dopamine, just as it might with a cocaine-like high. And that was just the beginning of BioShock and its city of Rapture. "Rapture" was so the correct word for this grisly and dazzling underwater city made by a wealthy madman drunk on his twisted dystopian ideas. He disdained the world above for its seedy politics, failed economics, and oppressive religious views. But Rapture had fallen into chaos. It was full of raccoon-eyed girls and robot monsters who had corkscrew weapons. Jack, the protagonist, injected himself constantly with a mutagen called ADAM, much like a heroin addict injects himself with junk. Beyond these grotesque creations, there were moments of Stephen King–like terror induced from the everyday, common tasks you encounter daily.

Yet this was not the game that videogame designer Ken Levine set out to make, not originally.

Ken Levine was born in the New York City borough of Queens, to an accountant father and a housewife mother with a penchant for attending Broadway plays. In addition to seeing plays as a child, Levine showed an early interest in games, often traveling to the Adventure Land arcade and restaurant in Flushing during trips to visit his grandmother. He was particularly attracted to electronic games, especially Maneater, which had full-motion video and in which you faced off against the Spielberg-inspired horror that was the Great White Shark. In Maneater, Atari made the fiberglass cabinet to look as if the behemoth was coming out of the floor itself—to get you. After that, if it had electricity in it and it was a game, Levine was drawn to it. Levine's brother had also influenced his appreciation of board games by showing him Avalon Hill's Panzer Blitz at age six. The game involved military tactics and strategy, and Levine loved it because you had to use your brain to play.

But Levine's appreciation became a full-blown revelation when he traveled to Connecticut to visit his sister at college. There, he found the text-based Star Trek game on a mainframe computer. He pored over the ten-by-ten-inch grid on a printout, trying to strategize, his mind all the while traveling like Captain Kirk to the Final Frontier. There, he fought Klingons as he took command of the starship *Enterprise*. Yes, the ship was identified only with the letter "e," the Klingons by the letter "k," and the stars by asterisks. But to Levine, it was a magic combination of monsters and mobility through different star sectors, an endless space opera. After the Star Trek game, life wouldn't be quite the same. Later, when Levine became entranced by Miyamoto's The Legend of Zelda, he played so much that he lost his first serious girlfriend to that fetching bride called game play.

At Vassar in Poughkeepsie, New York, Levine immersed himself in literature and plays. He worked—and was fired from—various menial jobs. After he was dumped from a busboy gig at the Vassar Alumni House, his friend Paul Bartlett suggested that he check out the summer theater scene at the college. The Powerhouse Theater was a magnet for up-and-coming writers and actors. There, Levine met John Patrick Shanley, who had won an Oscar for *Moonstruck* and would later pen *Doubt,* which won the Pulitzer Prize and became the award-winning movie with Meryl Streep. He also met actors David Straithairn and Mary McDonnell. It was the perfect milieu for anyone who loved language, as Levine did, and he worked away on his own plays. Finally, his friend Bartlett convinced him to show his plays to Jon Robin Baitz (later the producer and writer for TV's *Brothers & Sisters*), who was already selling his scripts to Hollywood. After reading Levine's *Waiting for Father,* inspired by Arthur Miller and John Steinbeck, Baitz passed it on to Tracy Jacobs, an agent who got Levine meetings with Paramount. He was flying to Los Angeles for power meetings as a college student, and eventually got an assignment to rewrite a terrible romantic comedy called *Devil's Advocate.* The movie, with singer Amy Grant attached as the star, was never made, although Levine purchased a Sega console and a VCR with the spoils of his work. After college, he moved to Los Angeles to write. But it did not work out well. Levine was still a student of literary writers like Arthur Miller, Tennessee Williams, and John Steinbeck, along with the German expressionists who made film noir and horror films. Ken so loved the movies of Fritz Lang, Billy Wilder, and Alfred Hitchcock that making something less stymied him.

"Why don't you just come up with something commercial and pitch it?" asked Baitz.

"If I knew what that was, I'd do it. But they want me to do comedies and I like different kinds of writers."

Levine left Hollywood and returned to New York City, living in downtown Manhattan as he wrote plays and founded a small company that performed them on the street, off-off-Broadway, way off. It depressed Levine when he realized that he couldn't make a living at the craft. During this time, he was still completely fascinated by games, often making hex maps and designing games on paper—just for himself. He didn't know exactly what a game inventor was. But he saw an ad in the back of *NextGen* magazine, one of the better gaming publications of the time. The ad Levine answered was for a "game inventor" at a small studio in Boston called Looking Glass Studios. Not only had it made some estimable games, like Ultima Underworld and System Shock, but the company name alluded to Lewis Carroll's classic *Alice* book, making working there all the more appealing.

"So you want to work in games?" asked Paul Neurath, who founded the studio in 1990 after working on a science fiction role playing game at Origin Systems.

"Fuck, yeah!" enthused Levine at the interview.

"And you worked in Hollywood writing scripts?"

"Yeah. I rewrote a couple of things. Wrote some plays, too."

Neurath went on to tell Levine that the company's Ultima Underworld: The Stygian Abyss was a role player that allowed the first 360-degree movement in a game. He exuded delight when he spoke of the potential within Looking Glass, which employed bright minds fresh out of MIT. Neurath suggested, "You should also check out [our game] System Shock. There's nothing quite like it. As someone who writes, you might like the story." It was from System Shock that BioShock would eventually be born.

Within three weeks, Levine had packed up and moved to Boston. He felt Looking Glass had hired him out of the naïve hope for convergence that was then sweeping both the film industry and the videogame industry. The idea of full-motion video that began with The 7th Guest continued with Phantasmagoria, the less admirable The Deadalus Encounter, and Hell: A Cyberpunk Thriller, which starred Dennis Hopper and Grace Jones. There was talk, however brief, that interactive movies like the one that Trilobyte's Rob Landeros had made would sweep the world. Short interactive features like *I'm Your Man,* starring an MTV VJ, actually had releases in some theaters. The audience would press buttons on the arms of their seats to move the film through various paths toward one of a couple of canned endings. But Hollywood and games didn't really get along in the nineties. Hollywood only appreciated linear stories. The game industry valued the bells and whistles of technology over narrative, whether it was a linear or even nonlinear story. Like arguing lovers, each industry complained the other didn't understand it. Never the twain would meet.

Still, Levine was the right guy at a decent company at an OK time, and he used his opportunity to the fullest. For him, Looking Glass was like college for videogames. (At the time, there were very few videogame programs and classes in colleges that helped students to get a job in the real life world. While there were the beginnings of videogame education at schools like DigiPen in Vancouver, British Columbia, which offered a two-year degree in computer animation, such institutions were few and far between. Like the many journalists and writers who had toiled at newspapers circa the 1960s and prior, Levine learned the art, design, and business of videogames by doing.)

Yet it didn't go swimmingly. Levine's first assignment, a game based on the *Star Trek: Voyager* TV series, came to a startling halt when the product was canceled. Then Doug Church, an MIT student who was overseeing the implementation of a design document called Thief, brought Levine in to brainstorm on the story. For months, Levine prepared a film noir–like backstory for Thief: The Dark Project, the people of which were going to bear resemblances to Raymond Chandler characters—even though the steampunk-inspired game, which focused on stealth rather than shooting, would take place in the medieval era. He worked tirelessly on a mystery that would make the player feel he or she had to solve the puzzle surrounding a ghastly gravel-voiced satyr with a third eye called The Trickster. Thief is still considered to be something of a classic by many critics. More, it's significant because Levine began to feel more comfortable with his story and writing chops as far as games were concerned. Yet after a year and a half at Looking Glass,

Levine took what he knew and left with two friends to form his own company.

It was an inelegant start-up, one that was run out of the living room of Ken's one-bedroom apartment in Cambridge, with his partners Jonathan Chey and Robert Fermier. Yet within weeks of its 1997 incarnation, they had a gig to work on a single-player version of an early multiplayer online game called Fire Team. Levine and his cohorts felt they were crazy to start a company, and that was why they called their venture Irrational Games. The trio, especially Levine, believed that everything they didn't like about the world, they would fix through games. In the back of Levine's mind, however, was a nagging thought. With this new control came the distinct possibility that the company could go belly-up at any time. In fact, three weeks later, Fire Team crashed and burned, and the high-flying trio was out of work. They had no money. They had little savings. And they were not the best at raising money. Worse, they had no self-created ideas for games.

Even though they were out of cash, they were not out of luck. The three had left Looking Glass on collegial terms. So Neurath gave Irrational a small office and a check for $70,000 to start work on System Shock 2. While Looking Glass's games generally were seen as pushing the envelope in terms of new technology and storytelling, few became the kind of hits that could lead the company to prosperity. Thief had sold more than 500,000 copies, making it the company's bestseller. Neurath hoped that System Shock 2 would be the polished gem that would make Looking Glass a major player in the world of independent videogame developers, a game that would pass the million mark in terms of sales. Meanwhile, Levine and his camp were thrilled. "Seventy thousand dollars," enthused Levine. "How are we going to spend all this?" In fact, the game would cost $650,000 to complete. Levine hired seven people and used some of Looking Glass's talent as well.

The original System Shock's story surrounded a computer hacker in the fictional New Atlanta who illegally viewed files for a space station and was caught red-handed by a multinational company. The vice president of the company, who was somewhat devilish, snidely offered up a deal. He would let the hacker off the hook—if he hacked into SHODAN, an alluring but stuttering female AI. Reviews for that first game were stellar. Sales were disappointing.

For System Shock 2, Levine wanted badly to meld science fiction with the horror genre. He also had some high-minded, almost literary ambitions for the game, which giant Electronic Arts would publish; he wanted it to be an homage to Francis Ford Coppola's *Apocalypse Now*. He told his able group of coders and designers, "It's like this. You're going up the river to this crazy place with a strange culture to see this incredibly amazing megalomaniac who's gone off the reservation. It's going to a dark place to meet a dark person. This happens to be in a spaceship. Whether it's Viet Nam or Africa à la *Heart of Darkness*, it doesn't matter."

"The thing," said Chey, "is to scare people."

"Right. Scare the pants off them," said Fermier.

"The key is, the genie is loose. Can you put the genie back in the bottle? And what are the ramifications of that?" There was a Frankenstein's monster element to the game as well; you couldn't control these incredible things you created. They took on a life of their own. While there was terror in the game, it also dealt with headier themes, like the meaning of government, governing, business, and economics. The question was, Would anyone care beyond the people at Irrational and Looking Glass? Levine, who was working as lead designer and president of the company, loved that he would be responsible for the success or failure of a big project. When the first review came out in the summer of 1999 via *PC Zone* in the United Kingdom, System Shock 2 was called "a masterpiece of modern horror."

Everyone felt redeemed, and Levine, Chey, and Fermier were elated. Levine told the team, "I didn't think anyone would like what we did. I guess we weren't totally high when we made the thing." Although the game received laudatory reviews, it didn't perform to expectations. In 2000, Looking Glass Studios went out of business. Irrational went on to work on The Lost, a videogame version of Dante's *Divine Comedy*. Unfortunately, The Lost was quickly canceled by the publisher, Crave Entertainment, a company that rarely could tell a good game from a bad one. But Levine kept thinking about System Shock 2, hating that he couldn't sell anyone on the idea of a sequel.

During the making of System Shock 2, he had learned that he didn't really enjoy many of the business aspects of running a studio, and those included dealing with the publishers of the time. Most independent studios have love/hate relationships with their publishers, and Levine had to go to great lengths to get money for the budget and to keep Electronic Arts from messing with the creative integrity of the game. Because Electronic Arts released so many games, he also had to fight hard for attention. And that meant occasionally yelling and screaming. In his Boston office Levine would say, "It's not always easy for the people who are writing the checks to see what's important in the making of the game. Because, why should they? They're looking at it from a different perspective, the bottom line. I'm like a fierce Momma Bear protecting my projects. If you don't fight, the odds are really stacked against you. I will go to any length to protect my team." Levine was not so unlike famous firebrand Harvey Weinstein, the once-high-flying cofounder of Miramax Films who would do just about anything to get his films noticed. But Weinstein's flaw while at Miramax was his mistreatment of creative talent, everything from verbal abuse to throwing tantrums and chairs across the room during meetings. Levine reserved his wrath and bile for business executives. A protective Levine, as with any company president who develops games, is in fact more of a necessity than was a ruthless Harvey Weinstein in his corpulent pre–Weinstein Company period. Performers in the film industry realized early on that the business needed the work of talent agents who could be tireless advocates for their clients. But the agent class in the game industry isn't yet well developed. While there were videogame agents at Creative Artists and William Morris at the time Irrational was planning another System Shock, the idea of getting such representation was still very much in its infancy. It was reserved for the proven superstars of gaming, not the up-and-comers with imaginative, compelling ideas. Top developers at independent studios had to be willing to lock horns with executives themselves.

Levine, war wounds and all, was now armed with an idea and a proposal that was more than somewhat influenced by System Shock 2. In late 2000, what would eventually become BioShock was more of a role playing game than a first-person shooter. It was pitched to Codemasters, a company known for both its crappy budget titles and creditable strategy games and which had moved on to produce full-priced sports and action titles. Marketer Tom Bass heard Levine hype a version of BioShock that involved Nazis. The package also included a video that took place in the galley of an underground base, a gross amount of scurrying cockroaches, and a distant island. Removing the Germans and the island were just two of the many major changes Levine and his team made during the pitching of what everyone wanted: a blockbuster game.

Initially, it was difficult to convince anyone to make the leap. Atari, which the French corporation Infogrames had purchased from Hasbro in 2001, thought BioShock might help to revitalize their long-tarnished brand name. But Nolan Bushnell's old company ultimately passed. Electronic Arts listened and was intrigued. They passed too. What Levine was finding was that lower level executives at game companies were fans of System Shock 2 and knew that

Irrational could produce a quality product. "But it was the damn bean counters," he complained. The money people couldn't see the sanity in giving the Boston company an amount of money in the low seven figures, the budget Levine was seeking. At the end of each go-round, the catch-22 was presented in no uncertain terms: Irrational had never had a breakout hit. The inference was piercing: It would *never* have a hit.

At the time, Irrational was working hard on prototypes of a passel of games. There was a new version of Freedom Force, a super-hero series lovingly based on the Silver Age of comic books. And there was a zombie game called Division 9, which Irrational believed would be the most well-crafted game it had ever produced. Yet there was something about BioShock. They were getting so close, it was stay-up-all-night frustrating. Levine and his crew could taste the money. More, they could see themselves making a stellar game, one that would be remembered for its mood and attention to detail. And then the doors would slam closed. One company that never said yes yet never said no was 2K Games, part of Take-Two Interactive, the same company that had Rockstar Games and the Grand Theft Auto franchise under its purview. At the time, Take-Two was mired in a scandal that saw the Securities and Exchange Commission investigate and sue its seniormost executives for inflating revenue and falsifying business records.

At the end of 2004, with Take-Two and other companies hesitating, Levine broke the rules by showing an unpublished, unfinished BioShock to the online press in order to tout what he felt could be one of the deepest, scariest games ever made. Irrational had put its own money into creating the small portion of the game that was demoed for the media. GameSpot, the most popular of the online videogame sites, published an unapologetically glowing article, laying out point by point why BioShock was "intriguing." The story was a marketing department's dream. The next day, BioShock became the talk of the industry.

When Take-Two got wind of a rumor that Electronic Arts was about to give Levine the money to make BioShock, it stepped in to preempt any such deal, offering Irrational a little under $2 million to complete the game. Then, in late 2005, when there was talk of another publisher buying Irrational, Take-Two and 2K Games again moved quickly, purchasing the studio for $11.8 million. At the time Susan Lewis, 2K's vice president of business development, said, "2K Games will provide additional resources and support to the Irrational team so they may continue to deliver cutting-edge games." On the surface, it sounded like pure PR-speak, the kind of spin journalists see every day and ignore. And maybe 2K never planned on spending more than $2 million for the game. But it turned out that Lewis wasn't just whistling "Beyond the Sea," BioShock's theme song. If Irrational hadn't been acquired by Take-Two, BioShock would not have morphed into the triple-A, detail-obsessed descent into terror it ultimately became. Two things made 2K Games realize the gem they had. *Game Informer,* the nation's biggest videogame magazine, with a circulation of one million, put BioShock on its cover. Then, when BioShock was shown at the bacchanal that is E3, the yearly videogame convention in Los Angeles, the game was, as Levine put it, "the belle of the ball."

2K Games was so thrilled that, shortly after the conference, Greg Gobbi, 2K's vice president of product development, asked Levine, "Do you want to make this a bigger game?"

"Fuck, yeah!" said Levine.

"What do you need to make this bigger? The money is there."

BioShock would become a $15 million behemoth by the time it was done a year and a half later. Few games at the time had such high budgets. Grand Theft Auto III was one. Madden NFL

Football was another. But throwing money at a game didn't necessarily mean marketplace success. Shenmue, a Japanese-made role playing game released in 2000 for the creditable but ill-fated Sega Dreamcast console, reportedly cost $70 million to make due to its painstakingly lifelike artwork. Because of its molasses-slow pacing and lackluster Dreamcast sales, Shenmue failed miserably; those who had Dreamcast would have had to buy the game twice to make up for its staggering production budget.

In a fascinating if wary marriage with necessity, where marketing informed game making, the Irrational team, which was growing to include a satellite office in Australia, listened closely to what the suits had to say. Sarah Anderson, 2K's marketing vice president, was certain that the right trailer for the game would make all the difference in the world to the hard-core gaming crowd and to retailers. Game trailers, mature and violent short films used to promote a game, were becoming ubiquitous in the videogame industry. In fact, GameTrailers, a site that featured these little promotional movies, was purchased by MTV Networks for $25 million—and MTV didn't even make games. To make the snippet Levine collaborated with an outside company called Blur. But when they saw the final product, 2K became concerned. One brief moment showed a swarm of bees emerging from a character's arm. The scene wasn't part of game play. It was the kind of thing that might enrage certain easily annoyed videogame enthusiasts. One cautionary example was Sony's second Killzone, a palpitation-inducing futuristic shooter franchise for the PlayStation the idea for which came in a dream-turned-nightmare of Guerrilla Games' Hermen Hulst. When the game was demonstrated at E3, websites and bloggers spun themselves into an angry frenzy when what had been said to be game play footage in the game's trailer turned out to be computer graphics that closely imitated the game experience.

Still, 2K was thrilled that the ocean itself was portrayed in the trailer with such violent, angry beauty. It dripped, flowed, gushed, and tossed you around like *The Perfect Storm* inside a videogame. "I always think of the water as one of the key characters in the game, one that is real," said Scott Sinclair, the game's art director. It's not unusual for a game developer to say something that's neither human nor animal is akin to a living, breathing being. It makes the designer into something mystical and mage-like. For example, each lead designer for Sony's God of War trilogy said that blood was an important antagonist in the series. But the idea that water could be a character was especially true in BioShock because the way it engulfed your senses was so unexpectedly fear-inducing.

When Levine asked again for more money and more time, there was some tension within the company. While everyone believed the game was groundbreaking, Levine had never spearheaded a project that was an out-of-the-box hit, one that sold in the millions. And that's what 2K expected from the game: big money beyond covering the budget; at the highest levels of Take-Two and 2K Games, executives hoped for Halo and Madden money. Yet as the game's development moved toward completion, BioShock's distinctive qualities made it difficult for gamers and retailers to understand. More than one marketer at Take-Two had doubts, complaining, "There's no log line, no pitch line you can tell someone in an elevator."

When he heard that grievance, Levine often retorted, "This is first and foremost a shooter." Truth be told, it wasn't. BioShock was its own new niche, a hybrid of role playing, shooting, horror, anxiety, terror, and the kind of literature that requires deeper thought to grasp. It was more mature, more freewheeling, more adult than System Shock 2 in every way. In conference calls between New York City and California, Tom Bass, then a senior product manager for Take-Two, felt that the way BioShock could become a megahit would be through viral marketing and the canny use of focus groups. In 2007, in the months before BioShock hit the market, the Web had not only become a tool that coaxed instantaneous responses from readers and forum trolls. It had become a tool for quick feedback for videogame executives. When there was a question regarding whether or not 2K should spend the money on an expensive collector's edition for BioShock, they asked the game community via a petition on the BioShock website. Within twelve hours, Bass had an answer for his boss, Sarah Anderson. More than fifteen thousand fans had signed the petition virtually, providing an overwhelming yes for a fairly standard package that would include an action figure and a "making of" DVD.

Yet even when the expanded BioShock was shown at E3, Levine, who was exhausted after days of personally showing the game in half-hour intervals, saw that some retailers remained unconvinced. Some, like the buyers at Best Buy, got it, and started calling other buyers at the chain enthusiastically. Others felt that the game might be a press darling and nothing more. Bass began hearing from store managers, and the news wasn't good. "The game won't sell beyond two hundred thousand copies," they said. The game needed to sell a million to recoup its budget. A year before the game was released, Bass began visiting retailers in earnest, one by one. By the time the game premiered in August 2007, Bass had met with more store managers than he had for any other game in a decade-long career that included stints at Acclaim and Codemasters. He would travel to their offices, pull up a chair, and talk about how 2K had tested the game.

"Everyone tests games. That doesn't mean you've got a winner," said a doubtful buyer for one of the country's biggest retail chain stores.

"This is one of the most tested games in history," said Bass, leaning forward and then standing up. "There are tests almost every day. There are game play tests. There are tests for the cover. There were ten possible covers. There are tests for the likeability of the characters. There are tests for the understandability of the story.

There are even tests for the demo that will go up on Xbox Live. Want more? There are focus groups, two to three every night."

"Yeah. So what? Everybody has focus groups." It was true. In the years since videogames were invented, in the decades since scientists like William Higinbotham used oscilloscopes as monitors for game play, testing code incessantly on potential consumers had become a way to allay fears that tens of millions of dollars might be flushed down the toilet. Gears of War, the popular sci-fi shooter franchise from Epic Games and Microsoft, not only had focus groups; it had psychologists who attended game play sessions to analyze how players felt when they played the shooter. Microsoft now analyzes almost every game it publishes this way, including Halo.

The reams of data collected for BioShock didn't simply lie fallow. The marketers parsed it, then used it to refine and hone their plans for the August 21, 2007, release. It was the kind of particular information that Ralph Baer could have used when he admitted that he needed a "marketeer" to help promote himself and the Odyssey in the 1970s, and the kind that might have given Trip Hawkins pause before foisting an overpriced 3DO upon North America in the early 1990s. Irrational wasn't thrilled by all of the marketing suggestions. But they were heartened by Sarah Anderson's attitude. The marketing vice president seemed to get it when she told Levine, "We know we're dealing with a core gamer, and that's a different audience, a typically cynical audience who doesn't like marketing for the sake of marketing. But they're receptive to marketing that's smart, which engages them and allows them to interact."

The marketing budget for BioShock was between 10 and 15 percent of revenue projections. It was a healthy amount of cash, but not as large as the huge stash for other marquee games, like Grand Theft Auto and Halo. In the months before the game's release, 2K began spending its money wisely, creating a BioShock website and community that allowed hard-core gamers before its release to connect to the ideas behind the most minute details of the game. And when they wrote about it on message boards, it was like the gamers were salivating over the rarest of truffles. The community wasn't as hard-core as the people who frequented community sites for World of Warcraft or even EverQuest. But it would be a tough audience to please. If the game disappointed, there would be instant furor online. Sales would tank immediately.

Meanwhile, despite the travails of the manic deadline period, the designers had the rare luxury of time to approach perfection. The difference between a middling game and a truly transformative experience is often extra months to polish the rough edges. Mistakes were made, but there was time allotted to fix them. It was the first time that Irrational had had the opportunity to make a game really shine.

Throughout February 2007, Levine called meetings in Boston to concentrate on some of the focus group issues. After watching evening focus groups from behind a mirror, Irrational employees would return to the office to start to work on the suggestions that were being made. But one morning meeting just six months before the game's debut was different. There were giant changes afoot regarding the beginning of the game. BioShock originally started at the shadowy lighthouse, not with a plane crash dropping the player into the blackened depths of a sea eerily illuminated by fire. But the people in focus groups didn't quite understand what was going on at the lighthouse or who the main character was supposed to be. Levine sat at the head of a conference table and talked about that character, Jack. "There are silly but important things like his job in the real world. Where did he come from? What can we do to address that? Why don't we show him on the plane, give a tiny bit of exposition, have him sitting on the plane, smoking a cigarette, and we'll learn just a bit about his family. It will be just a moment, but there's a lot of exposition because there's a lot more to it that you learn about later on. What artist do we have who can build an airplane?"

One artist raised his hand. A lone individual, though talented, wasn't enough, however. It was clear they would have to outsource. But the first company to which they sent the project came back with work that was merely passable. It was money down the drain. Everyone at the studio was crestfallen and, worse, nervous. The deadline was looming, and Irrational didn't have a huge amount of resources remaining in the coffers. Yet both the marketing people at 2K and the creative department at Irrational agreed that the opening had to include their best work—even though the staff still had to finish their other tasks, like testing for bugs. Levine and his producers changed the schedule to accommodate the extra work. "How much does it cost?" asked Levine rhetorically. "Well, it ain't free. And the faster you want to do something, the more expensive it is."

All told, the opening sequence alone took the equivalent of two years in man hours to complete. In addition to the Boston studio, designers at 2K Australia in Canberra and at 2K Shanghai in China built the old propeller-driven, fifties-era airplane. Stephen Alexander and his team created the aircraft's interior and some human animation, which showed no face, just two thin-looking hands and a cigarette, its smoke traveling in crooked tentacles through the cabin. (If you looked closely, you could see that an Irrational Games business card had been placed in Jack's wallet.) Then, there's the sobering line: "They told me, 'Son, you were born to do great things.' You know what? They were right." With screams in the background, the plane crashes and the dreadfulness of being trapped underwater begins.

Through all this, Levine kept writing and rewriting. Levine knew that the videogame industry was still too young to understand completely how writing works. In his office, he would say, "If you work on a play or a movie, they say to write and rewrite, right? In games, you're lucky if you can get the first draft done right. They expect you to write a draft and throw it over the fence and the dev team makes a game out of your story. Or they take your story and adapt it to the game."

Until BioShock, the art of writing had been given little respect in the majority of videogames. Other than the prose that flowed during the adventure game era, there was no heritage of even mildly literary writing in games. The standard was just a notch above "The president's daughter has been kidnapped. Are you a bad enough dude to get her back?" Even today, game designers expect that words won't mean much in any game because high-resolution graphics and interacting with enemies rule the roost. Therefore, they postulate, a script doesn't deserve much effort. As head of Irrational, Levine was able to convince everyone at Take-Two that if writing mattered to him, it should matter to them, too. But in BioShock there were hundreds of actors, production people, and animators, such that each change in writing involved exponential amounts of new work. Take-Two and 2K may have rolled their eyes with each request for more money, but the checks still came, even as the expenses cascaded in heavy sheets just like the game's anthropomorphic waters.

Levine also learned lessons from the ABC Network's smartly plotted, long-running *Lost* TV show. He became engrossed in the series, taking it apart, learning how to pace a mystery over time and applying that to BioShock. In an odd confluence of plotting, Levine's original plan for BioShock in 2000 revolved around a plane crashing on an island, although the game design document involved a religious cult that dwelled there. Both were classic story tropes based on Daniel Defoe's *Robinson Crusoe* and both got their heroes to a place rife with the unknown via the modern day equivalent of a shipwreck, a plane crash. Levine had also been influenced by Stephen King's novels and his book on writing in his quest to answer the question, Although everyone can dream up a monster, how do you make that monster, in this case BioShock's Big Daddy and Little Sister, impactful and meaningful in a modern context? King's writing taught Levine that horror is really about the fear of loss—losing your family, losing your job, and finally, losing your humanity. In BioShock, the characters are terrifying because they are living representations of loss. They have lost their minds or lost their daughters or lost their livelihoods or lost their dreams. Early on you meet a demented, haunted-looking woman with a baby carriage. The moment is as affecting as seeing someone having a heart attack on a city street. That was why BioShock got under people's skin. It could have happened to you. It wasn't just a monster coming out of a primordial swamp with tentacles ready to grab, suck, and chomp. BioShock didn't just play with the eyes; it played with the mind, the dark crevices where you hide things away from your closest friend or relative.

As the deadline approached, Levine became nervous about the animated TV spot for BioShock that showed no game play whatsoever, just CGI graphics with a bit of the "Beyond the Sea" music behind it.

"I don't know," he told Tom Bass in the hall outside a small room where one of the focus groups was to take place. "It's risky. We could alienate hard-core gamers."

Bass tried to be empathetic. "Tonight, we're going to show the TV spot followed by a game demo. If it doesn't resonate, we'll do a spot with game play."

Levine nodded. After the game and commercial were shown to the focus group, the moderator came out, shaking his head. Levine feared the worst. "I've never seen something like this," he said. "When we put the two together, the commercial and the game demo, we have everyone saying they'll buy the game. One hundred percent."

Irrational and 2K really knew they had a hit on their hands when a free downloadable demo with forty-five minutes of game play appeared on the Xbox Live Arcade on August 12, 2007. They knew that any game could die on the basis of a badly coded demo, and they had spent months refining what they would reveal to fans. In the end, the healthy amount of gaming on the demo, announced on *Game Head,* Geoff Keighley's late-night Spike TV cable show, was a surprise to viewers. Fans moved with such hurricane-like speed to their game consoles that the whole Xbox Live network was blown offline for a while. Within a week, a million people had played the free portion of BioShock. It was simply one of the most unsettling, goose bump–inducing console game experiences ever offered in a demo.

By the time the game was released and through the fall, 2K Games had mounted more marketing campaigns than its lean ten-person staff had ever before engaged in. They had ensnared the hard-core crowd. Then they targeted with print ads the mid-core crowd, the people who read *Wired* but didn't follow the game scene religiously. They also scheduled television ads to run on the Fox Network's *24* and during football games, both on Sunday with the NFL and on Saturday with college games. In the end, BioShock sold more than four million copies. Sales almost compared with the landmark Halo: Combat Evolved, which sold 5.5 million, so good that 2K was talking about the game as a franchise that could last for a decade or more. But Levine didn't want any part of the sequel or novelizations or movie option deals. BioShock 2, much less thrilling, would be made elsewhere. Eventually, Levine would find sufficient inspiration to propose a completely new BioShock, set far above the undersea world of Rapture, high up in the clouds, in a sprawling city called Columbia. The new game, BioShock Infinite, would be loosely based on the political and economic events of the 1893 Chicago

World's Fair (and perhaps on Erik Larson's *The Devil in the White City*).

With the literary writing, the painstaking, detailed graphics, and the carefully constructed dramatic arcs of each level, Levine and Irrational Games had set the bar high, not only for games, but for games as popular art. Even if the art world's hard-core Realists would protest that it did not fit their strict definition of art, the Relativists and even the Objectivists would probably agree that it did. BioShock affected your emotions through words, music, pictures, and video. It not only was skillful, it was created by masters of the craft.

Renoir once said, "I'm not interested in the relationship of color or form or anything else. I'm interested only in expressing basic human emotions: tragedy, ecstasy, doom, and so on." BioShock succeeded in expressing those emotions. It made people who eschewed videogames see the art in an entertainment that dealt with profound ideas and twisted emotions. Reviewers singled out the writing and the literary allusions to Ayn Rand. They made analogies to Stephen King because of the successful tension that built to horror as you progressed through the levels. BioShock expressed its ideas clearly and deftly, like the best movies, music, and books. It was art for game's sake and it opened up a whole new realm of possibilities—proof of the concept that art and commerce could successfully and happily coexist in the world of videogames.

13.

THOSE MOVIES SUCK

When Gore Verbinski, the director of the billion-dollar Pirates of the Caribbean series, got hold of the movie rights for BioShock, he began to talk to his coworkers and friends. He said, "I want to make this movie so scary, so creepy, that kids will tell their friends, 'Don't go see that movie. It's too scary.'" Verbinski wanted to do the film so badly that he decided against doing the fourth iteration of *Pirates*. John Logan, who wrote the scripts for *Sweeney Todd, Gladiator,* and *Star Trek: Nemesis,* had worked out a script that was true to the terrifying nature of Ken Levine's baby. But when the budget ballooned to $160 million, Universal Pictures balked, suggesting that the movie be shot outside the United States in order to cut costs. Unable to create his detailed, graphically moody vision of Rapture, Verbinski put the project on a long-term hold to work on another Logan screenplay, this time an animated movie called *Rango,* starring the voice of the director's favorite lead, Johnny Depp. Had Verbinski directed the BioShock film, it likely would have been the first significant videogame adaptation to find its way to theaters.

Studios also hesitated and ultimately passed on an adaptation for the landmark shooter Halo, which was at first reported to have Denzel Washington as its star, an odd choice. Microsoft resold to Universal for $10 million a screenplay it paid Alex Garland $1 million to pen. That inflated fee certainly annoyed the high-powered executives in Hollywood. But Universal's and Fox's decision to pull the plug was also likely due to the director Peter Jackson's box office failure with the 2005 remake of *King Kong.* Had Jackson had a megahit with the oversized gorilla, Halo would have in all likelihood been made and might have been the first important videogame-to-movie adaptation.

There has never been a standout movie, one with a compelling plot and A-list acting, made from a videogame. Compared to the best action movies from the world of comics, such as *The Dark Knight* or *Spider-Man,* videogame movies have sucked. The question always has been, Whose fault is it? Is it the gaming companies, whose technology nerds don't understand the linear nature of movie storytelling? Take the sad Final Fantasy movie. Hironobu Sakaguchi, the mastermind behind the games, muscled his way into the moviemaking process with a story of his own making. He also fussed with the screenwriters' interpretation of his story. The series of Final Fantasy role playing games is often brilliant, but difficult to comprehend story-wise. Sakaguchi could have created a compelling treatment that was a tasty bite from the universe where good fights evil, and where a character named Cid seems to morph into someone different with each release. Instead, he authored a story that was as hard to follow as a cockroach in a dark room. While *Final Fantasy: The Spirits Within* had perfect-looking animated characters, thanks to meticulously detailed CGI animation, reviews like Kenneth Turan's in the *Los Angeles Times* were typical: "The sight of these characters getting romantic is about as involving as watching two expensive mannequins kissing in a Macy's window."

Or should the blame be placed on the movie companies, whose executives are only in it for the synergy of branding, trying to cash in on the latest trend?

It may be that videogames are already their own movies. Forget for a while the movielike scenes between play that make games feel like they possess a linear narrative inspired by film. Each videogame is a twenty-to-one-hundred-hour experience, often one that inveigles the mind. In the end, the experience is affecting, almost the way an intimate human relationship is affecting. As you go to sleep, your mind muses upon the time spent with the characters and environments beyond the game play. In the best videogames, the interactivity, the movement forward through forests or space or a post-apocalyptic nightmare, makes you the protagonist too. Constructing a movie from BioShock can almost be seen as making a movie of your own life. Jack didn't seem like that when *you* played him. In fact, you might think that Jack wouldn't do such a thing because you yourself wouldn't do such a thing. How could a movie ever live up to that experience? In that way, movies based on games have their work cut out for them, even more than those based on books. Beyond the long immersion, a fan's first encounter with a work becomes a gold standard, and all other incarnations often suffer in comparison. When games are the first medium, movies *really* suffer by comparison. That also can apply when movies are turned into games. The games are rarely as engrossing as the movie, because you already have a preconceived notion of what the movie is.

It's not as if filmmakers haven't at least feigned concern for doing things right. Sam Raimi, the horror movie auteur who became the Spider-Man series director, was a ravenous player of World of Warcraft with his son, so much so that he signed on to direct a film version of the massively multiplayer online role playing game. Many WoW gamers believe it's impossible for any film to live up to their videogame standard, simply because the World of Warcraft story branches out in so many directions and has so many characters and side quests. The mythic story of Sylvanas Windrunner's hate for Arthas could be a movie in itself. Sylvanas was the tough Ranger-General of Silvermoon, a sylphlike beauty who was turned into a banshee by Arthas. She was also a military genius on par with George Patton. The tale of Arthas Menethil, even before he becomes the Lich King, is even more complex and wide-ranging, so much so that it was the subject of a hardcover tome. And the story of the Lich King's reign is full of more twists and turns than the novel about Arthas. So it may be that the Warcraft movie is an undertaking of infinite proportions, a black hole of tale upon tale upon tale. People who know Raimi have said that, while he appreciates and likes the Warcraft ethos, he is mainly engaged because of the bonding he has had with his son during game play sessions, and not because the game cries out, "There's a movie in here," or even a "series of movies." And can Raimi raise the nearly $200 million he would need to do Warcraft at least some semblance of justice? After being taken off of the Spider-Man series because Sony wanted to cut his budget and he refused to do so, it remains to be seen whether Raimi has the clout to do such a sprawling movie.

Blizzard itself had a certain level of nervousness about what a movie would do to the integrity of the game as a whole. Without a healthy World of Warcraft, Activision/Blizzard would see its stock plummet. Chris Metzen, who himself reached out to Raimi in November 2008, was stoked about the director's potential involvement. Raimi had succeeded three times over with a complicated license that, like World of Warcraft, had rabid, critical fans. While he was sensitive to the demands of the fans, he still made the movies his own. When Metzen talked with Raimi, he felt immediately that the director was ready to tackle something on the great scale of World of Warcraft, which has nine separate cultures that are in constant hostile confrontation against one another.

"I don't want to trip you up with story conversations this early. But what would you do with World of Warcraft?" asked Metzen.

Raimi, who actually did play a lot of WoW and worked on a character to an impressive Level 72, knew that there were as many as one hundred different linear stories in the MMO. Trying to tackle them all would be an exercise in madness. "I think it's about theme first," replied Raimi. "It's about why war is so unceasing in this unique world. Why do these cultures keep on fighting? What is it about their nature that never lets them live in peace? And what common values do these characters share with the people who will watch this film?"

Metzen left the meeting sure that Raimi was the perfect person to helm the World of Warcraft movie. Raimi was on board and Blizzard was thrilled. And yet the question remained: Even if the money could be raised for the film, and even if the film was expertly shot and edited, would discriminating WoW fans feel the final product was genuine?

Steven Spielberg, an avid gamer who loved the classic The Syndicate, and who was so juiced about games that he let Dream-Works Interactive produce a dozen PC games for five years in the 1990s, including three middling reimaginings of *Jurassic Park,* never saw fit to take a videogame to the big screen. Spielberg's friend John Milius, the jocular *Apocalypse Now* screenwriter, also worked on one of Electronic Arts' Medal of Honor games. While he enjoyed the experience, even as the game was being released he shook his head and said that videogames do graphics well, but they don't do story well. He indicated that Spielberg felt the same way. If Spielberg won't touch videogames because of what's seen as their inherent lack of story, the future of videogames as box office victories isn't bright. It's a genre full of poorly made movies, like the Milla Jovovich series *Resident Evil*. Resident Evil, the game franchise, is a series in which your very soul seems possessed by its zombies and general tenor of impending doom. The movies, on the other hand, are predictable and poorly acted. And you can say the same thing about every movie made from a videogame.

If you were to drive the circuitous roads high up into the Hollywood Hills, where the wealthier folk reside, you'd come across a fancy but somewhat hidden abode. Inside, children would be playing videogames. Outside, you'd sit on an expensive chaise lounge at a lavish Labor Day barbecue. The glamorous home overlooking Los Angeles belongs to the most significant maker of television movies in the world. He made Brad Pitt into a movie star, and he discovered Hilary Swank as well. As the smell of grilling burgers and chicken wafted through the unusually clean air, the producer would walk over to an area far from the pool, the only place the many children could not get to with their water blaster guns. The producer, who is whip smart and affable as a host but tough and savvy as a businessman, would sit down nearby. He would look out over downtown Los Angeles and then look you straight in the eye, asking, "Did videogames really earn more money than movies last year?"

If you knew a little bit about videogames, you would nod enthusiastically and say, "And they're going to make more money this year. Some of the games cost upward of twenty-five million dollars to make. Sometimes they sell, like, hundreds of millions of dollars' worth of games."

The producer would shake his head, unbelieving, and there would be just the merest hint of fear in his eyes. He would look over to his young son, who is blasting with water as many young girls as he can find at the party and who, like every son there, cares more about games than movies. "I could make four TV movies for twenty-five million dollars." And as you listened, you would think, "Nice, but they wouldn't take you on the same trip to the same places that just one videogame would." He would shake his head again, get up, and walk off, returning to tend the food on the barbecue. Maybe, just for a moment while he was shaking his head, he believed he was in the wrong business.

But perhaps television is where some of the videogames should go, to become TV movies at HBO or Showtime. If executives kept the budgets and expectations low, hired an up-and-coming director with heart and knowledge of the industry, one who worked hard and carefully, then a success might well come seemingly out of nowhere. Then again, if one, just one, of the videogame movies in theaters became a blockbuster, the lemminglike producers in Hollywood would fall over themselves to imitate that success. And some, the conscientious ones, would even try to do better than make money. They might try to make a movie that meant something beyond action; they might try to make a movie that was memorable beyond the genre. You can dream, can't you?

14.

UNDER THE GUN:
THE KIDS IN THE SANDBOX

They were nerds, but nerds of a different stripe, the kind that often felt severely out of place, even among other outcasts. The Houser brothers were not computer geeks. They didn't code games in their bedrooms in their spare time. They weren't geniuses of math or whizzes of computer science. They didn't want to take apart a game to see how and why the code worked. And they would grow up to become outsiders in a business full of computer whizzes and egotistical suits.

As angst-ridden teens, they sometimes felt they didn't even understand each other. At age fifteen, Dan Houser stood on the balcony of his parents' house in London, angry at his brother Sam. Sam, two years older, walked by below. Like a character out of an action movie, Dan leaped down onto his brother and started whaling on him. Sam was down, but not out. He fought back, hitting Dan with such force that Sam broke his hand.

"Enough is enough. This is bollocks!" yelled Walter Houser, breaking up the fracas. Their jazz-playing father, who toiled as a lawyer by day, had seen this kind of scenario too many times as the boys were growing up. And the boys knew it too. They were becoming too mature for childish fisticuffs. After all, how could they keep hurting each other when both were ambitious and both had big plans? Sam, the assertive one, wanted to start his own record company. Dan, the athletic one, wanted to be a writer or a journalist. At the time, they had no idea they would do these things together and create a sea change in the world of videogames.

Both were taught to stick up for what they wanted from an early age. In the Houser household, you had to tussle for a bigger portion of steak or to watch your favorite TV show. That boisterous, scrappy quality would serve the brothers well when the world seemed to be against them. At the prestigious St. Paul's School, the two would fight back when the other kids gossiped about their actress mother Geraldine Moffat when the classmates saw her on TV in the sometimes brutal British gangster film *Get Carter*. The beautiful Moffat spent much of the film naked, and the next day Sam and Dan would be mercilessly teased. They could have wimped out and wilted in the face of their aggressors. Instead, Sam, initially embarrassed, saw it as an opportunity to curry favor with the cooler kids at school, who ultimately left the brothers alone. That is what their stubborn, loving parents had instilled in them, a relentless ability to remain self-reliant, confident, aggressive, and argumentative when they needed to state their cases, fight for their causes, and win.

During their formative years, they devoured popular culture like one of those over-the-top, ghost-sucking vacuum cleaners in Nintendo's Luigi's Mansion. As kids, the brothers played Action Man, the English version of G.I. Joe, together. They watched movies like *Apocalypse Now* and *The Long Good Friday* with Bob Hoskins and Helen Mirren. They grooved to the music of the late seventies and early eighties. And they played games with zeal. Sam in particular enjoyed the Sinclair Spectrum, manufactured by Sir Clive Sinclair, a tough eccentric who also produced one of the first inexpensive pocket calculators in 1972. The Sinclair was a tiny, inexpensive computer with rubber keys that often broke, but man, when Sam loaded something like Jet Pac or Underwurlde, with their lurid colors and tough game play, he was transported elsewhere to the point of elation. Another game, Elite, would later serve as a template for the open world genre Rockstar would help to pioneer.*

The kids at Sam's school would have bags full of the inexpensive or pirated games to sell and trade. As children of the videogame age, the brothers loved games as much as they loved film and music. Sam would go from playing Pong and Space Invaders to spinning the latest seven-inch by ABBA or Bowie. To Sam and Dan, no medium was lesser or greater. Games could in fact be popular art in their eyes. And unlike anyone before or after them, they would soon meld together movies, music, and games in a magical, satirically evil brew.

Sam also immersed himself in games made for every console he could find and haunted the local fun festivals in search of arcade machines to play. But he always would return to the Sinclair, enjoying code that was transferred to the computer via a cassette tape and eagerly waiting to play during the long ten minutes it took to load onto the system. He loved the games from British publisher Ultimate, which later became Rare (the company that would make Donkey

* This first sandbox game was a space simulation made in 1984 by Ian Bell and David Braben. It boasted 8 galaxies and 256 planets in which you could get your Buck Rogers on. Graphically, it wasn't much, but the game package included a Flight Manual and a novella to get you in the mood to explore the universe. Bell and Braben in turn were influenced by a space opera RPG called Traveller, an intricately written game based on a 1977 guidebook. Traveller began 300,000 years ago, during a time in which a group of Ancients had the power of high technology. So complex was Traveller that one version included a twenty-sided die to help you resolve your fate.

Kong Country and a dozen other memorable games). Perhaps the brothers were most thrilled about life's possibilities when their father took them on the weekends to Ronnie Scott's, the legendary jazz venue that in its heyday was akin to the best New York clubs, like the Blue Note. There, the seductive world of jazz unfolded before their eyes as the world's greatest players would gig and then come to the Houser home in southwest London to hang. Sam and Dan appreciated jazz more than they were fans of the music. Mostly, they loved the trappings of it—the clothes, the varied characters, and the stories of musicians' lives on the road in the United States. They were entranced by the glamour of it all. Fashion as a release from the mundane would return to inform their games.

More than jazz, it was hip-hop that had Sam intrigued. To him, there was nothing better than the way Russell Simmons and Rick Rubin meshed like brothers to fuse rock, metal, and rap at Def Jam Recordings. Sam mooned about the medium, had his mother sew Def Jam patches on his sweatshirt, memorized all the lyrics, and saved up his pounds for a time when his father would take him to the promised land, New York City. When the time came, in 1988, Sam unleashed himself on the city like a whirlwind. He shopped Orchard Street on the Lower East Side for leather puffers and Air Jordans, both of which were so rare in the UK, they were like gold. At dinner with his father and German record executive Heinz Henn, Sam peppered Henn with questions: "Why is everyone in the record industry so old? Why don't you have young people working in this business?" For the rest of the dinner, he argued persuasively about what he could do for BMG. Henn whispered to Walter, "Your son is an utter lunatic. But he has some good ideas."

Soon, Houser had a gig as an intern at BMG. He quickly moved up the ladder there, while at the same time commuting to London University. He sometimes worked for Simon Cowell, who long before *American Idol* was scheming to jump-start the European boy band trend. With Take That, a pop group that spawned English solo artist Robbie Williams, Houser toured and taught himself to shoot video. His footage became a bestselling behind-the-scenes video. Sam was earning a mere 120 pounds a week, but he told Dan that the job gave him a sense of pride that no amount of money could buy. In his spare time, he was wowed by the games of the time—Myst, The 7th Guest, and the utterly insane, creepy, Flannery O'Connor-esque offerings by the cult band the Residents, Freak Show and Bad Day at the Midway (which featured Dixie's Kill-A-Commie Shooting Gallery, Lottie the Human Log, and Dagmar the Tattooed Dog Woman). As the CD-ROM trend became the big deal of the nineties, Sam pushed his way into BMG's multimedia department to work on odds and ends, in everything from David Bowie's *Jump* (not a great moment in multimedia) to the Le Louvre museum CD-ROM (an artful tour de force). But the suits of BMG were somewhat late to the party, and multimedia was expensive to produce. They wouldn't be in the game for long.

BMG was working with a gem of a game company out of Scotland called DMA Design. The DMA team, led by David Jones, was contracted to make four games. But they couldn't seem to make their deadlines. Sam saw BMG producer after producer let go because he or she couldn't get DMA to finish its games. When tapped for that role, Sam found he had the talent to persuade the game designers to bite the bullet and finish—on time. Sam told his brother, who was still in college, "If the game isn't coming together properly, I'll apply focus, drilling it in and pushing it through. I don't lay down the law. I'll just go in with enthusiasm and energy and do it in a pleasant but aggressive way. I don't take no for an answer. I don't do it by being difficult. I do it by putting the right effort in."

In the middle of 1997, a decision was made to shutter the BMG games division. Dan, whom Sam had convinced to come to BMG to localize games, was as bummed as Sam. Nonetheless, Dan was beginning to hone his creative skills, researching and writing hundreds of new questions for the popular You Don't Know Jack, a mix of television game show kitsch and trivia. After some begging, BMG allowed Sam and two executives to travel through Europe and the United States to try to sell the games unit. To various companies, they proposed a $9.5 million package deal that would include BMG Interactive's assets, rights to games and multimedia projects. At every meeting they took, Sam felt out of place, as if he were from a different planet. He didn't speak the same language as the suits from THQ or Electronic Arts. Luckily, Sam hit it off with Ryan Brant, the brash young CEO of a new game company called Take-Two Interactive. Take-Two bought BMG Interactive and offered to make Sam the head of the games division. But at his moment of triumph, Sam suffered from a serious case of cold feet. Fear sucker punched him: Could he do the job right? Should he leave his mates and parents in England? "New York is a different world," he thought, "and I don't want to exit my comfort zone. Here, I'm not paid that well, but I get nice seats on planes, the best hotels, and all these other perks."

Sam asked Brant, "Can I do two weeks in London and two weeks in New York City?"

Brant would have none of it. "Don't fuck around. Get over to New York or do something else."

In Manhattan, Houser went from the accoutrements of a mega-corporation to the fits and starts of a small company. There was no cushy office, just a large and creaky attic space in New York's Soho district. And there was the culture shock to deal with. Manhattanites whizzed by as they walked like they were on a combination of speed and coke. Early on, he told Dan, "What the fuck am I doing here? Take-Two isn't even in the top twenty-five game publishers. They're nobodies. All they have is a few corporate guys and a bunch of accountants. That's it." Despite his doubts, Sam dug in hard at Take-Two, building the publishing infrastructure, the game

development teams, and the marketing and public relations units. He
was insatiable in his need to prove he could do the job right.

More important than getting the business up to snuff was the
popular culture trend that Sam and Dan saw on the horizon. They
had this strange, innate ability to see gaming's future, a prescience
that would inform everything they would do in games. Part of this
wacky ESP was informed by the outstanding releases of the time.
During 1997 and 1998, some landmark games were launched.
Tim Schafer's Grim Fandango melded droll humor, ideas about
death, and film noir mystery into a richly detailed adventure game.
Hironobu Sakaguchi's Final Fantasy VII was arguably the very
height of slightly strange role playing games done Japanese style.
And Half-Life proved that imaginative eeriness and high-concept
sci-fi paranoia could be brought to a PC game. There was a buzz
on the street about all these games that was at once idyllic, fanatical,
and adoring. But Sam and Dan looked beyond games as they sat in
the loftlike attic and brainstormed. They believed, in the parlance
of Monty Python, that it was time for something completely different. For inspiration, they looked to the swaggering attitude the
US division of Sony displayed in promoting the PlayStation. Even
Crash Bandicoot, pooh-poohed as just a funny animal, had guts and
dynamism in that anti-Nintendo commercial. Beyond an admiration for Sony's marketing prowess, the Housers had early word of
the elegant-looking PlayStation 2, which would be released in two
years. They felt that the PlayStation 2 and the vast amount of storage
space available on the DVDs it used would change everything in the
game industry. Characters could have nuance in their personalities.
Graphics, detailed and lifelike, would be closer to the movies. The
PS2 would change their lives.

Beyond hardware, the change they saw was about a groundswell
of emotion within the nation's youth. Sam said to Dan, "The way a
seventeen-year-old is talking about and relating to games is the way

I was feeling about rock 'n' roll and hip-hop when I was their age. When I look at the other companies, they're made up of toy or technology people. Where is that company that is standing up, representing games, showing that they're rock 'n' roll and that they're willing to push the boundaries?"

Dan agreed, adding, "It's like they're not proud enough of their games."

Sometimes the brothers could still be argumentative and downright disagreeable with each other. But this time, Dan was on the same page. There was a huge need for a gaming company with a real edge, said Dan. "There's a massive disconnect going on here. It shouldn't be the way it is. There's definitely a hole that can be filled."

They were gunned up and couldn't stop brainstorming. Sam said, "Let's create our own company that has its own attitude, its own image, so that like Def Jam, when you see the logo on the box, you'll know that it's a quality product."

Some companies did indeed have the attitude, but it wasn't quite enough in the Housers' eyes. A certain kind of punky pride came from within the culture that made first and third person shooters—and within the games themselves. By the mid-1990s, when Intel scientists engineered processing chips that made computers *zoom, zoom, zoom* like a Porsche 911 CT3, the graphics had become more expansive, extroverted, unrestrained—and so had the game designers. If you didn't know game culture, you might have thought that John Carmack and John Romero, the makers of Doom, were delinquents, bad boys who would hurt you and cut you and then tie your cat by the tail to a telephone wire. But gamers knew they could free them from suburbia's banality as they shot vile Nazis in Wolfenstein 3D and destroyed the dangerous Pain Elemental that shot burning, horned skulls in Doom.

Wolfenstein 3D, Doom, and other first person shooters were teen rebellion personified, the bane of overprotective suburban mothers everywhere. And the more she yelled, the more you played. Doom was perfect for the defiant gamer who secretly wanted to spew four-letter words all over his parents, but who wanted a slightly subtler, less verbally exhausting way of sticking it to them. That first person perspective let you skulk through miles upon miles of long, dank chambers, the crazy mazes of the damned. Around every corner lurked evil. Whether you did it by running and gunning or whether you tiptoed stealthily to get the full effect, Doom was a seemingly endless haunted house and *Halloween* rolled into one. Each time you encountered a demon, you'd exclaim, "Oh, crap. I'm gonna die. I'm gonna DIE. This is hell; I didn't sign up for this. Oh . . . OH! I got him. Damn, I'm good! . . . Oh, nooooooo."

Also important in the canon of landmark shooters was Halo, with lines of dialog like "Marines! We are gonna pump the enemy full of lead and drown them in their own blood!" In Halo, you could almost smell the gunpowder, almost inhale the assorted stenches of combat. Like some nerdy Lieutenant Colonel Kilgore from *Apocalypse Now*, you could sit there amid the fiery trance of explosions, thinking, "I love the smell of Halo in the morning."

Still, the attitude Doom and Halo evoked was a highly fictionalized, stylized defiance. The Housers wanted to explore a visceral feeling that was more like real life—even with what they called their company, even with one of its early names, Grudge. Sam and Dan felt the name worked because, as outsiders, they both had chips on their shoulders and could hold on to and remember resentment for quite some time. It seemed like the right kind of name for the time because it sounded like grunge, the post-punk, vitriol-filled alternative music that had burst out of the Pacific Northwest with Nirvana and Pearl Jam. But someone said the name was too negative. As Sam, Dan, and Terry Donovan, Sam's pal from St. Paul's School in London, were driving near Marylebone and High Street, Sam blurted, "What about Rockstar? When you say the word 'Rockstar,' in my head I get the picture of a disheveled Keith Richards at his absolute lowest point. Living the life, the dream—and the nightmare, too. It's got edge and attitude and passion. It's not about us as stars, but what we make. Our games will be the rockstars of the twenty-first century."

"*Whhhhaaat?*" replied Donovan, who would become the take-no-bullshit head of marketing for the company and eventually its CEO. He snapped his neck and looked straight at Sam. As the son of one of Britain's savviest, most talented fashion photographers during the Swinging London period of the sixties, Donovan knew he'd heard something special, saying, "I don't like many of these names. But this one I can unequivocally say yes to." It didn't just have the punk, alternative essence. The name was positive and aspirational as well. Sam, Dan, and Terry Donovan pitched the idea of starting their own studio to Brant and some other Take-Two suits. The company was presented to Brant with such frantic eagerness, he thought the Housers and Donovan were somewhat unhinged. Brant gave them the green light, but he wouldn't put much money into the start-up. The Houser brothers would have to prove their worth. For many reasons, that would not be a walk in the park—unless you expected to be beaten up and blamed for all the country's ills while having your picnic in the gazebo.

15.

ROCKSTAR GETS PILLORIED

They would make many open world games, but Rockstar would become best known for a genre-defining project that DMA Design had been working on called Grand Theft Auto. The game was about 50 percent completed for the PC when Sam arrived at BMG. Even when it was finished, the first in the series gave you little of the gutsy underworld graphics that are now a Grand Theft Auto hallmark. Rather, you looked from high above down on the action you controlled in a kind of predator's-eye view. The original GTA was the brainchild of David Jones, a wry Scottish game developer who began his work in 1988 with a science fiction shooter called Menace. Three years later, Jones worked on the venerable Lemmings game, in which you as a kind of Pied Piper made bridges for as many as one hundred eminently commandable creatures, so they could move past hazards like rivers and canyons to an exit that always seemed too far off.

The game that would become Grand Theft Auto was originally called Race 'N Chase, and your primary goal was wholly different from that of the finished product—and not that new: You'd play as a cop speeding to catch criminals. That conceit began to transform during development, when everyone involved felt it was more of a kick to run over pedestrians on the streets than to avoid them. While Grand Theft Auto didn't look too spectacular, it was a miracle of game design that would popularize the sandbox/open world genre.

The deceptively simple formula would go something like this: Role playing game plus shooter plus driving equals a sandbox game. Here, you could make your world, not live in someone else's. The effect is a little like what My Chemical Romance describes in their gruesomely alive rock anthem "The Sharpest Lives": "There's a place in the dark where the animals go. You can take off your skin in the cannibal glow." But it's also about Brian Wilson's old-ass Beach Boys gem "In My Room": Here, he retreats into his lair to deal with his most dangerous private thoughts—"In this world I lock out all my worries and my fears—in my room, in my room." Except this world could be full of almost infinite contemplation, emotion, and action, as-big-as-your-brain-could-imagine-it big.

In GTA, you could complete heart-pumpingly frantic timed missions given to you by a crazy array of gangs. Or you could just simply drive, groove to one of seven radio stations, and explore the vast city below. You could even add your favorite CD to those stations to make the experience familiar and more about you. Yet even as the game was being finished, the Housers realized that the next salient trend in games would be the illusion of 3-D. They were sure that a Grand Theft Auto in 3-D would be a game changer. But they were planning ahead with a little too much exuberance. First, they had the debut game to worry about.

Grand Theft Auto took center stage in 1997 in the UK (before it was released in the United States), with the dynamic push of tabloid-minded PR whiz Max Clifford (who was O. J. Simpson's flak during the former football hero's sordid murder trial). The game was prominently featured in *Edge*, the well-regarded British game magazine, but it was a love-it-or-hate-it kind of game. Some reviewers praised it for its complexly brilliant game design, but critics who were more appreciative of detailed graphics dissed the game. Still it was a bona-fide seller for BMG Interactive, making purchasing the company's assets a fairly attractive proposition.

Meanwhile, there was drama on the business end. Instead of being made part of BMG Interactive's portfolio, DMA Design was sold to financially troubled Gremlin Interactive, which in turn sold it to an equally distressed company, Infogrames, in 1999. Finally, after much championing by Sam Houser, it was purchased by Take-Two in September for around $11 million. By then, DMA founder David Jones, frustrated that the company was constantly being sold, had left to form a new development house in Dundee, Scotland.

When Grand Theft Auto II was released in late 1999, Sam was primed and ready for success on a higher level. He was stoked about the refinements, the wide-open-world-ness full of freedom and the ability to choose and cultivate your own badass adventure. He loved the fact that if you were favored by one gang of thugs, you were not liked by the other. You would be hated, stalked, run down, and attacked when entering their well-guarded territory. There were puns galore, too. For instance, some vehicles were called Wang Cars (as in the British insult "wankers"). But Rockstar didn't account for Driver, a PlayStation game released four months earlier, which gave the illusion of speeding along in 3-D. Via a clunky old answering machine, Driver encouraged you to take on a titillatingly illegal driving mission. You would immediately become thuglike, picking up your masked pals, who robbed the local bank and screeched away to a safe house. If you avoided the out-of-control police cruisers, which sometimes flew over your hood like hulking metal turkey vultures, all the better. Ultimately, the sometimes gruesome evil that your man did was balanced by the fact that he was an undercover cop. Driver set a benchmark for games in the future.

A week after Grant Theft Auto 2 was released, Sam still believed sales would be of the blockbuster variety. Then Take-Two executives walked into Sam's office. They were sullen. "It's tanking," said one.

"Completely stiffing," said the other.

Sam thought they were playing a joke on him. "How could Driver be the game with the stellar reviews?" he wondered. "It looks better, but I can't get past the difficult tutorial level. And there are never more than two cars on the road at the same time. This is just a tech demo. Grand Theft Auto II is a real game." But it was true. The initial reviews for GTA II were bad, and sales were flat as a pancake. Sam, the proselytizer who felt Rockstar could be the most innovative company on earth, was forced to eat his first bit of crow. He said to Dan, "That was a humbler. Don't count your fucking chickens. Don't take anything for granted. That's what we learn from this."

To complicate matters, David Jones was raiding what remained of DMA Design for his new company. Of the eighty employees who were left after the Take-Two acquisition, only eighteen remained after Jones sank his teeth into them. Then Jones offered the most talented group within DMA a deal they had to take seriously. Sam had worked closely with these designers from Edinburgh on a satirical Nintendo 64 game called Space Station Silicon Valley, a radiant send-up of the sci-fi genre in which animals had evolved with technology to produce, say, a hippo powered by a steam engine. Sam firmly believed that the Space Station designers were the most talented of the DMA lot. And he actually clicked with them, saying, "These are the only guys who don't make me feel like a freak as the unwanted publisher guy." If he lost the group to Jones, designing a Grand Theft Auto in 3-D would be an impossible task.

"We don't want to go with David," said Leslie Benzies of the Edinburgh team. "But he's offering us all this stuff, money, creativity. We'd rather work with you. But you've got to match what he's offered, man."

Sam and Jones were no longer friends or even colleagues. In fact, they have not talked since the incident. Within days, Sam had a deal ready, which the Edinburgh team promptly signed. They had shown Sam and Dan the demo of their latest baby on the Nintendo 64 console, one that showcased monsters like Godzilla and dinosaurs roaming a city in which the buildings could be decimated with one or two whacks of a giant paw or claw. The graphics were minimal and the demo was presented as a wire frame model, basically a 3-D representation of the level design possibilities, made with rudimentary lines. When Sam saw it, he thought, "Why would I want to stomp around and destroy this city? I'd rather drive around it and check out the city and go inside the buildings."

By early 2000, Sam, Dan, and the other unique spirits at Rockstar came together as a thunderous force of nature to create what is thought of today as a Grand Theft Auto game. Their labors would result in one of the most memorable games in videogame history, Grand Theft Auto III. Because Jones and his team had gone their own way, the Housers and Rockstar North were now free to brainstorm in no-holds-barred fashion. As the ideas flowed forth, the game turned into something more inspired and subversive than before. But there was a pressing challenge. The Housers were essentially living hand to mouth, and Take-Two didn't have a lot of money to budget an expensive game from its twenty-four-carat-quality developers in the UK. To remedy the situation, the Housers helped to keep their company afloat by taking work they otherwise wouldn't have, like the Bass Hunter fishing game and ports for the commercially unsuccessful Sega Dreamcast console.

Dan traveled often to Scotland to write the violently compelling plot and ever-branching story. He created a crazy conglomeration of all of the best gangster movies he had seen. He would think, "If I did this scene, how could I make it even better than it is? How can it be grittier? How can I push the envelope?" As Sam saw it all come together, he could barely contain himself. He saw in Rockstar a motley crew of weird personalities who had all worked as one to create something that was countercultural, yes, but might, just might, resonate with a very large audience. Together, they all clicked like a sleek, magnificent machine, although they weren't always on time for their deadlines. "Every convention was put aside," Sam explained to the execs at Take-Two. "It isn't about furry creatures, and it isn't like Indiana Jones. It is a contemporary urban game with gangsters. The faces of the characters have these affectations that are so blatantly Dan. The city has a look to it that is so blatantly Aaron Garbut [the obsessed-with-minutiae art director]. And Leslie Benzies [the detail-conscious executive producer] is getting all the right things out of everyone else." Each had found his respective voice, but the whole was greater than the sum of its parts. It was like a band that had toiled for years on a grassroots level was finally ready to break into the Top 10—with a vengeance.

When Sam viewed a demo of one of the essential game play tropes, he was certain the Grand Theft Auto III would be a runaway success. In fact, everyone at Rockstar believed that the ability to carjack any vehicle a player found during his or her escapades was an inventive step forward, not only for the series, but for games in general—especially because it was set in a 3-D world this time. It made you feel like an absolute monster of crime, but in a good way. Stealing virtual cars would permit you to feel independent, wild, free of guilt, even sin, because that was what you were supposed to do in this gangster-filled world. But it wasn't just about jacking. For the game to feel more real, the team, always editing and re-editing, changed the cut scenes. Instead of being 2-D, they became little 3-D movies enhanced by motion capture, a technique in which a computer and camera record an actor's movement and translate it into a digital representation. Rockstar didn't have money for actors, so workers themselves donned mocap suits and "acted." But celebrities were involved in the voice-over. Kyle MacLachlan, Debi Mazar, Joe Pantoliano, and Michael Madsen, working for a very low day rate, added their distinctive talents to the game. Because of his work in the record industry, Sam (with the aid of Donovan) was able to cut deals to license Giorgio Moroder's *Scarface* film soundtrack and music from the estimable English jungle drum and bass label, Moving Shadow. The enthusiasm in New York and in Edinburgh was palpable.

Six months before the game arrived on shelves, a very proud Sam and Benzies took Grand Theft Auto III to E3. At the demo booth, they waited to show their baby off to the world's press and retailers. They waited. And waited.

"Where are the people, Les?" Sam asked in exasperation with the game controller in his hands.

"Shit. Dunno," said Benzies, looking around. "Seem to be at the State of Emergency kiosk." While State of Emergency was a decent game, full of terrorism, political assassinations, and populist unrest, Sam couldn't see why it was getting all the kudos when it was clear to him that GTA III was so much better made. After the E3 debacle, Sam never really had a substantial presence at the convention again.

Sam tried his best to turn the perceived slight into a hunger that he could use to drive the team to make the game even better. But just as he began readying his fiery personality for the game's launch, he and Dan, from a Thompson Street apartment, watched the World Trade Center attacks on September 11, 2001. In the early moments of the disaster, Sam feared that the buildings might tip and cause a domino effect right into SoHo and farther up into Greenwich Village. For an intensely nerve-wracking two weeks, during which the country as a whole was on edge, the Housers talked about bagging the game altogether. Like everyone in Manhattan at the time, they didn't know when terrorism would strike again. Manhattan smelled noxious, like burning chemicals, and there were posters of the missing plastered everywhere. Sam told Dan, "This beautiful city has been attacked, and now we're making a violent crime drama set in a city that's not unlike New York City. My God, I'm terrorized where I live, and on top of that, we've got this fucking crazy game that is not exactly where people's heads are at right now." But they had done so much fine work. In the end, they simply edited the game. Since Grand Theft Auto III was based in a fictional New York City called Liberty City, Rockstar immediately removed any vestige of the World Trade Center's Twin Towers from the game. They changed the paint on the police cars from NYPD blue and white to LCPD black and white. And they completely excised a character who was an activist hell-bent on bringing down Liberty City's economy.

When the game was released on the technologically advanced PlayStation 2 in October, it sold 80,000 copies in its first week. In the second week, it sold 150,000 copies. The game received nearly universal acclaim and *Game Informer* wrote, "It's a game you could play for weeks—maybe even months—and still discover something new every day." As time passed, it just kept selling and selling, like vinyl out of the seventies, when music was the only thing that mattered. It kept selling like Pink Floyd's *The Dark Side of the Moon,* more than fifteen million copies.

Sam, Dan, and Rockstar North had approached game making with a granular rock 'n' roll intensity that has rarely been matched by designers. Their mission was to make movie- and music-inspired games that they were certain would have a great supremacy in the

gamer's mind, games that made action films look puny in comparison. Stating that Dan Houser's writing is merely influenced by film,
especially the gangster genre, is to offer only a couple of scenes from
the whole movie. Mentioning that the writing often wins because
of its grinding, gnashing satire and searing social commentary gets
closer to the point. Dan Houser can occasionally be long-winded.
But he is among the better narrative writers in our popular culture
today, not only in videogames, but in any medium. He and his team
are not writing a linear story. Rather, the narrative is like a 3-D chess
game of sorts, often very different from the linear structure of a
movie and fairly different from even a narratively experimental book
like Peter Carey's *My Life as a Fake*, which frequently moves around
in time. So he is a master of popular writing, especially because he is
dealing with a genre of games that is open-ended. You can go anywhere, and wherever you go, treading down whatever dark alley you
choose, you are eventually funneled through the story to its conclu-
sion. And once you hear the words spoken, watch the action that
ensues, and then participate in the story, exploring Liberty City, San
Andreas, or Vice City becomes more than a game. The rough, tough
Bukowski-esque dialog sticks with you just like opening paragraphs
of Truman Capote's *In Cold Blood*, where shotgun blasts are heard
as "somber explosions." Therefore, you don't play the game as much
as you get to know a world and its people. And you feel as though
you are the first to do so. You live it and you dream it. That's what
makes the game's endings all the more satisfying and breathtaking.
There is a sad joy in the final mission of Grand Theft Auto III. After
hearing the venomous invectives of the harpy-voiced Catalina, the
game's antagonist and possibly a cannibal, you speed away and ultimately shoot down her helicopter over the sprawling Cochrane Dam
in Cedar Grove, in an explosion one game character calls "better
than the fireworks on the Fourth of July." You know you've done
what you have to do, but there's not much joy in it. Even when you

get the girl, she talks and talks inanely. As the game ends and the screen becomes black, the crack of a gunshot pierces. Did you kill her? Did she kill you?

Not everyone saw Grand Theft Auto III as a jewel of popular art. Walmart was so worried that kids would play the game that it began checking the IDs of every buyer. For a while, Australia banned the game due to its violent and sexual content. Politicians like Senator Joe Lieberman railed against it, saying the violence was horrendous and that the Housers "have a responsibility not to do it if we want to raise the next generation of our sons to treat women with respect." After seeing GTA III, Jack Thompson, a conservative activist lawyer, made it his crusade to ban the spread of violent videogames. The Housers didn't react publicly, but privately they shook their heads. They had made the game for adults. Through the Entertainment Software Ratings Board, they had labeled it with a Mature rating, hopefully ensuring that no one under seventeen would purchase the game.

"I don't get it," said Dan of the controversy. "This isn't a toy. It's expressly not for kids."

"It's clearly for older people," agreed Sam. "It's relevant to me. I'm older now. I don't want to play as penguin. I want to play as a man and do things that a man does."

With Grand Theft Auto Vice City, Rockstar added new ingredients to what Sam began to call The Vibe, which, he said was "like injecting blood like Tina Turner did to [The Who's] Tommy as the Acid Queen. They put Tommy in that weird sarcophagus thing and she starts injecting him, and he comes out happy" as a blissed-out baby for the good part of the drug trip. Then, he goes in again and comes out covered in snakes for the bad portion. So à la Tommy in that film scene, the game would be rife with these supreme emotional highs and lows. Sam, a fan of the 1980s pop culture, suggested that the team create a game that melded the TV show Miami Vice with

Scarface with the music of the era. He was greeted with "Everyone's trying to *forget* the eighties. This is idiotic." But he had watched every episode of *Miami Vice* again and was certain a game that took place in the culturally maligned decade would be perfect. So Rockstar moved into a licensing deal with Epic Records that included a call to Michael Jackson to convince him to add "Billie Jean" to the game and to a separate, seven-disk box set of CDs. Sony's record chief Tommy Mottola came by Rockstar's SoHo office to confirm that the eighties still resonated with Americans, and not always in an ironic way. It was as though Sam finally had his record company, except it was tucked neatly within Rockstar Games.

With Lazlow Jones, a former radio host, Dan created in-game radio stations that featured well-known DJs and commercials brimming with parody. Some programs could be so humorous, you had to pull off to the side of the road during a mission to avoid crashing. Rockstar continued to add celebrity voices to the GTA experience as well, including Dennis Hopper as porn director Steve Scott and Burt Reynolds as the corrupt real estate tycoon Avery Carrington. Dan, a fan of Reynolds since the Smokey and the Bandit movies, went down to the recording session in Tribeca expecting to find a guy so affable, they might raise a glass together. For some reason, Reynolds was uncomfortable with Dan in the studio, and began crying, "Get the limey out of here. I'm not going to work if this limey Brit is in here!" The atmosphere became so tense that Reynolds and Dan were chest to chest and fisticuffs were about to break out. The two had to be separated by the studio's engineer.

In all its games, Rockstar continued to enrich a dark but lively underworld with essential humor. That hilarity in the writing was even more a part of The Vibe during the ambitious Grand Theft Auto: San Andreas when, on Bounce FM, DJ Funktipus spews the barb, "I'm the Funktipus and I got my tentacles wrapped around your San Andreas. Ain't my fault." And you wonder, "Who the hell is this guy? I wanna hang with him, buy him a beer, and get him really loaded so he can spill some tales. Come on, Funkitpus. Tell me about that crazy night with George Clinton. Oh. Wait. You *ARE* the voice of George Clinton." Beyond the radio stations and their over-the-top on-air personalities, the adventure within the state of San Andreas was inspired by four real states: California, Nevada, Arizona, and Oregon. In a way, San Andreas was the ultimate road trip, one that was menacing and rapturous at the same time.

It was also a role playing game inspired by the old Tomagotchi toys. Sam once took a friend's virtual pet and sadistically overfed it until it died. His friend was angered, but Sam never forgot the almost mad scientist feeling of experimentation he got when watching what would happen as he stuffed more food down the little monster's gullet. Similarly in San Andreas, tough thug CJ's demeanor and physicality would change if he chowed down too much. Sam saw that one game tester had made CJ become massively fat. Like a character out of Tod Browning's *Freaks,* this CJ wore tighty whities, a cape, a bandit's mask, and an Afro. In a kind of a media bridge of game to old-school fiction, the tester crafted a short story around all the things he was doing with CJ in San Andreas. All this RPG-ness was completely integrated through his actions while playing. It was incredibly subtle game design. There were no on-screen buttons or sliders you could use to change your character's size. But it was still there. While there was evil and violence everywhere, like Doom gone urban and hyperreal, it was The Sims and SimCity as well. It was life in a blender spawned by game genres in a blender.

But as the game continued to pile on the sales, and the media attention, life outside the game took a treacherous turn for the brothers. The Securities and Exchange Commission charged Take-Two and founder Ryan Brant, the son of billionaire publisher and horse breeder Peter M. Brant, with severe accounting irregularities, pointing to income that had been inflated by $60 million in 2000 and 2001.

(A disgraced Brant would eventually resign from Take-Two, pur-portedly for medical reasons.) Brant's troubles hit Sam hard, because the executive had believed in him enough to give him a life-changing break.

Sam had been living in San Diego and working at the Rockstar division there since May 2005 and was witness to the beginning of a fascinating open world game called Red Dead Redemption. He still was riding high from the success of San Andreas and felt the follow-up to 2004's Red Dead Revolver, a Western-themed offering about rough-riding cowboys, was something he always was meant to do. Sam immersed himself in work, trying to enjoy the fact that he was creating art with a hardworking team that was taking the sand-box genre to a different time in history.

Then, lightning struck a second time. When an incident that occurred in June became public in early July, those who disdained Rockstar for its game content found more reason to become un-hinged. A Dutch techie named Patrick Wildenborg had used some self-created code to open up the PC version of San Andreas. Inside, he discovered a locked portion of the game that featured the gangster character CJ having what amounted to R-rated sex in various posi-tions with a girlfriend. (Without Wildenborg's software key, all you heard were the sounds of passion.) Soon, the modder's program was all over the Web. It went viral and thousands upon thousands were playing the sexual mini-game called Hot Coffee.*

In San Diego, Sam had been thinking what a good life he was living. His son had just been born. He had just bought a country house with his brother. Maybe now he could relax a bit. And so could all of Rockstar. Then he read about Hot Coffee on a message

---

* It was hardly the first time that explicit sex had been seen in a game. Multimedia companies had made far more explicit games with full-motion video. In 1994, Virtual Vixens from Pixis Interactive had you satisfying various women in a sci-fi setting. If your rhythm was off, you'd be verbally dissed by your companion.

board. Immediately he had a sinking feeling. Everything moved in slow motion. Hot Coffee tore away the short-lived feelings of peace and accomplishment. He called up the New York office of Rockstar. Was this true? How could it be? How could this have happened? Sam remembered that a level designer had proposed the addition of the mini-game in question. But when the content was seen, the code had been nixed by all involved in making decisions, especially those at Rockstar North in Edinburgh. The snippet shouldn't have remained on the disk—no way, no how. But there it was, and critics were coming out of the woodwork to lambast Rockstar. Sam called Dan. "They're acting like this was meant to be in the game. It's unfinished. Not meant to be in the game!"

Dan said, "You can see the usual quality isn't there. Everyone should see that this wasn't intentional."

Sam continued, "This not how CJ would be with a girl. This was a very crude initial implementation. Had we completed it, it would have been more stylish, dare I say it, more romantic, more chic, a little bit more Barry White. But what's there—it's crude and embarrassing and childish, not what we as a company are about." Indeed, CJ was a well-rounded character whose sad backstory included the murder of both his mother and his brother. He was also being blackmailed; in essence, CJ was trapped in a gang world he never made. It makes sense that a finished Hot Coffee would have shown CJ's softer side.

The Housers and Rockstar were trapped, and the nightmare had only begun. Take-Two asked to see all pertinent Rockstar e-mails—including all of Sam's missives—as they searched for a smoking gun that might prove the Housers had intentionally added the mini-game to spark controversy. They found none. By mid-July, New York senator Hillary Clinton had called for the Federal Trade Commission to look into the genesis of the game material and how it got on the game disk. She assured her constituents that she was calling for a full and complete investigation in order to keep "inappropriate videogame content out of the hands of young people." Politicians around the country condemned the game, including New York State attorney general Eliot Spitzer, who, while campaigning for governor, called the release of the game "irresponsible behavior" from which our nation's children needed protection. The Los Angeles district attorney called to obtain the Rockstar e-mails. The scandal was feeding upon itself. Powerful conservatives throughout the country feared that the game's content could cause irreparable damage to kids.

Sam told Dan, "These guys are out to get us. They'll garrotte us whatever we do. They don't give a shit. This is *crazy*. They're throwing serrated-edged boomerangs like the little kid in *Mad Max 2*."

Sam had always been a little neurotic; he would probably agree with former Intel CEO Andy Grove's famous motto, "Only the paranoid survive." Worry was an essential part of his personality because it helped him to get things done, a quality that allowed him to drive the various divisions within the company forward to complete deadlines. But when the FTC hauled nine Rockstar employees, including Sam and Benzies, down to Washington, DC, for their investigation, it changed Sam forever.

Like a character in his own game, Sam had become Public Enemy Number One—except in real life it wasn't nearly so much fun. In January 2006, Sam sat down in an uncomfortable chair in a small-ish room at FTC headquarters. Behind him was his cadre of three lawyers. In front of him were three agents of the commission. To his left in front of the agents was a two-foot-high stack of paper, including thousands of his e-mails to employees during the making of San Andreas. The fussy FTC agents went through the highlighted portions of each page, grilling him for nine hours. When they saw certain words he used in his correspondence, they would raise their eyebrows and ask, "What do you mean by this language?"

Sam, fearing that his use of the "F" word would make the FTC believe he'd surely done something wrong, explained that he used salty language in an effort to get the job done during crunch time. Then the agents came across a more recent e-mail that read, "Why are they so concerned about what we're doing in the game when we're bombing the hell out of people in Operation Enduring Freedom trying to keep our freedom, and they're back here trying to curb the freedom that we're paying the taxes to fight for?" Sam stood by his statement, saying he wasn't particularly political. "But if you're blasting people over there in the name of freedom, why are you clipping our freedom of speech over here? Those things seem to me to be at odds with each other." The FTC eventually found nothing out of order with the e-mails and no grand conspiracy to pervert the youth of America with Grand Theft Auto San Andreas.

Even after it was over, Sam was powerfully affected by the ordeal. For some time, he had spells during which he felt terrified. He wanted to leave the country. Some of his friends, who'd been with him since the beginning, began to bail on the company. Terry Donovan left his CEO position because of the emotional tumult the investigation had caused in him. While in the UK on business, Sam had an episode on a train from Scotland to London while heading over to visit his parents. After he heard via his cell phone that the New York City district attorney was thinking about investigating Rockstar, he felt a desperate need to drop out. In what he dubbed his Black Dog period, he literally wanted to give everything up, leave Rockstar, leave his brother and his family to go live in isolation in a cave, well, somewhere. Back in New York City, his doctor said the Hot Coffee incident had left Sam badly injured, like a victim in an emotional car crash. In the end, it was the making of GTA IV that fueled Sam's recovery. Sure, he and the others at Rockstar were outsiders again, maybe even more so than before. Sure, they were reviled. But Rockstar would come back because they had a point to make. Rockstar did not let Hot Coffee chill their speech. They would pull no punches with GTA IV, which would be hailed as the most grittily brave game they had ever created. It would sell 3.6 million copies on its first day and earn $500 million in its first week. The success showed throughout popular culture. Coke riffed on the Grand Theft Auto theme, except the grungy lead in the extravagantly animated commercial gave back an old lady's stolen purse, put out a fire, and gave away the soft drink as the motley cast of characters broke out into the "Give a Little Love" jingle. Comedian Dave Chappelle parodied the series with spot-on humor (and an Uzi). And in the off-Broadway play *The Common Air,* a loquacious DJ tried to be hip by talking to a kid in an airport terminal about GTA III.

Rockstar had sped through the blackness to continually make the finest games for adults on the planet. With their dangerously anarchic edge, cynical humor, and hip-hop swagger, Rockstar's creations resonate with legions of the disaffected across the world to an extent that no games before them have achieved. And if Rockstar bottles the spirit of rebellion for the young and old-ish who feel browbeaten, subjugated, and downtrodden, well, that's fitting enough—for that's what the Housers feel they still are and always will be, no matter how much money they make. Because they had almost lost it all, Sam and Dan will always have that haunted edge, that gnawing suspicion and lingering fear that combined with their innate creativity to stimulate greatness. Just as a Jedi can always count on the Force, The Vibe will always be with Rockstar.

16.

THE POPCAP GUYS AND THE
FAMILY JEWELS

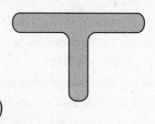

It was hated. It was disdained by the gamers who loved Grand
Theft Auto and, really, by anyone who called himself a hard-core
gamer. Those hard-core gamers said the new genre of casual
games was generic, repetitive, and thoroughly unexciting.

In 1999, much of Sony Online Entertainment's early work
was with casual games. The seasoned gamers on the team hated
them too. In addition, the editorial staff initially abhorred
what it saw as a lowest common denominator audience. Sony's
PlayStation 2, which played games and DVDs, had been released that past March to great acclaim; it was this console that
almost everyone cared most about, and the online videogame
space where people played bridge or bingo inside their Web
browsers was anathema to the serious gamer's sense of what was
paramount in games: to find and seek out the new. But Sony's

market research was showing that the people who flocked to games such as online poker and *Jeopardy!* were *non*-gamers—middle-aged women, busy housewives, or single mothers who had a few minutes here and there to play games that were not terribly involved as far as game play was concerned. And Sony had found that these middle-American gamers were loyal and hard-core in their own way. Women were the driving force behind Sony's huge, caring community, and they comprised the majority of the eight million registered members for the company's gaming portal, The Station. When The Station held contests, the floodgates opened and thousands of entries were received.*

Even though game critics looked as if they'd been sprayed by a skunk when the phrase "casual games" was mentioned, no one could ignore the immeasurable potential of these small online applications. Truth be told, many of these offerings weren't so very unlike the classic games of the eighties—like Pac-Man. As casual games blossomed, they were geared to women more than men—even though most were still made by men. By 2001, a billion-dollar industry had been born. Since the cost of making the games wasn't high, eager young game designers could set themselves up in a dorm room to work solo or with two or three fellow henchmen. The only problem was the inherent similarity among the games. Like Nolan Bushnell with Pong, the game makers seemed to want to release endless versions of the same game. The conundrum was a little like Aesop's ancient "The Crow and the Pitcher" fable. You had to add "pebbles," the games, to bring up the water consumers would drink. But the pebbles couldn't be too different or they wouldn't fit in the pitcher, in this case the niche of casual games. Would different pebbles change the taste of the water? Would those who wanted to drink even care if the water tasted too different?

* Some of this chapter is informed by my firsthand experience in working with the casual genre while employed at Sony Online Entertainment.

Flashback to 1997. In the wilds of Indiana, two teenage college students who epitomized the word "slacker" met in a computer science class in Indianapolis. They would soon find out more about casual games than behemoths like Sony would learn over the next decade. John Vechey and Brian Fiete were teenagers who didn't quite fit into the Purdue University milieu. Fiete had already learned more about computer coding on his own than any instructor could teach him. He'd been mesmerized by games ever since he could remember. As a child, he was drawn to the most violent games he could find in the Sumpter, South Carolina, backcountry. He spent hours in Aladdin's Castle, Bally's arcade chain, playing the vengeful ninja in Shinobi and thrilling to flying games where planes bombed vessels below into smithereens. In school, he amused himself making Pac-Man clones and text-based role playing games. But what Fiete really wanted to do was to make a game that many people could play at once via a modem. He felt that playing games online with others was the future.

For his part, John Vechey wanted to plunge into game making headfirst—forget the books. For him, college seemed to slow things. He had come from a lower-middle-class family in northern Wisconsin that occasionally ate government-provided cheese during hard times. His mother, an independent spirit, married many times. Once, she and a stepdad built a cabin in the woods to save money. John, too, inherited his mother's freewheeling, do-it-yourself mentality. At Purdue, Fiete and Vechey met as freshmen in a computer programming class and immediately started talking about games. It was clear within minutes that they were on the same wavelength.

"You want to make a game?" asked Fiete even before the third class of the first semester was over.

"Hell, yeah," enthused Vechey. "I don't know anything about it, but just tell me what you want me to do."

"Well." Fiete often spoke in measured tones, carefully choosing his words. "I have this idea for an Internet game. I need someone to do graphics."

"I can do it. No problem. I mean, I don't know much of anything about art. But I can try. I can start right away. I mean, the Internet! Let's do it." Vechey wanted everything to happen yesterday. He was impatient, even with the progress of the Internet. He became puzzled when he saw America Online for the first time. He liked the service, but he was flummoxed that you couldn't play games against another person online. He thought that was a slam dunk.

Vechey started working on drawings right away, finishing them in a day or so. He showed Fiete his sketches, including one for a spaceship.

Fiete perused the drawings for a minute, and his eyes stopped on the spaceship. "That doesn't look like a UFO," he said, scratching his head. "It looks like a woman's nipple!" Both started cracking up.

The two holed up in their dorm rooms, taking about four months to make the first version of their online game. After changing the game from a turn-based strategy effort to an action game, they changed its name from Ambush to ARC. The trickiest challenge was pounding out networking code so the game could be used on the Internet without choppiness. Both Fiete and Vechey had played games, like Quake, online that were perfect for higher speed connections but slowed appreciably with a dial-up modem. Fiete's clean code combined with Vechey's rudimentary graphics added up to no latency, even on slow connections. They found a cheap host and bought a used 486 computer because those with Intel Pentium chips were too expensive at the time.

ARC wasn't a huge hit; it had no marketing behind it. But it garnered an enthusiastic cult following, however small. That following was vocal, and it led to an e-mail that read

So, I was playing this game, and I see that you guys
made this game, so, like, I thought I'd write you and
see what you're doing with it and stuff like that.

−Jason Kapulka
  Senior Producer,
  Total Entertainment Network

Vechey scratched his head. "You think he really works in the
industry? He sounds too cool for school."

Fiete snapped back, "He writes like he's fifteen years old or
something. Plus, he sounds like a dick."

"TEN is like the biggest multiplayer gaming site in the world,
though."

"Whatever. He still sounds like a dick."

Until that moment, the guys had held those who worked in games
in high esteem in the same way a rabid music fan worships, say, the
lead singer in his favorite band. They imagined that any contact from
their heroes would be a godlike experience and not so hipster casual.
It didn't make sense to them that the man from TEN sounded like
just another dude with an attitude. But Jason Kapulka wasn't much
older than the teens, a transplant from Vancouver, British Columbia,
whose father was a park warden and whose mother worked as an el-
ementary schoolteacher. In Vancouver on an Apple II PC, he had
begun programming his own crude shooter games with odd, humorous monikers like Toxic Waste Marauder, a game where you stopped
sludge from coming up from the manholes and sewers in the streets.
Kapulka also penned some reviews for *Computer Gaming World*, a
monthly magazine that prided itself on being the *New York Times* of
gaming magazines.

"We'd like to publish ARC on TEN," Kapulka told Fiete and
Vechey in a phone call.

Greg Harper, TEN's head of business development, called them next. He assured them there would be no pressure and lured them with a trip to San Francisco and a tour of the offices. Vechey had never been west of the Mississippi or south of Tennessee. He thought San Francisco was close to New Orleans. He and Fiete both agreed to the free trip immediately.

When the pair arrived in the Bay Area, they marveled at the bustle of Union Square, eventually strolling into the lobby of TEN. The well-dressed Harper took one look and handed them off to Kapulka because they were just gawky, geeky kids with long hair, not the kind of people Harper wanted to talk business with. They couldn't even drink legally, which didn't stop them from sucking down booze—until the local watering hole carded them. By the time they left San Francisco, Fiete and Vechey had made a deal with TEN to license ARC for play on its site for $45,000.

"We're rich!" cried Fiete.

Vechey nodded, adding, "In Indianapolis, we won't have to work for, like, ever!"

But times were changing. While ARC did well, sometimes amassing hundreds of players at a time, TEN saw the writing on the wall when it came to the increasing popularity of casual games. Without warning, Kapulka began getting directives from the higher-ups to drop some of the site's hard-core focus and to research games like mah-jongg and bingo. "One day I'm working on Total Annihilation and the next day I'm on bingo," a stunned Kapulka told Vechey and Fiete. Other sites, like Sony's The Station and RealNetworks, were already licensing dozens of casual games, launching sites that aggregated everything from tic-tac-toe to Wheel of Fortune. At first, the very idea of these games made Kapulka sick to his stomach, especially bingo. There was no skill involved in bingo, just dumb luck. Then he traveled to some churches to see what the bingo crowd was all about. What he saw was groups of women having a raucous time,

drinking, playing, and being social. The experience was totally unlike the bingo games on the Web at the time, primarily single-player
affairs that made you refresh your browser each time you wanted a
new bingo ball to drop.

Kapulka, an avid reader and thinker, was concerned with what's
called the Third Place, which Ray Oldenburg, an urban sociolo-
gist, so succinctly espoused in his 1989 book, *The Great Good Place*.
Kapulka thought, "You've got the home, work, and this public area
where you socialize, a pub, a restaurant, a bingo hall. There's a big
difference between sitting in a bar drinking by yourself and sitting at
home drinking by yourself, almost like the difference between alone-
ness and loneliness." For TEN's bingo game, he told executives,
"Let's slap on a big chat room so you have fifty people in there and
it feels more alive, like a real Third Place." Kapulka's idea survived
when TEN became Pogo and completed its transition to a casual
gaming site. That didn't mean he liked the job any more. In fact,
the bureaucracy and inability to implement new games quickly made
him begin to think his job sucked.

Meanwhile, Fiete and Vechey dropped out of college and moved
to Seattle after getting a job with King's Quest and Leisure Suit
Larry maker Sierra On-Line, thanks to a phone interview arranged
by Vechey's aunt. Both were in awe of Sierra CEO Ken Williams,
who, with his wife, Roberta, was responsible for making and publishing some of Vechey's and Fiete's favorite adventure games. The two
began to work in the company's burgeoning WON (World Opponent
Network) online games division. But both were frustrated, especially
Fiete, who often complained to Vechey, "They're just slapping some
network code onto their games and calling it multiplayer. Half the
time it doesn't work well and the other half it doesn't work at all."

"And they're depending on people clicking on advertising to
pay for things," agreed Vechey. That was no way to build a business;
it seemed like smoke and mirrors. And both were adamant: if you

don't design a game to include multiplayer functions from the design document onward, it's not going to feel right or play well. Both
thought WON had already lost the battle.

It all came to a head when Fiete and Sierra cohort Brian Rothstein
began to imagine a casual game called Wordox in which the player
matched tiles on a grid featuring various animals. Once the tiles
were matched, the screen would clear and points would be amassed.
Fiete's bosses nearly fired him for ignoring his assigned tasks. Yet
after a heated discussion, the game, which was soundly designed,
was put on the network. Within weeks, it was the most played game
on the site, sometimes garnering forty thousand players at one time,
as much human traffic as half of Sierra's online games put together.
But Fiete was disgruntled. Even though Wordox was really a hit, he
only received a small bonus—a laptop—out of the deal. Frowning,
Fiete grabbed an envelope and calculated on the back that Sierra was
making thousands of dollars from Wordox every day. It didn't have
to be as big as the legendary ones Ken bestowed upon the early Sierra
inventors like John Harris, but he wanted a real cash bonus. He told
Vechey, "It's making me kind of jaded on the whole gaming thing.
I'm pretty burned out on games."

Fiete and Vechey were becoming cynical; Kapulka already was.
Like Nolan Bushnell and Graeme Devine before them, the three
didn't like the idea of making money for others, and they knew that
Williams had paid staggering royalties of up to 30 percent for games
back in the 1980s. The trio had learned much about the emerging
online games business while at their respective positions, and they
thought they could do better. Realizing that the late nineties was the
Era of Start-up Mania, they put out a shingle under the moniker
SexyActionCool, based on a poster for the movie *Desperado* they saw
at a bus stop. The ad featured a pistol-packing Antonio Banderas
dressed in black and a breathless quote from overexcited *Rolling
Stone* movie reviewer Peter Travers: "Sexy. Action. Cool."

After much discussion, the trio decided to enter the world of online pornography with a strip poker game called Foxy Poker.

"So how sexy action cool do we get?" posed Kapulka.

"I don't know about nudity," said Fiete. He considered what his relatives might think, what his mother might say.

"The money could be decent, though. And we could finance other projects," said Vechey. But Vechey agreed that he, too, was uncertain about doing a game with nudity. Ultimately, they didn't have the balls to go all the way; their poker ladies never really took off their clothing and the game didn't include photographs of real women, just cartoons. And getting the character to strip was difficult. You had to score so many points to get the women to take off the smallest piece of clothing that it almost didn't seem worth the effort to achieve the minor thrill. The trio didn't like the personalities involved in the X-rated world either. Kapulka said to Fiete, "Everyone we deal with at those sites seems sleazy. They give off this vibe of extreme untrustworthiness. I don't have any big compulsions about being family friendly, but I still feel kind of dirty fooling around with that stuff."

Licensing wasn't bringing in much revenue, so Vechey and Fiete cut corners on meals, eating only cheap fast food. They vowed not to travel by plane and not to pay too much for girls' dinners when on dates. Sometimes they ate only once a day. Yet they were happy; they kept telling themselves they weren't in the game industry to become millionaires, just to have fun, earn a living, and live life on their own terms. Kapulka was now doing artwork and design for the games, while Fiete continued to write code. Vechey admitted that he had no particular talent except for one thing: He was a guy for whom the stars always seemed to align; he'd always been lucky.

In April of 2000, Vechey was surfing the Web when he thought he'd come upon something unique in its simplicity: a crude Javascript game called Colors Game. He matched the colors. When they paired up, the colors disappeared, only to be replaced by new colors after he refreshed the Web page. It really had him hooked. He excitedly e-mailed the link to Fiete and Kapulka.

"It's pretty addictive," agreed Fiete.

"Yeah, but how do you make something like this compelling enough that anyone would want to play it?" asked Vechey.

Kapulka came up with the idea of making the colors into fruit shapes. He tossed that thought away because he wanted to include seven different shapes and colors of fruits, but too many looked alike. Settling on jewels, Kapulka drew seven distinct shapes on a notepad. Along with a few other game ideas like Money Maze, Alchemy, and Atomica, they proceeded to work on and off for four months on the jewel game, constantly tightening the design and graphics. As the game ended, players were in a cave (a trope that had spread widely since the days of Colossal Cave). Thunderous roars were heard as the cave crumbled in as a kind of animated payoff for playing.

Before they went further, the team had to ascertain whether they should include a timed mode to quicken the pace and spice up the action. When showing the timer-less version to game designers, they received negative feedback, including a rude response from a Pogo executive: "This stupid thing isn't a game at all." More and more professional game designers offered snotty and snooty remarks. They were almost viscerally opposed to what the three were doing, seeing the jewel matching game as an example of exceptionally poor game theory.

Yet when Kapulka traveled home to Canada, he performed what he described to John and Brian as the Mom Test. He gave Roma, his mother, a laptop to play on, and he noticed that she enjoyed the game when it wasn't timed, so much so that once or twice, he couldn't get her away from the computer. It was strange to witness; his mother had developed a videogame jones. Kapulka speedily reported back to his partners, "When she plays it in timed mode, she doesn't much like it at all. When it's not timed, she plays it a lot. She says it relaxes her. The timed mode stresses her out."

Diamond Mine, as they christened it, was licensed to Microsoft's MSN Gaming Zone with one caveat. The executives in charge didn't like the name and asked its staff for various suggestions. In the end, it was named Bejeweled by a slick in-house marketer named Eddie Ranchigoda, who previously had worked at Sierra as a public relations flack. The new name didn't go over well with the game makers.

"They're changing it to *what*?" asked Fiete in disbelief.

"That sounds just like that crappy *Bedazzled* movie with Brendan Fraser that just came out. This sucks balls," proclaimed Vechey. Yet within a month, more than thirty thousand people were playing Bejeweled simultaneously. Though it was a hit for Microsoft, the corporate giant paid the developers a measly $1,500 a month to carry the game. Yet because the revenue model of the nineties was about getting users to click banner ads, Microsoft had a good argument for keeping the licensing fee on the low side. Meanwhile, the trio felt they should change the name of their company to one sans the word "sexy." They were, after all, now in the business of making family-oriented games, not something even vaguely pornographic. Still poor, they searched for a Web address for their company that wasn't already taken—they couldn't afford to buy a domain name from someone already using it. Jason liked the word "Pop," for it suggested that they wanted to make popular games, not something quirky and hard-core. And they wanted something with six letters, easy to remember and easy to type. If PopFrog or PopSlap had been available URLs, they might have taken those first. But PopCap was available, and it seemed to have the right kind of feel. When Microsoft agreed to allow PopCap's Web address to be featured on a screen before players started played Bejeweled, the three thought it would be good for business. They didn't know how good.

None of the PopCap principals wanted to charge too much for

the game on their own website and alienate what they hoped might be potential lifelong customers. After all, the game was already free to play on the Microsoft site. The trio agreed they needed to add something valuable to the game before they charged for it. But adding fees was tricky at the time, especially for a new company, because of the big dot-com implosion of early 2000. During that period, trillions of dollars in technology market value was lost, and no one wanted to gamble on anything even remotely related to the World Wide Web. Figuring out how much to charge proved to be more difficult than choosing a name for the company, and far more difficult than making the game itself. They knew games. But they knew about as much about selling games on the Web as Mario the Plumber knew about Kenyan economic policy. The trio thought about fixing a price for each download and, after some beer, came up with $4.99 for a fuller version of Bejeweled.

Despite their success, the PopCap guys were still kids who liked to party. During work hours, Vechey and Fiete would often take breaks and escape their monitors. They bought motorcycles and sped through the piney back roads of Seattle to clear their heads. As they sped, Fiete would rag on Vechey for buying a used purple Ninja 250 starter bike, mocking him with "Dude, that's a chick bike." As long as they got their work done, they weren't going to worry too much about prices and marketing. Fiete and Vechey even took some time off to go to Argentina to party while Kapulka toiled in the States. Sure, sometimes they would work on games, and once, Vechey closed a licensing deal with Yahoo. But for most of the three months after they launched the site, they soaked up the sun, drank, and chatted up the local girls. Their philosophy of life wasn't too complex: They didn't need to get rich quick; they just wanted to live life their way, on their own terms. Yet inside they knew that the $12,000 to $15,000 a month they were bringing in from Microsoft and Yahoo wasn't enough to run a company, at least not for very long.

Then Howard Tomlinson, an executive at Astraware who was converting the game for use on the PalmPilot portable digital assistant device, suggested that they put up a shareware version of Bejeweled on the Web. Tomlinson told Kapulka to sell the full version for $19.99. Kapulka called Vechey and Fiete explaining that Tomlinson had a theory that essentially held that if it isn't expensive enough, people will think it's a crappy game that's not even worth the cheap price.

"Crap, that's expensive," said Vechey.

Fiete was quiet. But then, he was always somewhat reserved. But this time he had something to say. "I think we should do it. We can always lower the price later." The full version included both the mode with a timer and the more tranquil untimed mode.

Within a month, the game brought in $35,000 from the PopCap website. The address became a kind of a viral grassroots slot machine that would not stop spewing money. Vechey kept shaking his head, saying, "Holy crap. Just holy crap!" every time he looked at the numbers. Fiete created a little app that would make a ka-ching sound when someone bought Bejeweled. At the end of the second month, it went off so much that Fiete disabled it.

The game was nonetheless pooh-poohed by game developers and critics, who said it required little skill to play. Reviewers ignored it and often refused to write about it. Yet those who didn't care about being cool could feel a Zen peacefulness when playing, like the feeling you got when indulging in hours upon hours of Tetris. Like Tetris, Bejeweled had something that had nothing to do with skill or tension or beating the pants off other gamers. The experience of playing Bejeweled was akin to things that calm everyone in life: vegging out in front of the TV, looking at the waterfall at Yosemite National Park, sitting and watching a river flow on a summer day. And Bejeweled was right there on the computer, waiting for you when you needed a break from the stress.

The kids at PopCap soon had other successful ideas for games, like Bookworm, which was a spelling game hosted by a bespectacled worm named Lex, short for "lexicon." Not long after came Peggle, which combined pachinko, pinballs with special changing powers, and cute characters. You even heard "Ode to Joy" from Beethoven's Ninth Symphony when you cleared a level. The money just kept flowing in, primarily from women gamers, so much so that they had offers to buy the company for $60 million. But unlike Trilobyte with The 7th Guest, and scores of companies that came after them, Kapulka, Fiete, and Vechey didn't care about taking the fast track to going public. They stayed private, hired an imaginative CEO, and methodically increased their staff to two hundred employees around the world, everywhere from Ireland to Shanghai. They licensed pro- prietary software to make PopCap-style games. Sometimes, when they were trapped in meeting after meeting that kept them cooped up for twelve hours, they complained about it. But behind those doors, PopCap was amassing tens of millions in investor money and slowly preparing for an IPO—if another colossal company didn't preempt the deal by swooping down and buying the guys out.

PopCap and its groundbreakingly simple games had opened the floodgates for a nascent sub-industry. The company's ideas for indus- try domination weren't that different from Nolan Bushnell's when he marketed Pong incessantly—even to doctors' offices. Like Bushnell, PopCap pushed hard to have their games on every platform imag- inable. Bejeweled and Peggle brought built-in cred to newer deliv- ery systems like the cell phone, the iPad, Web browser Flash games (and games on airline flights with those horrible controllers attached by a stupid spring-loaded wire). Wherever games could be played, there was PopCap with a new port. Their seemingly overnight suc- cess encouraged the formation of dozens of small studios in garages, apartments, and student dorms, for independently made games. The venture capital coffers opened up, but the beauty of casual gaming was that the new entrepreneurs didn't need much venture money. They saw where PopCap had gone, and they wanted to make small games that made fistfuls of money for little or no investment, too.

Each year the industry grew by leaps and bounds, to become a $3 billion force within a decade. The development costs, according to the Casual Games Association, could be as low as $50,000 (less if you paid your employees on the back end and worked out of a dorm room), a fraction of the cost of a popular console game, which was budgeted at $20 million or more. And unlike the console game making machinery, where hundreds worked on a game in almost an assembly line fashion, the casual teams were small and full of camaraderie. The risks were small enough that casual games companies could try fresh and forward-thinking games, more so than the console giants. The developers of the latter games worried about risking millions on offerings that didn't have defined, already-existing audiences. They were often caught up in a kind of Hollywood-itis, where the idea of propping up and supporting the popular series—or making a new game with a known audience—was more vital than innovative advances in game play. The indie game visionary, however, could dive headfirst into any wild idea with gusto. If it failed, he or she could try something else, having lost only some man hours and not much money. In that sense, casual gaming harkened back to the Williamses in the early days of Sierra, when a game on a floppy disk could cause a major industry furor. (These games also spawned the sub-sub-industry of a new kind of critic who reviewed casual and browser-based games only.) Few of these nerds would reach the heights of PopCap, which was formed early on in the revolution. But they all would try to lure the female gamer. A lucky few would even hit that sweet spot, the one that brings in moms the world over along with seasoned console gamers. And even if those hardworking nerds lost a few dollars, they sure had a lot of fun—and gained a lot of experience—trying to make game.

17.

THE THEORIST GOES GLOBAL

"Will Wright is leaving." The news reverberated throughout the videogame world on April 8, 2009.

Will Wright is gone. Oh, God. Oh, God. Oh, God.

Just the day before, Wright had sat with his elite one-hundred-member Electronic Arts team, the hardworking men and women who had developed his magnum opus, Spore, for more than half a decade. The game had sold more than two million copies since its release the previous year. After everyone had gathered, Wright spoke in measured tones, thanking the staff for their contributions over the years. The reaction to his departure ran the gamut from stunned silence to grudging understanding to shock to sadness. It was like Derek Jeter leaving the Yankees in his prime. Wright just zipped up his leather jacket, walked down the hallway, and out the door. There were no speeches from

Electronic Arts honchos, no lavish dinner, no going-away party, no videogame equivalent of a gold watch. In actuality, the higher-ups at EA had known for nearly a year that the brilliant designer of SimCity and The Sims was going to leave, but they had kept it a secret from stockholders, industry analysts, and, especially, the press. Outside of the Emeryville offices, the spring weather in the Bay Area was crisp, nippy. Wright lit a Marlboro Light, and as he drove away in his black BMW M3, to his home high in the hills, he began to reflect upon his long, successful career in videogames.

In the late 1980s, the videogame industry had emerged from its stasis to become huge once again. But the majority of personal computer games had become less than exceptional, at least to Will Wright. With a mind like a vacuum cleaner that sucks up complex pop culture and scientific theories, Will Wright was the kind of guy who left no stone unturned when researching a game. If something intrigued this inquisitive generalist, he became obsessive. For instance, he read *Zen and the Art of Motorcycle Maintenance* at least ten times. Then he absorbed every bit of information he could find about the book itself. Of all the videogame changers, Wright was the truest individualist, an unusual, alternative-headed thinker who was taught to take ideas apart the way hackers analyze the code of a videogame to see how it works. And then, like the most intelligent hackers, Wright riffed on the ideas he had absorbed. If he had not been an insatiable bookworm, researcher, thinker, and scholar of human nature, the genre he helped to create would not have progressed so exponentially, so scientifically, and so beautifully.

When Wright began his work, a handful of game designers had begun to dabble in what would become known as God Games, games in which you could control the lives and fates of humans. Journalists and game makers weaned on fantasy described these games as if players had become deities themselves, perched upon the puffy-cloud-filled heavens, looking down upon their minions, deciding whether they would live their lives through free will or pre-destination or a combination of the two. With a tap on the keyboard, you could alter their fates, their routines, the way they moved, and the way they intermingled.

At the time, three of these game creators were doing similar things. Peter Molyneaux from the United Kingdom made Populous. While ominous music played, you built a world that included vast mountains and deep blue seas that you yourself would design. Magically, you influenced the world's busy beings and chose whether they would be bad or good. There was even an Armageddon button to push to end everything, if you dared. Sid Meier made the Civilization series, based on highlights from the history of man. Civilization bit you hard and didn't let go; there was even a quick lesson in evolution during the two-minute-long opening sequence. You were the unseen but powerful Great Leader, whose job it was "to unite the quarreling tribes to harness the power of the land to build a legacy that would stand the test of time, a Civilization." Mesmerized, you traveled from the Bronze Age through the Space Age, and even constructed the world's Seven Wonders.

But it was Wright's games that set the stage. In Wright's inventions the literary-minded, the sociology-minded, and the science-minded could discover fragments of their most beloved theories. In Wright's games one could see the slow, sad suburban irony of Raymond Carver and John Cheever, and even the transcendent hope of Ralph Waldo Emerson. In that sense the moniker "God Games" was a misnomer. Wright's creations, especially SimCity and The Sims, were more about the human condition, about evolution and about the meaning of play, than they were about simply taking the role of an omniscient being. These games were Human Games, not God Games.

Wright, an atheist, might well agree. A lanky Ichabod Crane of a man, who often wore a black lambskin leather jacket, Wright was born in Atlanta to an engineer father who attended Georgia Tech and started a profitable company that made plastic bags. Boyhood conversations with his father made young Will enthusiastically muse about science, NASA, the planets, and every child's hope in the 1960s—to be an astronaut one day. But how Wright played as a child in solitude made him into what he is today. There was nothing he liked more than opening a colorful Revell plastic model box and putting together the pieces of a car, a tank, or a ship. Then he would sit on the couch and watch Godzilla movies in black-and-white. Thinking the movies were real because the national news was also presented in black-and-white, he hid behind the couch in utter terror, positive the scary monster was going to get him. It was only when his mother bought him a Godzilla model kit that he realized the monstrosity wasn't going to harm him; he felt that something he made would never turn on him. Yet his mother, Beverly, had ambivalent feelings as his life beyond school became a mix of model building, board games like Panzer Blitz, and *the* strategy game of many future game designers, Go. "You'll never amount to anything if you keep that up," she would say.

But he kept on building, graduating to bigger things, constructing dioramas and model trains. His mother would just shrug. And he loved robots, not just those in his favorite sci-fi movies, like *2001: A Space Odyssey* and *Star Wars,* but toys you could control remotely. It was his mother who gave him the creative genes. As an amateur actress and magician, she would have as many as thirty magicians over to the house to perform their tricks. Will became an ardent Harry Houdini fan, intrigued by the way the magician opened locks and seemingly controlled his audience's emotions. Houdini was a hacker before there were computers. It was probably thanks to Beverly that Will was sent to Ashton Hall, a huge Montessori school in Atlanta. And she became both father and mother when Wright's dad died of leukemia when Will was eight years old and the family moved to her hometown of Baton Rouge.

Wright's major videogame influence was Miyamoto's Super

Mario Bros. for the Nintendo Entertainment System. Ask any video-game designer that question, and Mario is probably one of the three answers he or she will give you. It's de rigueur. Yet Wright's reasoning was a bit different from the others. For Wright, it wasn't Mario's longing to save Princess Toadstool that captivated. Wright wasn't thinking about the game's simple objective: travel through eight crazy fantasy worlds and thirty-two levels to save the girl. He didn't focus on the strange tools that Mario used, like flowers turned into weapons that would shoot fireballs. What rocked Wright was the way he could take his time to explore that mushroom- and monster-filled seriocomic universe as he encountered a variety of quirky characters. It all made him sit back and consider who the protagonist was and why fans could not turn away.

No matter how much he appreciated Miyamoto's game design, Wright didn't want to make platformers. He was more inspired by and attracted to an Electronic Arts game designed by Bill Budge called Pinball Construction Set. Wright loved pinball as much as any nerd anywhere. Playing pinball not only freed Wright's mind, it made him wonder at the joys of physics and math, made him muse about the arcs and angles of the pinball itself. Budge's Pinball was ideal for Wright. It opened a door that let him make a contraption in his very original way. More, it let him feel like he was a pioneer of sorts. For a nerd, Budge's game was like what freshly cut logs were for a pioneer of the American West. You could make things from this software—not a cabin in the clearing, but what looked and worked like an electronic entertainment machine. You did it your way and it had your signature. You could say to your friends, "I made this. Can you beat it?" In real life, you probably couldn't be a designer of pinball games—no matter how much you loved them. But with Budge's game, you could live the dream, at least on your computer screen. For Wright, it was the ultimate model kit. Forget Godzilla and plastic hot rod cars.

Figuring out what to do with his life didn't happen easily for Wright. He didn't want to take on the family business, which was a dead end to him and entrapping. So his mother sold the company. He didn't quite finish college, so being an astronaut was out of the question. But he did study urban planning at Louisiana State and at the New School in New York City. Part of him still wanted to get his hands dirty, to make those models real at a real world job, like an architect . . . maybe. And he wanted to make games . . . well, maybe. But then again, he liked robots, which he could control with the Apple II computer his mother bought for him. He also loved the idea of racing cars. With a pal, he tricked out a Mazda RX-7 with an extra tank, night vision, two radar detectors, a computer system, a radar jammer, and a refrigerator. He sped across the country and was stopped late at night in Indiana for speeding at 104 mph. The shy Wright's heart pounded as he told a gullible cop in Indiana that he was a journalist test driving a souped-up car. The cop let him pass, and Wright and his partner sped from Long Island to Southern California to win a cross-country rally. But like many students, Will still could not for the life of him figure out precisely what he wanted to do with a young, somewhat scattered and haphazard existence that led him to go to college for five years and to leave without a degree.

For Will, setting up digs on the West Coast was like being reborn. The skinny, self-effacing intellectual was psyched when he moved to the Bay Area in California, a place where technology was treated as art or, at least, artful. Inspired by the new era of personal computer gaming, Wright began to design a kind of science fiction war game on his cheap Commodore 64 in which you piloted a helicopter to save a world of islands from treacherous science fiction marauders. As you flew, you bombed the bridges, power plants, and roads below you (along with protecting your aircraft carrier from bomb-dropping enemies). Broderbund, a company perhaps best known for its interactive software for children, published it. The company let Wright know in no uncertain terms that any humans should be changed to aliens to eschew parental concerns about violence. The game became known as Raid on Bungeling Bay and featured the evil Bungelings that appeared in other Broderbund releases like Choplifter. It was not a remarkable game, nor did it push the envelope. Yet people bought more then 800,000 copies in Japan alone. Suddenly, Wright didn't have to worry about money . . . for a while.

More salient, he felt he had found his calling in life. Because Wright enjoyed constructing the minimalist terrain and architecture in the game more than making the souped-up helicopter and its exploding weapons, the game made him realize his immediate future was in simulation games, not in games of destruction. He enjoyed devising his island environments so much that he wrote the code for a mini-program to help him in the building process. But what should he do next and how should he do it? He did not possess the marketing wizardry of Nolan Bushnell or Trip Hawkins. He wasn't even as garrulous as the generally reticent Ralph Baer. How could this introvert break into the gaming industry?

Wright faced another obstacle in his quest to make sim games: The videogame industry, still in its infancy in the middle 1980s, had some rules from which CEOs and designers would rarely stray, perhaps because they believed their audience was primarily young and male. Games were often still viewed as nothing more than toys. So there was a child-influenced golden rule in games: They had to be about winning. In this atmosphere, Wright's City Planner 1.0, which asked you to develop a detailed city and its accompanying infrastructure, stuck out like a sore thumb. Wright had been inspired to create the game when his neighbor, an Oakland city planner, suggested that Wright read a stack of books on city planning theory. Broderbund ordered a prototype of the game—without any pay for Wright. That was the way it worked for many freelancers back in the day. You worked primarily for royalties down the line, with nothing upfront.

But when they saw the actual game in action (if you could call it action), the decision makers at Broderbund were perplexed.

"How can we market this?" wondered cofounder Doug Carlston. "There's no proper end to it. And there's no way to win."

Wright countered, "It shouldn't have to be about winning. It's about making things. People like to make things. It's about society, how people make communities and live in them." He went on for some time with lucid, logical arguments. He brought up the success of LEGO and Lincoln Logs in the toy industry as analogies. Kids and adults alike loved to build. But he could not convince Broderbund.

Carlston didn't like to reject any designer, but he looked down and shook his head. "We don't want to experiment this way. We don't think people will buy it. So we can't buy it. And we can't put money into it." Wright understood and appreciated the way Carlston made him feel like part of the Broderbund family even as he was rejecting his work. But, after so much time invested, he was crestfallen. He knew he owed a huge debt to Doug and Gary Carlston for giving him his big break, not to mention a direction in life. Yet he wished they shared his vision. Maybe he needed a better name for his game. City Planner 1.0 seemed too much like a college course, as dry to the uninitiated as the dozen or so city planning tomes he'd been reading. Micropolis, his other idea for the title, was already taken.

Perhaps Wright had gotten too complex while stating his case in those meetings at Broderbund. He'd brought up a book that inspired him, MIT professor Jay Wright Forrester's 1969 tome, *Urban Dynamics*. Forrester put forth an engineering theory that led him to create computer models to simulate the way cities behaved. Forrester was intrigued by information feedback, which happens "whenever the environment leads to a decision that results in action which affects the environment and thereby influences future decisions." In other words, the many assessments that have to be made by a city can be converted into variables so city planners can simulate what might happen in everything from the economy to low income housing as a city grows or contracts. In the seventies, Forrester's theories of system dynamics became a pop culture trend, so much so that they were even employed to predict worldwide economic havoc, mainly due to starvation, that would happen in 1981.

Yet even after Broderbund's rejection, Wright was hooked. He couldn't stop thinking about his game. Luckily, at the same time in the mid-1980s, an aggressive young go-getter named Jeff Braun had had a taste of success in making and selling Calligrapher, the first color computer font program, for the Amiga. Braun wanted more. Like many before him, he had played SpaceWar!, the Asteroids predecessor, on a giant mainframe computer at UCLA and felt that the game industry was no fad. With the money he'd made from Calligrapher, Braun decided to court game developers by helping to host a series of beer and pizza parties at a friend's apartment in Alameda. Will Wright didn't want to go to the techie mixer, but a young neighbor goaded him into it. Once there, he sat in a corner by himself, looking uncomfortable. Braun worked the room and eventually came upon Wright. Braun brimmed with enthusiasm about fonts, so much so that Wright thought he was trying to sell him something. At the end of the oration, Wright mentioned, "I have a game that I really want to do. But nobody wants to do it. And I don't blame them. It doesn't fit the mold."

"Why's that?" asked Braun.

"Because there's nothing to win. You don't become the hero. You don't save the world. You probably wouldn't like it either."

Braun was intrigued and invited himself over to Wright's house in Piedmont. As Wright led him into the basement to see his small tech setup, which featured a Commodore 64, he said again, "I'm pretty sure you're not going to like this." At first Braun watched a demonstration of another game Wright was working on, ProBots, to which he took an instant dislike. While Wright saw ProBots as an homage to graphic artist M. C. Escher and was working hard on its artificial intelligence, Braun thought it was just a run-of-the-mill matching game and "pretty ridiculous." On the other hand, Jeff saw limitless possibilities in the city planning game. He couldn't contain his ebullience. He wasn't talking fonts anymore; he was talking games to anyone who would lend an ear.

Everything looked brighter then. Just as Henk Rogers envisioned the unlimited potential in Alexey Pajitnov's Tetris, Braun saw the potential in SimCity (the game's new name). He and Wright went on to retrieve the rights from Broderbund and to raise $50,000 to start their new venture. To name their company, Braun decided to hold a contest, asking friends and family for a two-syllable name that meant nothing (like Kodak or Sony), but sounded good when you said it. Braun's father won after coming up with Maxis. Wright and Braun liked the word's techie "X" sound, and Braun loved that it really was shorthand for his mother and sister, Ma and Sis. While Wright had amassed some money from Bungeling Bay royalties, the four years it took to find a publisher took their toll; every company he and Braun met with agreed with Broderbund. Yet, in 1989, it was actually Broderbund that agreed to copublish SimCity with Maxis. Broderbund had just launched an experimental affiliate program that allowed Wright and Braun to keep 80 percent of the profits, instead of just 15 percent of the royalties, and was eager for guinea pigs. Every game would be given on consignment to Broderbund, which would distribute SimCity. Maxis would do the rest of the work, including boxing the game and manufacturing the disks.

Initially, Wright and Maxis sold the game themselves at Bay Area computer fairs at which they also passed out flyers. Sales were so slow that Wright himself easily handled all technical support. But then, the media came to the rescue in the form of Newsweek. Writer Bill Barol said glowingly that experiencing SimCity was "thrilling," that it gave you "the exhilarating ability to change your environment." When *Newsweek*'s photographer found Maxis to be housed in Braun's condo, with just a few computers around a furnished apartment, he shook his head and apologized, thinking he was at the wrong address. Then he snapped a shot of the game on Braun's computer monitor and left the fledgling operation posthaste. The publication of the full-page article was one of the first instances in which a videogame was reviewed by a major newsweekly (the first two were reviews of the interactive text adventures Zork and A Mind Forever Wandering in 1985). The SimCity review was a sign that games were slowly going mainstream and legit.

Suddenly, Wright was the "it" designer, and SimCity became the Game of the Year. It had earned approximately $3 million by the time Christmas rolled around. As the PC version sold 500,000 copies and the Nintendo version added sales of 1.3 million more, the phone rang off the hook with requests for Wright to work on simulations. Entities as diverse as the CIA and Chevron wanted sims for their own agencies and companies. Maxis bought a small company called Delta Logic to deal with these contracts so Wright could concentrate on game making. (The business contacts didn't amount to huge money and the deals took a long time to wangle, but SimRefinery for Chevron eventually brought in $75,000 to the coffers.)

The hits just kept on coming for Wright. Thoughtful hits. Yes, there were SimCity sequels, which were Maxis's bread and butter. But there was also SimAnt: The Electronic Ant Colony, based on the studies of the Pulitzer Prize–winning myrmecologist Edward O. Wilson. While the box featured a cute, Disney-esque ant with soulful black eyes, in the game, the player got graphically primitive ants to work together in centralized societies in an almost socialist way. By mobilizing workers, soldiers, and queen ants, you fought off the oncoming hordes of red ants and occasional arachnids. To the danceable strains of some bass-heavy funk music, you took over the yard as if it were a raging battlefield. Sometimes your ant "writhes in burning agony" when bitten by a spider. Eventually, you took over a suburban house, driving out the annoyed human owners.

There were inevitable growing pains at Maxis, which in 1994 was readying to go public. They had $1 million in venture capital from William Janeway at Warburg Pincus, primarily because Janeway wanted to seem hip to his son who played computer games. With the money, Maxis expanded quickly, cobbling together a staff full of the inexperienced. For instance, a secretary was promoted to be head of human resources, but she didn't have the proper training and wasn't up to the huge challenge of managing personnel at a company in the throes of an IPO. Braun and Wright spent months and months courting venture capitalists—instead of making games. Like Landeros and Devine's Trilobyte, Maxis incurred pressure from investors to diversify its lineup and earn big money. Along those lines, Wright worked on a game that explored the various ideas behind the *Hindenburg*'s tragic explosion. But the game never was released.

Maxis went public in June 1995. Though that success placed $35 million in company accounts, it was the beginning of the end of the pure, childlike fun of game making with a small group of buddies. Just as in the later years of Atari, arrogant idiots were brought in as bosses. They knew nothing about games. While the company netted a healthy $6 million that year, there was no way it could continue on that course, because the next SimCity was years away from hitting shelves. In 1996, bean counters forced Wright and his crew to release a quartet of generally unfinished, unpolished, sometimes untested games. Life just got worse for Braun and Wright. While working on SimCopter, a programmer who was secretly annoyed that there were no gays in Maxis products surreptitiously added two guys who kissed each other—often. That did not sit well with Wright and Braun, who had made certain that Maxis did not discriminate and had health care benefits for gay partners. The employee was shown the door, but the damage was done. SimCopter had to be recalled, which hit the company's stock hard, not to mention the harm it did to its reputation.

By 1997, Maxis was seriously in the red; it lost $2 million. The pressure from industry analysts and stockholders was constant and tremendous. Wright himself felt a combination of utter stress, frustration, and bemusement. He kept trying to look at the troubled times objectively. "This is a learning experience, nothing more," Wright repeated to himself. But keeping on an even keel was trying; the business sapped much of his strength and his patience.

What had started as a lauded company now seemed to be something less, something that was joked about as having games that were a couple of steps above shovelware. When the payroll ballooned to 450 employees, many of whom the two did not know personally, Wright and Braun felt like strangers at their own company. And the stock was in a tailspin. Maxis needed serious help. Wright and Braun agreed that they were in a precarious position—their company was not big enough for them to go it alone or without a publisher, but they were not small enough to be left alone to simply do their own thing.

Braun let it be known that Maxis might be interested in being acquired. Activision was interested. But it didn't understand Maxis games, nor did it have the deep pockets needed to satisfy investors. There was, however, another possibility. Depending on how Wright and Braun looked at it, there was either a savior or a wolf at the door. Because it wanted to have a more diverse stable of PC games, Electronic Arts, which always seemed to be in expansion mode, offered $125 million for the troubled company. Under extreme pressure from investors, Braun and Wright agreed to the sale. But it all came at a price. EA cleaned house with alacrity, firing executives and most of the Maxis sales and marketing employees. Braun was moved from the Maxis studio in Walnut Creek to Foster City, away from any influence at Maxis. It was a shark pit, and Braun left the company within a few months, saying to Wright, "These guys are out for blood." But EA recognized Wright's brilliance and hired some of the country's brightest designers to help him out. In 1999, they released SimCity 3000, starring the shoot-from-the-hip former mayor of New York City Ed Koch. By that time, Trip Hawkins was no longer involved in the company, but his edict to corral superstars for EA games had not been forgotten by what was becoming the world's biggest videogame software maker. At the time, the crotchety Koch was a bigmouthed star with a series of bestselling books and was featured semiregularly on NBC's *Saturday Night Live*. He was the perfect celebrity for SimCity 3000.

In part, it was SimAnt that gave Wright the idea for his next series of games. But Wright was also inspired by mathemagician Martin Gardner's game page in the back of *Scientific American*. Gardner, who had been a puzzle lover since his first requests to Santa as a child, wrote the column for twenty-five years, until 1981. A game called Party Planner, in which you used variables to simulate the likes and dislikes of party attendees, also fascinated Wright. He thought about it for months. As well, when Maxis was still a public company, Braun had shown Wright a 1985 Activision game for the Apple II called Little Computer People. Little Computer People was occasionally hilarious and featured a slow-moving cartoonlike character called Darren who would write you letters saying, "I have many hobbies that occupy my time." To prove it, he watched TV, exercised, and searched for someone to live in his computer with him. Finally, Wright was impressed with John Horton Conway's theories of cellular automata, which were espoused in The Game of Life. In his 1970s simulation game, Conway showed that you could emulate the complex patterns of the birth and death of organisms living together in society—and everything in between. All these combined to influence Wright as he dreamed up a project whose working title was Home Tactics, the Experimental Domestic Simulator. Wright later tweaked the name to the slightly more appealing Dollhouse. In Dollhouse, you controlled a human being, everything from his or her leisure time to work time. It was a miserable failure in focus group tests. Wright told his coworkers that it got "the worst response of any single game we've ever tested. Every person in the room said, 'There's no way I'm ever going to touch that.'" From that moment on, Wright harbored a distrust of focus groups (especially those that relied on people's imaginations to fill in the blanks about specific play elements, as had been the case with Dollhouse). He would even bring up the story in future lectures and speeches. Truly, Dollhouse was a hideous name for a game. Wright wasn't creating a toy with which only girls would play.

Then Wright received more disappointing news, news he refused to believe. EA's sales prognostication for the game was a mere 300,000 worldwide. In the designer's mind, the estimate suffered from a reliance on the tried and true over the innovative and interesting. Wright complained, "If it's something like a successful game out there, their numbers will always be equal to the success of that game. If it's something that's radically new, the numbers drop off substantially."

Eventually, the game became The Sims. EA dubbed it "a new way of life," and gamers agreed, making it a phenomenal hit. When you first try The Sims, you likely play by the rules of society, by the straight and narrow. You go to work every day, and you do your chores when you come home. All told, you generally keep up with the Joneses. As time passes, you change. Your Sim becomes an extension of you and your passions, perhaps your need to be a slothful couch potato, a playboylike Lothario, or the lampshade-wearing drunken life of the party. And you're thinking, "Hey. Maybe I can do the nasty in this game. That woman over there. She looks great. I mean—her eyes. I know she's just an avatar, but that smile. Maybe it's not about sex. Maybe it's the big one. Maybe it's love. Wait—this is just a damn game. Is that a *Star Wars* shirt she's wearing? It MUST be love." You might go so far as to steal a kiss from her, and be slapped upside the head for your brashness. But you keep trying.

You might even try to have an illicit affair or dip in the hot tub naked with the person of your dreams.

The Sims would become one of EA's most popular games, eventually selling more than six million copies. It would become beloved by millions of women gamers, who would proudly outnumber male players by two to one. It would also be the first game to have its own official Visa credit card. The Sims was a brand. Riffing on McDonald's signs, EA even sent out press releases saying, "10 million people served."

Bubbling beneath the surface of The Sims were heady theories about computer science, popular culture, psychology, and education. By combining these theories just right, Wright was like experimental molecular gastronomist Ferran Adria, the famed Spanish chef who mixed contrasting tastes together to delight the daring foodie. For instance, if Wright hadn't attended one of Maria Montessori's schools, which taught self-sufficiency in education, The Sims might not have been so enthralling. Wright was a firm believer in the ability of a person to educate himself at his own pace. All he needed, according to Montessori, was the basic materials to build his own path of learning in a nonlinear format. At its core, that's what The Sims was about: your own style, which is not like someone else's, got you through life in the simulation. Individuality beckoned. Wright wanted those who indulged in The Sims to imagine this was their own world, one in which they had a creative stake in the outcome, just like when they were kids and reimagined *Gunsmoke, Miami Vice,* or *The Brady Bunch* in the backyard.

Wright believed that people would play The Sims in their own mind even when they had no access to the game, just as they would relive a movie or book they had enjoyed. In movies, you might ask, What if Harry Potter kissed Hermione early on in the series? What if Batman's parents were still alive? What if the James Bond women were only evil and never good? Stellar story experiences are deconstructable into little pieces that evoke a great variety of game play. Conversely, the most memorable playtime experiences are "generative": They can take us through the looking glass to a nearly endless variety of stories.

Like life in the best of times, The Sims is an exercise in balancing material needs with social needs. Yet it includes the full range of human emotions. Most games address base feelings like fear, aggression, and violence very well. But it's in Wright's (and Peter Molyneaux's) games that you get a sense of human compassion, empathy, even reflection. Partly, this is due to Simlish, the gibberish that the Sims use to talk. Simlish is never understandable, so the player ends up interpreting what the characters are saying. That projected story can be the subject of endless speculation. The danger, of course, is that some people take better care of their Sims, their virtual selves, than they do their real life selves.

To The Sims, Wright also added what he distilled from some of his favorite fiction, like Philip K. Dick's *The Three Stigmata of Palmer Eldritch*, in which the pioneering inhabitants of a planet used Barbie-ish toys called Perky Pats and a drug called Can-D to make themselves believe they lived the sex- and love-filled lives of dolls. Wright wasn't exactly saying that his game was love and that love was the drug, although he wasn't denying it. He was saying that "in a lot of ways, that's what we do in games, allow people to project themselves into these worlds."

Wright's next signature game, Spore, was on the other hand criticized as overly ambitious. For six years, Wright oversaw an ever-growing design team that was trying to make a simulation, a real-time strategy game, and a first person game that led to a kind of massively multiplayer experience. Every creature you created in this game of evolution had its own animation, and the combination of parts made each character move with its own personality. While it took a seemingly endless half hour to install on your computer, the first experience as a young cell under the sea was peaceful and sublime . . . and harrowing when another cell tried to eat you. But when you find your girlfriend cell and hearts bubble up around you, you're hooked by the cuteness. Adding a poison puff appendage to your cell, you could survive, even thrive, and swim happily to land. Spore was an enticing look at evolution that you controlled. You become master or mistress of your own planet and then move into the galaxy to conquer parts unknown. Then you upload the experience that amazed you to the Spore website, to share it with the like-minded online. And you can choose tens of thousands of other people's planets to download and play in. It seemed that you needed a completely extra or separate existence to live in this game world. But it was not the blockbuster that Electronic Arts had hoped it would be after the long years of production. Sales of the collector's edition, with a making-of DVD and an art book, were lackluster; the price went from $80 to $40 to $20. Nonetheless, the game without the extraneous extras sold more than two million copies and spawned various expansion packs along with a kids' series called Spore Heroes, a far more mainstream version with easier, more traditional game play.

As a designer, Wright succeeded because he didn't copy other games and because he didn't go with the trends. He was not an imitator. He was an innovator, in part because he had interests beyond videogames, compulsive interests. He was able to take these multifaceted tenets from other disciplines, streamline them, and make them accessible to the public at large. Like Spielberg in film, Miyamoto in games, or David Foster Wallace in books, he knew humans better than we know ourselves.

Wright didn't think of such things as he stepped into his car and sped away from the Emeryville offices. He didn't have that kind of ego. Instead, Will Wright just left. The game world would never be the same. The greatest living American game designer had left the building.

He wasn't idle for long. Even as Wright was preparing to leave EA, he was thinking of the next, new thing. In his start-up company, Stupid Fun Club, Wright took two people from EA with him to a five-thousand-square-foot space so a small, intimate group could work on the convergence of movies, games, TV, and social networks. While he was secretive about the exact content, he made a deal with the Science Channel to work on TV programs that would have online and game aspects. Another deal, with Al Gore's Current TV, the Creation Project, was a fascinating idea that had the Web community creating plotlines for a show. It seems clear that Wright has set his sights on merging games with TV. His challenge now is greater than ever: to pull it off in the old medium where structures for shows like sitcoms haven't changed in forty years. TV is a place where they don't understand Simlish, just old-guard gibberish. But who knows? In five years maybe Will Wright will become as well known as J. J. Abrams, Damon Lindelof, or David Chase in television circles.

But there was a greater, more wide-ranging concern to be reckoned with when Wright left EA. In a videogame world where it's becoming more and more difficult and financially hazardous to do something that's big *and* new, a young, brilliant game maker will rarely (if ever) get the chance that Will Wright got, to make something newfangled that tens of millions will play. If a young version of Will Wright approached a big company today with the fascinating idea of making a game that you couldn't win, it just wouldn't get the green light. In fact, he probably would be laughed at. That is indeed sad, far more affecting and depressing than having your computer crash and your Sim wiped out of his or her virtual existence.

18.

WII NATION

By the mid-2000s, videogames had become a mainstay of nerd popular culture and were grudgingly accepted by the nation's media elite. To complement the pop art medium, which was expanding its boundaries monthly, there needed to be a new kind of videogame executive, affable but tough-minded, personable but full of bluster—especially since a landmark console was about to be introduced throughout the world. Reggie Fils-Aime was perfect for the role, for he had guts, swagger, smarts, and a gift of gab. It was as though Ron Popeil, that slick but smiling pitchman of late night TV infomercials, was selling a videogame console.

Although Nintendo was as recognizable as Disney as a company, it had never had a face beyond Mario in the United States, never had a go-to person who had style, if not grace. In the past, Nintendo would depend on occasional appearances by

Miyamoto, certainly a smilingly enthusiastic superstar developer, but one who always needed a translator during interviews. Similarly, Nintendo in the United States had never been known for flash, had never been known to promote the hip, cool lifestyle that the Xbox and PlayStation executives felt was essential to their marketing plans. When Sony would hire Beck or the Foo Fighters for its parties, Nintendo would go a quiet jazz route with Diana Krall or George Benson. That all changed in 2004, when Nintendo decided to remake its image with a brand-new gaming box, code-named Revolution. The very name had the whole industry abuzz. What did the box do? How would Nintendo make a Revolution, especially after the decidedly cartridge-based Nintendo 64 and the low-tech GameCube, which used half-sized CDs as media? Sony executives like Kaz Hirai secretly laughed when they heard what the Revolution was all about. Sony marketing guys like Andrew House felt that the PlayStation 2's dominance was unassailable. And their upcoming behemoth of a PlayStation 3 had WiFi, Bluetooth, Blu-ray movie technology, everything a technology-loving gamer could want in a machine. Nintendo couldn't come back. It was in third place in the Console Wars, a sluggish, dawdling turtle struggling against the sleek racing cars of Gran Turismo.

To introduce the machine at the E3 trade show, Nintendo had hired this new personality who was in charge of sales and marketing. In the past, a fairly staid George Harrison (not the Beatle) would hit the stage, armed with facts and figures. Harrison was an intelligent guy who cut a gentlemanly figure. But to say Harrison was the life of the party would be like saying George W. Bush's favorite book was *Infinite Jest*. It just was not true and it never would be. Reggie Fils-Aime, on the other hand, shocked the world's media and game developers, who had gathered in Hollywood to witness the magic.

Backstage, Fils-Aime was pumped up. He would make no mistakes, he promised himself. This was The Big Show, and there was no room for error. As his pulse quickened, the Haiti-born executive was introduced to the media that had come to Los Angeles from all over the world. The former Pizza Hut marketer strode onto the stage with the confident gait of Bill Clinton. From a teleprompter, he read an unforgettable speech that was one of the most energetic in video-game history. Fils-Aime must have taken one of those executive training classes for public speaking as well; he kept moving his hands when he hit his primary talking points, like a magician pulling a rab-bit out of a hat. "Voilà," said his fingers, as if they were throwing off magic dust. Reggie's unwavering deep voice told the crowd all about the new console's wow factors. The audience was spellbound from the get-go as he proclaimed, "My name is Reggie. I'm about kicking ass. I'm about taking names, and we're about making games."

Fils-Aime talked a big talk. The release of the Wii console, no longer dubbed Revolution, would not be just another console launch. It would change the nature of gaming. It would be so mo-mentous that everyone would want to play, not just kids, not just adults, but grandparents, too. He stood straight and tall as his voice boomed. "Our strategy is based on one core belief: that the next step in gaming is bringing gaming back to the masses. . . . It is literally that simple—appealing to current gamers as well as broadening that indus-try to new gamers, people who today don't even consider themselves in the gaming industry." What Fils-Aime had to say on that early Los Angeles morning was not original, nor was it particularly thoughtful. But the way he said it, with a combination of awe, aggression, friendli-ness, and self-assuredness, made the media prick up their ears and nod their heads in approval. Fils-Aime knew very little about videogames, except to say that he played Nintendo with his kids. It didn't matter.

Overnight, Reggie became the face of the New Nintendo in America. Within days of his debut in the videogame industry, he was seen as neither a nerd nor a marketing wonk. He was treated as a ce-lebrity, a businessman entertainer who was full of power and puffery.

Yet Reggie knew how to keep secrets. In subsequent interviews with the media, he kept to the Nintendo ethos of never saying too much, never giving anything away. Often, the confident executive said nothing at all of substance. But through a combination of passion and glittering generalities, he always seemed to have said something of gravitas. Reporters couldn't even get a game release date or a game release month out of Reggie. But that was *so* Nintendo. Even before Bill Gates made institutionalized paranoia one of the prime tenets of Microsoft philosophy, Nintendo had been suspicious of every other competing company in the world—whether it made playing cards or videogames. You couldn't get a job at Nintendo in Japan or in the United States if you had loose lips when it came to company secrets. Even after many Nintendo of America executives had left the company, they refused to talk about their time in Redmond. It was as though the Nintendo console itself could grow killing hands that would seek them out and choke the life out of them if they did spill the beans.

Everywhere he went, from G4TV to the *Today* show, Reggie extolled the brilliance of the Wii and its motion-controlled Wii remote as if to say, "Look, Ma, no wires. Just move your arms and hands and you control it all." It became the Gospel According to Reggie. It should not have been an easy sale. Nintendo was down to third in sales because of the GameCube, a toy-looking square thing with a lunchboxlike carrying handle, which was the worst of the three big game consoles when it came to graphics. And the Wii should have been seen as a stupid name. Indeed, it sounded like a lisping Elmer Fudd had a hand in the marketing when all Nintendo honchos began to refer to the wireless remote control as the Wiimote. Snarky reviewers everywhere began to make sex jokes about the change of the console's name from Revolution to Wii: "Play with my Wii." "Touch my Wii." "I love my Wii."

But Reggie was right: the remote and the console would become a worldwide tsunami that left nothing but gaming glee in their wake. The new machine was all about simplicity, about refining old wireless technology into a system so easy to use that sexagenarians would be able to play without much instruction. Yes, Nintendo used the old adage espoused by Game & Watch designer Gunpei Yokoi so many years ago: "The Nintendo way of adapting technology is not to look for the state of the art but to utilize mature technology that can be mass-produced cheaply." Unlike the Sony and Microsoft consoles, there was nothing cutting edge about the chips in the Wii. There was no Blu-ray technology to play DVDs. Unlike the PlayStation 3 and Xbox 360, there was no concentration on filmlike graphics that were supposed to give the movie industry a run for its money. The only nod to techies in the Wii was the wireless online capabilities. Nintendo would not even have a game that would be playable online for some time after the console's introduction. What you would be able to do online immediately was to download old, sometimes hard-to-get Nintendo and Sega games, a library of classic games that would grow by three to five games each week. Nintendo fans would purchase these gems by the thousands.

As it turned out, none of the shortcomings mattered one iota. Nintendo was about to find the ultimate sweet spot, with a mix of tried-and-true tech and something that felt new to the heartland of America. A low-tech chip didn't matter. State-of-the-art graphics didn't matter. *Play mattered. A wireless controller mattered.* Remember the way writerly raconteur Jean Shepherd waxed rapturous in *A Christmas Story* when the hapless Ralphie finally receives his coveted BB gun? That's how Nintendo hoped middle-class American kids and their parents would feel en masse when they opened and played the Wii on Christmas morning. Their hopes would be answered in spades.

But first, Nintendo had to get the Wii on the shelves. Just one year before the launch, it was not an easy sell for the company. In early 2006, they began to formulate a $200 million marketing plan that focused on families and not gamers. Perrin Kaplan, a crabby but hardworking marketing executive at Nintendo since the GameCube days, already expected that jokes would be made about the Wii name. She didn't care. Nor did Reggie. The Wii would be pitched to the American public not as a luxury, but as something as essential as food. You had to have it. Like the healthiest food, it would help you to live right. The name Wii said, "Forget them, those executives with the high-tech boxes who yearn for the eighteen-to-thirty-four-year-old hard-core gamer." The Wii, posited Reggie, was about the rest of us, the silent majority who'd left games when they became all about shooting and violence. This wasn't Doom or Columbine or Grand Theft Auto. This was a gaming experience for *us*, Nintendo would say. The Wii wasn't about me-ness. It was about we-ness. Those who bought the Wii would come together in a tight social network that was all-inclusive. Nintendo targeted the blogosphere, particularly the so-called mommy blogs, and the moms loved it and the word spread virally across the Web. The philosophy was as cult-y as anything Mary Kay could have imagined. But like the cosmetics company, its popularity would go beyond a small sect of believers. Nintendo preachers physically went to the houses of moms who had invited other moms to house parties of about thirty people, many of whom were bloggers as well. Nintendo would bring Wiis, and they would deal with the wires and the setup, too. They might even bring some food. At the end, people would order two or three Wiis each. Then, they would blog about the party. Had the company done this for journalists, the writers would have thought they were being bought. But the mommy bloggers loved getting things for free, for they had not been schooled in the rules of ethics and journalism, which were now being blurred by the excited amateur writers who would post at length on Blogger. They weren't part of a machine pushing the hard sell, either; they were part of something special and magical, we-ness in all its warm, fuzzy glory. It was the new videogame religion in which those who were lucky enough to get a Wii (for Nintendo had faked a shortage to enhance its desirability) would sermonize this gospel to others, especially the unfortunates who weren't converts.

Meanwhile, Sony was about to release the PlayStation 3. In the last decade, Sony had lured so many gamers with its PlayStation and PlayStation 2 that it had the same dominant share of the market that Nintendo had had in the eighties. But Sony was about to suffer from Trip Hawkins–itis, a hubris in which Sony executives from Kaz Hirai to Sir Howard Stringer couldn't foresee that people around the world would have trouble paying $699 for the fancy, high-tech machine. Even its lavish celebrity launch in a former department store in Hollywood was plagued by celebrities like Lindsay Lohan, who spoiled the mood of celebration, which featured a performance by Sean "P. Diddy" Combs. On the red carpet, Lohan, still a rising star at the time, complained loudly enough for the press to hear, "I'm just here for the machine so I can give it to my brother. I just want to get it and get out." To complicate matters, Sony did not manufacture enough of the shiny black consoles. As many as 150,000 of the promised 400,000 consoles did not reach stores on November 11, 2006. Of the twelve games ready on launch date, only three were available exclusively on the PS3, and none of them were deemed must-buys by most game critics. The word "Sony," which had been associated with innovation and quality, was suddenly synonymous with "Fail." And even at the high retail price, Sony was losing at least $100 per PlayStation 3 sold because it was so complicated and costly to manufacture. Outside developers and executives, including Activision's powerful Bobby Kotick, complained about the difficulty of making games for the system with the tool kit Sony provided. Even Kaz Hirai fessed up to the problems. (The PlayStation 3, with the exception of a few yearly gems, would remain a fiasco until Sony cut its price to less than half in 2009.)

In an effort to beat Sony and Nintendo to market, Microsoft's Xbox 360 had gone on sale a full year prior to the PS3 and the Wii. A self-assured Bill Gates had said that the machine would sell ten million by the time the other boxes got to market. Yet, like Sony, Microsoft couldn't manufacture enough of the machines initially. The 360 was indeed a worthy machine, one that easily connected to home WiFi setups. It featured a wide array of forward-thinking, downloadable games. It soon added Netflix so you could download movies from the virtual store that was the Xbox Live Marketplace. That in itself made it arguably the best console to hit the market. And the machine had Halo 3, an eagerly anticipated shooter that would finish the trilogy of Master Chief and the Covenant. Microsoft also spent tens of millions on exclusive downloadable content from Rockstar Games' Grand Theft Auto series. But there was a problem ingrained in the Xbox 360: It kept breaking down.

Initially, Microsoft tried frantically to downplay the number of consoles that were plagued by the Red Rings of Death, so named because when the front of the console displayed three flashing red lights, the machine was unusable, fried. As the machine gave up the ghost, you'd exclaim, "Oh God. Oh God. Oh God. What fresh hell is this? I call bullshit." It was a horrible, sinking feeling of loss. Sometimes the hard drives, with all the saved games, were wiped of information as well. Microsoft claimed a failure rate of 3 percent, but technology journalists, like VentureBeat's Dean Takahashi, reported that the problem was far more widespread. Then, of five thousand *Game Informer* readers polled, more than half said their Xbox 360s had failed. Microsoft would spend well over a billion dollars on repairs alone. While hard-core gamers loved the 360 and would remain loyal, the Red Rings of Death were a disaster of monumental proportions for Microsoft. The Xbox 360 should have been the leader, far ahead of the pack in sales because of its year-long head start in stores around the world.

Both Sony and Microsoft had shot themselves in the foot. Nintendo would make no such missteps. It was primed and ready for world domination. A weary Shigeru Miyamoto was traveling the world to talk about the joys of the Wii. He had spent years overseeing the mechanics of the product, sending the Wii remote back to the design department in Kyoto time and time again to simplify the experience.

How hard should someone have to move the remote to get it to, say, roll a ball down a virtual bowling alley? If it was too hard, Miyamoto surmised, the Wii remote would go flying out of children's hands from the force of movement. If it was too little, the experience wouldn't feel real.

"Not ready yet. Try again," he would say over and over again.

Then it *was* ready. On November 19, 2006, the Wii was premiered on store shelves worldwide. The bundled Wii Sports game was a winner even though it had rudimentary graphics that weren't even as good as the best of the last generation GameCube games. But its variations on bowling, baseball, and boxing let families everywhere use the motions of real life sports: swinging the baseball bat, rolling the bowling ball, punching with their fists. Reggie went on TV and played, sometimes losing, but always breaking into a bit of a sweat. He extolled the importance of the Wii to exercise as if it were a kind of robotic Richard Simmons. No longer would kids or young adults be couch potatoes. The Wii could engender an aerobic workout. Like Guinness, where Reggie had been head of marketing, the Wii was good for you. At a Nintendo press event in San Francisco, a well-regarded blogger from *Wired* used the Wii exercise program to get in shape prior to the press conference. Nintendo garnered the seal of approval from one of the world's finest tech culture magazines— without paying Condé Nast one penny in advertising money.

Again, Reggie was right. Playing Wii Sports was fun for the entire family, an experience that would quiet and entice the most inebriated of annoying uncles at a Thanksgiving repast. But there was more to the Wii than Wii Sports. The Legend of Zelda: Twilight Princess, in addition to its traditional boy-saves-girl conceit, allowed you to attack enemies as if you were swinging a real life sword. Some preferred a more solitary experience of sitting by a lake and using the remote as a fishing rod. Amazingly, the fat fish would crowd around and bite a hook that had no bait on it whatsoever, just a lure. You would sit there, thinking: "Man, this is so boring. I could be fighting a boss. I could be saving a princess . . . Whoa. WHOA. That's one mother of a fish. How cool is that?" If you stuck it out and were lucky, you could bring in a thirty-five-pound Hyrulean loach, a bottom dweller that was a true fighter.

There were videos on YouTube showing black eyes that people had received while playing virtual boxing. Frantic playing had led the overenthusiastic player to release the Wii remote—into his opponent's face. There were photos of expensive flat-screen TV sets displaying a Wii remote stuck in irreparably broken glass. Perhaps, in their must-play-now ardor, kids and adults hadn't tightened around their wrists the strap that came with the Wii remote, even though a message on your TV screen tersely reminded you to do so before every game. Somehow, all this damage only added to the wow factor.

From Thanksgiving to Christmas, lines of parents hoping to get a Wii at stores were the norm. Sales on eBay sometimes soared to three times the retail price. By the end of the holidays in 2006, Nintendo had sold 3.2 million of its $250 machines, and there still were shortages in every country. One executive for GameStop posited that the shortages were manufactured by Nintendo itself to keep the Wii frenzy going. Of course, no one but Nintendo knew if the shortages were real, and they weren't telling. Whatever the case, it worked; though there was lack of supply for *years*, the demand didn't let up until the spring of 2009. And then it didn't let up much. Even better, unlike the other boxes, for which Sony and Microsoft saw losses, Nintendo was making a profit of $40 on each Wii sold, and its stock skyrocketed from around $25 on release day to more than $78 a share at its peak less than a year later. Nintendo hadn't been on the top of the console heap since it sold the Super Nintendo Entertainment System, and it wasn't about to let what it saw as a healthy trend become a mere fad. The Wii became part of cultural history. It was portrayed on TV shows that wanted to seem hip. Superstar pop singer Beyoncé claimed she used Wii Fit as part of her exercise regimen. Whether she was paid to say this or not was the subject of some speculation. Barack Obama's kids played Wii Sports too. (Obama's people knew the value of videogames during the presidential campaign; they even advertised in Burnout Paradise, the Electronic Arts racing game, with a virtual billboard that touted the website Vote for Change.) Just as Atari did in its early days, Nintendo released specious but well-received surveys showing that the use of the Wii games in its Brain Games line made you smarter.

In May 2006, Reggie was promoted to president of Nintendo of America, where he thrived just as the Wii juggernaut thrived. Shigeru Miyamoto requested release from his management position because he disliked the constant paperwork and employee evaluations that came with the job. His new role allowed him to go back to his roots of making and overseeing games. There was a new order of marketing people in the United States, for longtimers Perrin Kaplan and George Harrison decided not to move to help start a new office in the Silicon Valley under Reggie's edict. They quietly left the company. It was a brand-new world for Nintendo, the age of the Wii.

Incoming was a parade of marketing people to take Kaplan's and Harrison's place, one with a résumé that included stints at Frito-Lay and Yahoo!, another from Reebok. Neither executive knew much at all about videogames. But just as Sony had with the PlayStation, Nintendo began to believe nothing anyone could do would defeat the Wii's supremacy. Then the backlashes began. Industry analysts began to say on background to journalists that the Wii indeed was a fad and that people were putting their Wiis in the closet because there wasn't much to the games. Others, like the brother of Cliff Bleszinski, the maker of the renowned Gears of War shooter series, claimed that the Wii was ruining gaming by dumbing it down. He was correct on one count: Storytelling was radically absent in many Wii games. Instead, disks were filled with up to thirty short, disjointed games of skill, like those on a carnival midway. There were hundreds of such games, and most played like clones of the others. On YouTube, there emerged tightly edited parodies of Reggie's hand and finger movements, which he still used during speeches. But through all this, the Wii retained its domination, even during the height of the recession.

While hard-core games never really took off on the machine, three Nintendo-made games sold massively: Wii Play, which included nine mini-games like billiards and came packed with a Wiimote; Wii Fit, a fitness routine, which included a wireless balance board full of sensors to track your exercises; and Mario Kart, a speedy arcade racing game that let you play online with people from other countries. These became three of the bestselling console games of all time. Wii Play alone sold more then 25 million copies all over the world. Even as all the consoles began to feel like old technology, Nintendo was still triumphantly leading the pack—much to the consternation and occasional anger of hard-core gamers. Microsoft and Sony, who had remained loyal to the hard-core gamers with their systems, would be playing catch-up by making casual games and motion-sensitive controllers through the life cycle of the Wii.

Nintendo had gambled hugely on introducing millions of new gamers to the videogame lifestyle. And they'd gotten filthy rich, pig-in-a-sty rich, in the process. But once again things were changing. If you didn't like Nintendo, Fils-Aime, and the Wii, you could just look to the horizon, where there stood within sight a panoply of new inventions about which everyone could become nerdily rapturous.

19.

THE FUTURE

In the lightning-charged world of technology, evolution is quick. Your eye blinks and there's a new game with astonishing ways of playing, a new console that's speedier and sleeker, a new platform that brings gamers together like never before. In the early 2010s, the target is still Nintendo; the Wii still reigns supreme. But that will change when some young engineering genius, maybe the next Will Wright, gives us our next innovation. The tens are poised to become the era of 3-D, and the first experiments were with clunky glasses, serviceable for games like Batman: Arkham Asylum and Resident Evil 5. But it's annoyingly intrusive to don glasses, especially if you're a nerd who already wears glasses. Microsoft's next big thing, Kinect, uses cruise missile electro-optic technology originally developed by Israeli company 3DV Systems to allow you to interact with on-screen characters without controllers. Peter Molyneaux touted its import with his signature British panache during demonstrations at various Microsoft press events. You could throw an off-screen ball to a hyper-realistic child named Milo on the screen. The boy would "see" how you tossed it and catch it accordingly. As you watched, you thought, "Man, which world is more real, that apple-faced kid's or mine in which I live in my living room long into the night, playing games?"

Farther beyond 3-D, there is the possibility of more massive change. Not far from a boring shopping mall in San Bruno, California, IO2 Technology manufactures what it calls the Heliodisplay. In one demonstration, inventor Chad Dyson showed that the survival horror game Sin could be displayed holographically, although not in 360 degrees. Seeing it was like stepping through a portal into the future—even though all that was displayed was two characters blinking and turning around. While the cost of the device is prohibitive at $18,500, and the technology has yet to be perfected, Heliodisplay successfully uses lasers and the condensation in the air around it to create a nearly 3-D image. Currently, however, you'd need a supercomputer to deal holographically with all the frenzied character and vehicular movement present in today's games. But it is completely conceivable that within two decades, the progeny of Madden and Halo will be played on TVs equipped with this technology. Crytek's CEO Cevat Yerli, the maker of the shooter Crysis 2 in 3-D, believes that holographic TVs and games will be in stores "within ten years." Imagine that the curtains are drawn, the TV is turned on, and the videogame characters appear like three dimensional apparitions before your eyes. But when you reach out and touch, your hand moves right through them as if they are ghosts from The 7th Guest. "It's just so real," you'll say, "so lifelike. May I just hug Lara Croft, please? Just twice? OK, all right. Just once, one long hug?"

There is one trend that shows no sign of slowing down in the future: There are so many kinds of games for so many platforms for so many tastes, that there's a vast wealth of choice. If Gamer Culture is a city, it's one with many neighborhoods spreading far and wide. Nintendo with the Wii and the 3DS gives you your Mario and Zelda fix. With the PlayStation 3, Sony gives you the eye-popping God of War, its online social network called Home, unusual downloadable games, and the über popular techie next door Veronica Belmont in a Web show to which you subscribe. The Xbox 360 brings you Kinect, Halo, and Netflix. Apple's App Store features games for the iPad and iPhone that are often worth more than the small price of admission. And your PC is your ticket to the mother of them all, World of Warcraft. It's such an embarrassment of riches, it's difficult to decide which platform to buy.

In some instances, the future recalls gaming's past. Beyond the gleaming multimillion-dollar advancements, enterprising companies or even individual nerds see fit to use the consoles to distribute down-loadable games and game content. Sometimes these are intensely emo-tional stories for hits like the post-apocalyptic psychodrama Fallout 3 and the scheming underworld criminals of Grand Theft Auto IV. Sometimes they are little strategy games whose later levels are al-most impossible to solve, like PixelJunk Monsters for the PlayStation Network. Sometimes, they are relaxing experiences, things to let you breathe in and notice beauty and feel peaceful after a long day, like the game in which you grow flora during sweet dreams, Flower.

Small enticements downloadable in a few minutes over a broad-band connection are the perfect remedy for the gamer who doesn't have a lot of money to spend. They cost less than $20 and often are sold for under $10. It is in these downloadable games that the most forward-thinking ideas are being implemented. Quirky and experi-mental, these are homages to the joy and invention of the early days of game making, when Donkey Kong or Pong was made by a team of a half dozen people at the most. These delights didn't need or want budgets of tens of millions of dollars; nor did they require hundreds of workers employed across the planet. Alongside the downloadable game came another venue—the social network. Simpler versions of casual games and stripped down role playing games like Mafia Wars and FarmVille appeared on social networking sites and became so engrossing that some of your friends became as avidly addicted as they had been in the early days of EverQuest. Zynga, the developers of FarmVille, claimed that eighty-three million people signed up to play their free game. Casual gaming had hit another milestone.

And there were independent Web game makers who, like the PopCap guys, just wanted to do games their way, forget about the cash. Scary Girl, a game that is free to play, has an opening movie that is better than many of the recent console games. It also boasts game play that features a fairy tale world so engrossing, you want to meet the Coraline-like Scary Girl in the flesh and go on escapades with her. It doesn't matter that some of these games were school projects intended to show off skills to potential employers, like interactive résumés. What's significant is that so many young people are beguiled by games. In them, they see a way to create and become recognized when they are in their twenties or even their teens. Working on games is so unlike the movie, TV, or book industries, in which you must be a proven moneymaker before you're given a job that means something beyond being a slavish production grunt. In games, you don't have to have Daddy's tens of thousands to make an indie film. In games, all you need is a program you can borrow and your computer. It's almost akin to the do-it-yourself aspect of the independent music scene, but without the need to buy instruments, microphones, speakers, a used van in which to tour the country, and coke to keep you rocking all night. In games, even though the industry is bigger than it ever was, young people can still hope for a successful career full of creativity early in adulthood. The snooty gatekeepers and numbers crunchers who judged content from on high are gone.

This new indie world, however, has forced freelance game makers to be their own marketers. Like it or not (and who would truly like it?), they must learn how to promote their products so that they don't become lost in an industry that increasingly relies on highly paid publicists to sound the trumpet call a year or more before the game is on the market. If you're not a creative self-marketer in today's indie world, you're dead, no matter how ingenious your game may be.

Kurt Vonnegut once said to a group of eager writing students, "Probably all of you are good enough to make it as writers. But it's likely that only one of you has what it takes to endure the constant rejection." It's the same with today's independent inventors. In a world in which there are more than fifty thousand games for the iPhone alone, a designer has to find a way to cry boisterously above the fray, "Play mine! Play mine!" It's what Ken Williams did when he hauled his butt from store to store to sell the wares that Roberta had placed in Ziploc bags.

If game makers can't stomach that arduous task, the job at the big company beckons, with its assembly line for action-filled games that have gargantuan budgets. They'll be paid generally well, drink a lot of coffee, and stay up all night when deadline time encroaches on sleep time. They will be implementing someone else's vision, and very few will ever know their names. Yet they will be living under the auspices of an agile industry that is forever in flux, forever changing with the trends and fads, forever creating its own history, every day and hour by hour.

One game in particular has bridged the gap between hard-core and casual gamers, between indie company and megacorporation, and between art and commerce.

In early 2005, Chair Entertainment was founded by two brothers who had almost megalomaniacal ideas. As the ten- and eight-year-old kids of an environmental engineer and an opera singer, Donald and Geremy Mustard planned to take over the world—as pro football players for the Denver Broncos. The two did everything together, from playing with toys like G.I. Joe, to reading books like Edgar Rice Burroughs's *Tarzan* and *A Princess of Mars*. By the time they got to high school, their plans had grown loftier. They fell in love with computer graphics and wanted to make the next *Jurassic Park* movie. Donald was always drawing comics, and Geremy had a mind for the technical. Beyond movies, both had loved games ever since they fell head over heels for one of the best Nintendo games, Super Metroid. They dreamed about the game all the time, for it made them feel like they were in their own science fiction movie. Donald spent his hours drawing Samus, the ever-helmeted female character, and her varied armor, which worked miracles like James Bond's gadgets. The Mustards were completely hooked on games by the time Hironobu Sakaguchi's Final Fantasy VII hit the stands in 1997. Its movie-like graphics made FF VII one of the decade's most lauded games. The Mustards scraped together all of their money (which was supposed to be for college) to buy FF VII and a PlayStation. In their haste to get the game home, they forgot to purchase a memory card and had no way of saving their progress. And they were totally out of cash.

"Let's just play it through," said Geremy, wired PlayStation controller in hand, ready for a sleepless weekend.

At first, Donald looked at him like he was crazy. Then he thought about it out loud. "The characters, the graphics. It's all here. You're right. Let's do it." The Mustards didn't stop playing for thirty-six hours, until the game was done. So well honed was the branching story that they nearly shed a tear when Aeris, the protagonist's upbeat, cheerful love interest, was impaled and died in the movie-filled role playing game. From then on, it was games, not movies, that got them going. They felt they had a brand-new map for world domination—except they didn't know exactly what kind of game they wanted to make.

After graduating from Brigham Young University, Donald

Mustard convinced Todd Sheridan, the CEO of GlyphX, the Orem, Utah, video production company at which he worked, to go with his grand idea for a science fiction shooter called Advent Rising. The movie-like game would feature a pesky race of aliens called The Seekers, who were out to exterminate humanity. Epic Games, a maker of everything from platformers featuring rabbits to a fast-paced and frightening shooter called Unreal, liked the demo enough to license their sophisticated videogame creation program to Mustard and GlyphX. While companies like Electronic Arts expressed interest in publishing the game, Majesco, a revitalized company out of New Jersey that had just gone public and had $70 million in its coffers, put up most of the $3.5 million budget. Majesco should have concentrated on putting more money into its two games with potential, Advent Rising and the humor-filled Psychonauts. Instead, it never put quite enough money into any of the dozens of games it published, and the money the Mustards had wasn't enough to finish the ambitious game properly, even with a staff that expanded from eight people to thirty-five. When Advent Rising came out three years later, in May 2005, some of it was just plain broken. The TV screen would sometimes freeze on a video frame, and the Xbox would whir and whiz as if in the throes of a mechanical black plague. Then the system would shut down and restart. Plans for a trilogy were canned by Majesco, which wanted nothing more to do with the Mustard brothers. The feeling was decidedly mutual.

The Mustards licked their wounds for a while, but they still harbored a hope for "world domination," albeit on a smaller level. Smartly, they eschewed efforts to make the Big Game, their version of the Great American Novel, right away. Instead, they decided to move into the relatively fresh genre of downloadable games. With a small game, they could employ a tiny staff of diligent workers, with no behemoth of a corporation breathing down their necks. They could take their time. They could polish their game until it was nearly flawless. They kept their business plan in the family and approached their uncle, Ryan Holmes, for help. Holmes was a tough, semiretired moneyman who liked to play golf and invest in real estate more than anything else in the world.

"Why would I want to do this?" he asked.

Carefully and enthusiastically, they explained that the next big thing was in downloadable games, not just simple casual games like Uno or Jeopardy!, but games that would attract the people who played Halo and Gears of War. Holmes, who was schooled at Stanford as an engineer, had a soft spot for cool, nerdy technology. As the brothers spoke, he became cautiously optimistic. After their spiel, Holmes began to believe that downloadable games could well be the next trend.

Donald ended with a zinger: "The main thing we want to do is leverage our ideas for games in other media. They could be books, or even comic books, and then movies, too."

"We really want to elevate the medium," said Geremy. Both brothers believed that games should be considered art and the best way to do it was to bring well-rounded, finished ideas to other media—even prior to a game's release.

Holmes came on board with plans to build the company up and sell it. The Mustards and Holmes went to work. On paper, they valued their company at around $8 million and received about $2 million in investment capital, which the Mustards felt would get them through a couple of years with a staff of eight people—if they were frugal enough. Unlike the Williamses with Sierra or Trilobyte's Devine and Landeros, their angel was close at hand and involved. He was part of the family, someone who would guide them and not rip them off. They called the new entity Chair Entertainment, a moniker based on Plato's theory of forms. According to Plato, when you identify something as a "chair," you're looking at its ultimate "chairness," a philosophy of perfection in your mind that may never be attained in real life. Chairness was the Mustards' goal: to make something as close as they could to the perfect videogame they believed was possible.

Their first game, a multiplayer side scroller called Undertow, cost $350,000 to make and was programmed by Geremy alone. Finished in just ten months, Undertow took place underwater, in a flourishing fantastical ocean world in which Captain Nemo and an Atlantis that emerged from an icy crypt were portrayed with gusto and pithy quotes from D. H. Lawrence. Because of its multiplayer functionality, which allowed up to sixteen people to play at once, the game went straight to number one on the Xbox Live bestseller lists in late November 2007, although it didn't stay there for long. Undertow certainly didn't break any records for sales, but it was a critical hit. The brothers had also proven that Epic's Unreal software, which would soon let the Mustards insert realistic-looking artwork and program a sharper artificial intelligence than in Undertow, could be used as the backbone for smaller, more casual games. Unreal wasn't just for BioShock or Gears of War anymore. Developers with teams as tiny as one person started lining up to license the software, and Epic's bean counters rubbed their hands together.

Then, while he was mowing his lawn in Pleasant Grove, Utah, a lightbulb went on in Donald's head. He remembered how much he'd enjoyed playing with G.I. Joes with Geremy back when they were kids. For a moment, he could even see the action figures on the lawn, ready to combat COBRA, the dominant, technically advanced evildoers. As he cut the grass, he began to conceive of a game in which a low-tech military drudge fights against a very well-funded enemy, a science fiction game not set in a fantastical world but in a realistic and modern setting. Donald felt that hard-edged realism was the way to go. There would be a primordial forest, rushing waterfalls, and craggy caves to explore. And deep beneath a lake, a maze-like, high-tech underground compound would lie, helmed by an angry madman commander hell bent on fomenting a new civil war in the United States.

Donald contacted science fiction writer Orson Scott Card, who had worked on the Advent Rising script. Card listened closely as Mustard described his story. Donald made it clear that he would prefer the idea to be a book before it became a videogame. Like the Mustards, Card liked the notion that videogames could, at some point down the line, be elevated to the status of popular art. He informed Tor, his publisher, that he wanted to flesh out the Mustards' outline and make it into a novel. As he thought about it more and more, Card believed the germ of a story would really become his ticket to not one, but a series of bestsellers. More energized than ever, Donald and Holmes took their pitch to Hollywood. There, they were utterly misunderstood. Studio after studio warmed to the idea, but after all the ass-kissing and back-slapping and lunch-doing, they all wanted to put their videogame directors and writers on the project to make it all action and little else. Mustard protested that *Empire* (now the name of the book) was about story first and videogame-like action second. From most movie executives, he received scrunched up faces or blank stares. Strangely, Joel Silver, the boastful action movie producer of the Die Hard and Lethal Weapon series, appeared to understand the concept immediately. An option deal was struck with Silver and Warner Bros. in October 2006.

With the movie and book deals under control, Geremy and Donald concentrated on making a game they called Shadow Complex, whose story would be a bridge between Card's first two *Empire* tomes. They wanted it to feel like Super Metroid. In other words, playing would be like exploring a great corn maze full of astonishment at every turn. But since there was no design literature about Super Metroid, the eight members of Chair spent a month playing it, all the time deconstructing it and thinking about how it could be made modern for a 2009 audience. Then, like old school

Shigeru Miyamoto with Donkey Kong, they mapped out the game on paper before attempting to code a computer demo with the Unreal engine. In February 2008, they took a short, action-filled trailer of Shadow Complex to the bustling Game Developers Conference in San Francisco. Early in its history, the GDC had been a fairly staid networking event for employees of game companies. By 2009, the event had as much buzz as E3, the yearly videogame convention in Los Angeles. Word about the game spread as quickly as the potent strain of the flu that infected convention-goers on the show floor. Chair's rapidly pieced together prototype looked spectacular on the little screen of an iPhone. Thankfully, no one asked to see it on a bigger display. Blown up on a television or even a laptop monitor, it would have failed to impress—because the graphics were no-where near complete. Yet it made Cliff Bleszinski, the designer be-hind Gears of War and an ardent fan of Super Metroid, joke to the Mustards, "This is so good, we're gonna buy you out. We're gonna buy you out tomorrow."

"OK. Fifty million dollars," joked Donald.

But in three weeks, there were talks, serious talks, at Epic's Raleigh, North Carolina, headquarters, with Mark Rein, Epic's co-founder, and Mike Capps, the company president. Capps, an army brat who was a child hacker, was a former professor at Monterey's Naval Postgraduate School. While there, Capps also proposed and worked for the military on the America's Army shooter, which became a well-regarded recruitment tool. Reins and Capps knew that others at the Game Developers Conference had approached the brothers to buy Chair. They wondered if it was the right time to strike.*

By the time Epic considered acquiring Chair, Bleszinski had be-

---

* Epic had come a long way since its early days in London, Ontario. Then, the young Bleszinski (with Arjan Brussee) was focused on making a kind of Rambo meets Mario platform game called Jazz Jackrabbit. But the game featuring the warhawk bunny wasn't Bleszinski's real call-ing. Gears of War was.

come a superstar of gaming. His Gears of War, informed by the classic Battlefield 1942, took place in a scary, desperate world in which chaos fought against order. In the military science fiction story, the macho Marcus Fenix was pitted against The Locust Horde, a hulking race of seven-foot-tall monstrosities hell-bent on genocide. The Gears of War series, with twelve million games sold, rivaled the success of Halo and had earned Epic enough money to buy anything or anyone it wanted. Its success made Epic one of a handful of very influential studios.

Epic did not know that the offers from other companies seemed to the Mustards like more of what Majesco had to offer with Advent Rising: Everyone required delivery on deadline whether or not the work was finished. After various springtime meetings with Ryan Holmes and the Mustards, in which Chair detailed its accomplishments in other media with the *Empire* series, Capps would ask Rein, "Like, who are these kids? They really have balls, not to mention a great sense of design." Following a trip to Utah to make certain that the ten-person Chair team was in good working order, Epic was impressed enough to make an offer. Significantly, Epic offered Chair complete creative control, thus freeing the Mustards from the specter of another Advent Rising disaster in which they'd be forced to rush a broken game onto the market. By late May 2008, Chair had been sold to Epic for more than the $8 million Chair had originally envisioned. And Epic had the finances and the cojones to tell any publisher to stick their deadlines up their butts if the game wasn't ready. Publishers would have to wait until Shadow Complex met Epic's high standards. (Epic's games weren't perfect, but they had far fewer burps and hiccups than other shooters.)

Microsoft was eventually chosen to publish the game, perhaps because of its frighteningly futuristic, statistics-based game testing laboratories in Redmond, Washington. These high-tech labs, formed in 1998, were used to great advantage for Halo and Gears of

War, although, as Capps would tell the Mustards, the whole process seemed "a little *Clockwork Orange* because you're basically wiring people up."*

When Halo 3 was under the microscope at Microsoft's testing lab, the early version was so confounding to play that testers couldn't find their way out of the tree-filled canyon area in the first moments of the game. The research that was accumulated resulted in a change for the better. Video cameras recorded the habits of every gamer. Cameras zoomed in on faces, then on the hands using the controller as the ups and downs of game play were dutifully recorded. At the same time, the team of twenty-five psychologists and researchers, watching from behind a one-way mirror, interpreted every move, blink, and facial expression. This is truly the focus-testing of the future. The audio is key as well: Game testers talked about every move they made, and their constant chatter was recorded and analyzed. Every year, eight thousand testers lumber into this laboratory, people of all ages, paid only in games or with a Windows operating system. They spent six hours a day in this usability lab with Shadow Complex and Microsoft's researchers, who noted dozens of game play stats about each user, from how they were feeling as they played to where they died.

As reams of data flowed back to the Mustards in Utah, Capps and Rein told the brothers that tweaking a game per the testing lab's recommendations could increase sales by as much as 100 percent. So the Mustards fixed, for example, a problem with an ice blue lake, because people were swimming deep underneath and not moving

---

* In fact, testing can get even creepier, with galvanic skin response testing. A company called EmSense specializes in wireless sensors to detect anything from sweat on the hands to increasing heart rate. They can measure your arousal level, your positive and negative emotions while playing, and the level of cognitive engagement with anything from the way you save games to your enjoyment of a harsh battle. If a gargantuan monster busts through a wall and the heart rate jumps twenty beats a minute, a developer might want to ratchet down the thrills to ten beats a minute for the sake of pacing. That's really *Clockwork Orange* stuff.

forward. Testers nosed around for too long, and to their dismay, their character gasped, breathed in water, and drowned. To remedy the situation, the lake was made shallower and the on-screen character was given more time to hold his breath before dying. Finally, a subtle beam of sunlight directed gamers to the shore on the opposite side, where a small, spiderlike robot shot at the gamer, unremittingly. You shot back, splashed your way out of the water, and moved on to the next breathless moment of adventure.

As they pored over the constant stream of metrics from Microsoft, there were some suggestions the Mustards ignored. Hard-core shooter fans kept saying, "Make it more like Halo," or "Make it more like a shooter." The game really wasn't about shooting; it was about exploration, about building central character Jason Flemming's powers by having him crawl through dank caves and squeeze through air-conditioning ducts to find power-ups scattered like treasure in nooks and crannies. The Mustards also discovered a little-known but stunning fact about the shooter genre: Only 25 percent of players of marquee offerings like Halo and Gears of War actually completed the game.

"We have to do much better than that," said Donald in a meeting.

"Bring it up to at least fifty percent," agreed Geremy.

Everyone at Chair agreed that their game had to appeal to two kinds of videogame players. Throughout the decade, especially since the Wii's ubiquity, there had been a seismic shift in the market toward what both Epic and Chair called the "visual tourist," the person who wanted to check out the experience, but stopped playing once he or she felt the frustration of failure over and over again. Super Metroid itself could be very unforgiving, at a time when many games were ball-busters. The Mustards felt being killed and starting again was punishment, not entertainment. They wanted every player to finish the game in less than fifteen hours. Their tip of the hat to the hard-core gamer who enjoyed the deeper challenge was to add certain goals that were very hard to accomplish—for instance, playing the game all the way through, without dying once.

When all was said and done, it worked amazingly well. Shadow Complex was released in August 2009, and more than 200,000 gamers downloaded the 835-megabyte package at $15 each. The game didn't work just because you had to eliminate hundreds of enemies. These sci-fi soldiers, guards, and robotic monstrosities were merely navigational roadblocks on a thrilling trek through the odd, ultra-conservative world of evildoers called The Restoration. They were so archly to the right that they would have made Sarah Palin seem liberal. And as you progressed from room to room and from cave to cave and swam beneath that lake, you were enticed to continue because regular guy Flemming evolved in strength and confidence every step of the way, as you peeled back the world's secrets like layers of onion skin. As you gathered an assortment of weapons and explosives, you began to learn more about a conspiracy that sometimes left you aghast. When you looked outside the window in real life, you might have thought, "Geez, is that guy on the street one of them? He looks so suspicious with that bulky ski parka. Is there a bomb under there? Crap. Is this guy the real Restoration? Is this the beginning of a new civil war?" You were grabbed by the balls by both story and play, neither of which would let go. Shadow Complex was that effective.

The ending, which was full of fire-filled explosions, an oversized spaceship, and a saw-that-coming-a-mile-away twist on the story of the protagonist's oddly lipped girlfriend, was not as gripping as the game play leading up to the epilog. *But oh, that game play.* You could almost smell the pine trees and feel the mist that sprayed from the waterfalls. In an underground war complex, you battled all manner of well-armored creeps and angry knee-high robots shooting foam that made you immobile for seemingly endless seconds while a soldier took aim at your not-quite-tough-enough armor. But the true joy of Shadow Complex was searching the hidden recesses for little treasure chests after you finished the initial mission. They were hidden deep in mountain caves or at the very tops of ceilings on obscured ledges that were treacherous to get to, even with your jetpack. All the while you had to be wary of sudden mishaps, like stumbling upon a fast treadmill that pushed you into nuclear reactors. Zap: you were killed by burning. You became nothing but cinders and ashes.

Shadow Complex was the way of the future: a small game that made money for a big company. Epic executives estimated that Chair, after its success with Shadow Complex, was worth three to four times the amount Epic paid for it initially. And a giant megacorporation like Microsoft was proud to have Shadow Complex in its stable of downloadable games, because it added a cachet of brilliance beyond the usual fare. It was part of a master plan for Microsoft that ultimately paid off; in 2010, the landmark Xbox Live service on which multiplayer games are played became a billion-dollar-a-year industry in itself. The magic behind this new form of game was, of course, its new means of distribution. With downloadable games, a developer didn't need a game disk, manual, box, or space on a store shelf. Such games would not see a Grand Theft Auto kind of return, but the monetary rewards weren't chump change, either.

Whether next year's or next decade's games will have colossal or infinitesimal budgets, whether they'll be mind-bogglingly high-tech or appear humbly in our browser windows, it's undeniable that gaming has already changed our lives and our culture. Blockbuster TV shows and movies are influenced by the action sequences in videogames— every week. But beyond the braggadocio and hype, beyond being trivial playthings that are mere toys for some, there is real depth in about 10 percent of each year's releases, and that's akin to the best of our major movies and TV programs. Sony's Heavy Rain proved that a serial killer story could be influenced by the subtler, sinister human emotions à la Raymond Carver. Uncharted 2: Among Thieves, with its nineteenth-century penny dreadful influence on a story surrounding Marco Polo's lost treasure, let you feel as though you were in a melodramatic movie with all the spills and thrills of an Indiana Jones adventure.

So these are more than toys, as educator and game designer Ian Bogost suggests in his book *Persuasive Games*. Games can have their own kind of rhetoric—not oratory, but a procedural rhetoric that lures us into thinking and changing our points of view. So-called serious games with low budgets are used in politics, education, and medicine not to make money or to be played by millions. Rather, they attempt to convince stricken children, say, that a kind of cancer can be defeated with chemotherapy. One question to mull in the future, beyond ideas for technology like holographic play, may be whether serious games can become subsets of more commercial games. Could a game like Gears of War take time to slip in some of the makers' inspirations from real war battles, kind of like a battle history–fueled featurette in a DVD? Could a portion of Madden take time in a mini-game or in coaching mode to help us better understand football plays themselves? And what if, in a series like Sony's brilliant God of War, which waters down the Greek myths, there was a section in which you could enjoy snippets of *Bulfinch's Mythology*? It sure would make games far more acceptable to the nabobs who say that they are throwaway ephemera. You could say, "Screw them, I just want to play," and you would mostly be right; but adding such stuff in a seamless way might well make the game a deeper experience. In the opening scenes of Rockstar's ambitious cowboy epic, Red Dead Redemption, you see John Marston, the game's ultra-cool but scarred protagonist, who's perhaps named after a fifteenth-century poet/ satirist, board a train to a dusty, nowhere town. Quiet and alone, he sits listening to the nearby passengers, including bigoted old women who talk about politics. Then, a teen girl tries to school a Luddite preacher about the coming technology that includes airplanes. Man will never do that, replies the preacher. "Flying is for the angels." It's an understated history lesson of a time when the United States was in utter transition in everything from politics to religion to technology. And it doesn't stick out painfully because it's done with wit. It's entertaining, but it's delicately stirred into the Rockstar recipe of Palahniuk-esque anarchic energy and social commentary. And it all works better than similar scenes in, say, Martin Scorsese's *Gangs of New York*, which tries to shoehorn history into the drama and often fails in the process. But game makers also have to stop falling back on the idea that the games industry is still in its infancy, a childhood that must be given a cultural pass even if its creations are full of cliché design and childish writing. The industry is not a baby anymore. Games have transformed from curiosities to a conquering form of mass entertainment. Do it thoroughly and thoughtfully or don't do it at all.

As I write these words, many critics and pundits are rubbing their hands together in glee at reports that the videogame industry has been hit by the recent recession, and they are pouncing upon this news as another opportunity to denounce videogames as shallow playthings. But if you look at the history of popular art, this is hardly surprising. Novels were once forbidden and considered deleterious, leading Voltaire to pen a parody called "Concerning the Horrible Danger of Reading." In the late 1800s, Anthony Comstock tried to ban everything from Whitman to Tolstoy, and critics were pooh-poohing the content within the popular penny dreadful novels. When movies became the sensation of the late 1800s, Maxim Gorky worried that in viewing them, "we will be increasingly less able and less willing to grasp the everyday impressions of ordinary life." When movies were finally considered worthy of being called art, the movie critics disparaged pop music from the likes of Elvis Presley and the Beatles. And when videogames came to the fore, all those established critics—book, movie, pop music—ridiculed this growing form of expression. That's what critics do—they sniff, they rail, they bellow and try to snuff out whatever it is they vehemently disagree with. But Transformation 2.0 is just around the corner as more and more developers elevate their games to something that's beyond action. Soon, there will come a time when the pundits can no longer hold their noses and shake their heads. Soon, they'll forget their concentration on the stupid shovelware games. As they look to the new diversity that will flourish, they'll no longer be able to deny that videogames are more than just toys.

Until then, those of you who love games will find the art of the game within yourselves. And until then, you'll sure have fun playing, fighting ever more malevolent grues and traveling to new worlds on roller coaster rides that allow you quick and satisfying escape, and sometimes profound thought, and sometimes, as that non-gamer Coleridge wrote in 1817, the "willing suspension of disbelief for the moment, which constitutes poetic faith."

Bring it on. Bring on more gems like Shadow Complex. Bring on 3-D without glasses. Bring on holographic gaming. Bring on the next generation of Will Wrights, Shigeru Miyamotos, and Houser Brothers—along with the startling, lambent genres they'll cre-ate. Bring it on. Bring it on. As Nightmare growls so ravenously in SoulCalibur II, "My thirst is endless."

ACKNOWLEDGMENTS

I want to thank the highly intelligent and always witty Helen Pfeffer, who listened to me bitch about this book for nearly three years and helped me with the editing. My agent and pal Adam Chromy was in my corner even before this was a book proposal. Julian Pavia, my thoughtful, long note–penning editor at Random House, really gets games and pop culture. He truly understands writers. I also want to thank my good friend Steve Kent, whose *Ultimate History of Video Games* was an inspiration. To Trip Hawkins, the first who gave of his time, and to all the game makers who listened and opened up, and the publicists who helped to make many of the two hundred interviews happen, I am forever indebted. Jennifer Kolbe, Sam Houser, and Rockstar came through big-time in the end. To the New York Videogame Critics Circle and all the game writers and game players who believe that videogame journalism and culture are about more than shooting, next-generation technology, and leveling up, this book is for you.

SELECTED NOTES

All Your Base Are Belong to Us is based on approximately two hundred interviews, along with three years of writing and research.

INTRODUCTION

PG. ix   I'm referring to SoulCalibur for the Sega Dreamcast console, released by Namco in the United States in September 1999.

PG. xi   The videogame industry statistics cited are from the Entertainment Software Association, circa 2010.

PG. xi   The Pokémon-branded milk was from a Bangkok 7-Eleven store. It was mixed with honey and tasted awful.

THE PRELUDE—
FIRST BLIPS ON THE SCREEN

The chapter is based on twelve interviews conducted with William Higinbotham's son, Bob Dvorak's son, Ralph Baer, and past and current scientists and employees at Brookhaven National Laboratory.

PG. xvi   The original Noughts and Crosses can be downloaded at http://www.adit.co.uk/html/noughts_and_crosses.html.

PG. xx   Goldman, Robert P., "Wonderful Willie from Brookhaven," *Parade*, May 18, 1958, pages 15–18.

PG. xxi   Higinbotham, W. A., The Brookhaven TV-Tennis Game, date unknown.

1.
A SPACE ODYSSEY

This chapter is based in large part upon a full weekend spent with Ralph Baer at his home in New Hampshire. Baer's basement was filled with memorabilia, including a toy shop and a working Odyssey. On the floor of his bedroom was a G4TV Legend of Videogames award.

The chapter is also informed by Mr. Baer's autobiography, *Videogames: In the Beginning* (Rolenta Press, 2005) and by a second, currently unpublished, memoir.

Also interviewed for the chapter were Bill Harrison and Al Alcorn, along with three others who spoke on background.

2.
SO EASY, A DRUNK COULD PLAY

AND

3.
HIGHEST HIGHS, LOWEST LOWS

Long interviews for these chapters were conducted with Al Alcorn, Ted Dabney, Mark Cerny, Todd Frye, Trip Hawkins, and others. An older interview with Nolan Bushnell was also used.

PG. 21   Loni Reeder's three-page e-mail is dated December 28, 2005.
PG. 27   Bushnell's memo was provided to me by Al Alcorn.

4.
OF MONKEYS, MARIO, AND MIYAMOTO

Based on three interviews conducted over the years with Shigeru Miyamoto, as well as interviews with Henk Rogers, Trip Hawkins, Al Alcorn, Minoru Arakawa, Howard Phillips, and five others who spoke on background.

PG. 7 0   The quote "to escape the cycles of worries I had" is from a Miyamoto interview done by Nintendo of Japan's president, Satoru Iwata. http://us.wii.com/wii-fit/iwata_asks/vol1_page1.jsp

5.
FALLING BLOCKS, RISING FORTUNES

Based on long interviews I had with Henk Rogers, early Nintendo maven and spokesperson Howard Phillips, Alexey Pajitnov, and Minoru Arakawa, and conversations with Jason Kapulka and others who spoke on background.

PG. 7 5   Russia was not an easy place to live while Pajitnov was growing up. See Hedrick Smith's *The Russians* and *The New Russians,* both landmark tomes, to read more about the tenor of the times during the Soviet Union's heyday and what came after.

PG. 7 8   Vadim Gerasimov tells his side of the Tetris story at length at http://vadim.oversima.com/Tetris.htm.

6.
THE RISE OF ELECTRONIC ARTS

Based on interviews I conducted with Trip Hawkins, Ray Tobey, Mark Cerny, and Jason Rubin, as well as conversations with Steven L. Kent, Mike Harvey from *Nibble* magazine, the football players Ray Lewis and Daunte Culpepper, and others inside EA who spoke on condition of anonymity.

PG. 1 0 3   According to *USA Weekend* magazine (August 27, 2010), Madden NFL has earned more then $3 billion in revenue since 1988.

PG. 104   The *New York Times*'s Trip Gabriel estimated Hawkins's financial
worth in an article dated October 27, 1993.

7.
GAMES, MYST, AND THE 7TH GUEST

Based on interviews and follow-ups conducted for the book with Graeme
Devine, Rob Landeros, Ken Williams, and others who requested anonymity,
along with older interviews with game writer Michelle Em, Rand Miller, and
musician George "The Fat Man" Sanger, and conversations with journalist
Geoff Keighley.

8.
THE PLAYSTATION'S CRASH

Based on interviews conducted with Andy Gavin, Trip Hawkins, Mark
Cerny, Jason Rubin, John Smedley, and various people at Sony who requested
anonymity, as well as older interviews and conversations with Kaz Hirai, Ken
Kutaragi, and Andrew House.

PG. 138   Though Kutaragi disdained the idea of a new mascot, the U.S.
marketing team paid no attention. A *New York Times* article
dated September 7, 1995, quoted a U.S. executive: "'We're going
after males 12 to 24, too, with a skew toward the high end, so
VMA is perfect for us,' said William Herman, Sony Computer
Entertainment's vice president of marketing, referring to the
awards show." If Kutaragi had heard the age of twelve bandied
about, he would have thrown a fit.

PG. 141   You can see the very mocking Crash Bandicoot
commercial at http://www.youtube.com/watch?v=mTi5EaocGaY.

9.

WHEN THE ADVENTURE ENDS

Based on long interviews with Ken and Roberta Williams. I also spoke with the PopCap guys, some of the Phantasmagoria team, and a few people who didn't want to be named here. I also drew from older interviews with Roberta Williams and Al Lowe.

PG. 156   It wasn't just Ken and Roberta who were fooled by CUC/ Cendant. Everyone believed the hype, from analysts who rated it a "strong buy," to *Forbes,* which, in a May 23, 1997, headline, called the company "The Procter & Gamble of Video Games."

10.

EVERQUEST: ORCS, ELVES, AND A CAST OF THOUSANDS

Based on interviews with John Smedley, conversations with seven of my former Sony Online Entertainment compatriots, and an older conversation with Kelly Flock. I also talked briefly about EverQuest with the makers of World of Warcraft and two videogame analysts.

PG. 163   In the December 20, 1999, issue of *Time,* an unbylined "Best of Cybertech" story stated, "EverQuest's superior software puts it sword and shield above the rest."

PG. 166   Shawn Woolley's sad story is dramatically portrayed by Lazlow (who would go on to work for Rockstar Games) in the May 2003 issue of *Playboy.*

11.

THE EVERQUEST KILLER

Based on interviews with Chris Metzen, Michael Morhaime, Frank Pearce, Rob Pardo, John Smedley, and others.

PG. 182   The complete WoW episode of *South Park* is still worth watching at http://www.southparkstudios.com/guide/1008.

12.

BIOSHOCK: ART FOR GAME'S SAKE

Based on lengthy interviews with Ken Levine, Tom Bass, Susan Lewis, and Sarah Anderson, and conversations with Warren Spector, Hermen Hulst, journalist/editor Ricardo Torres, Geoff Keighley, and employees at Take-Two Interactive and Irrational Games.

PG. 185   Seth Scheisel's piece in the October 31, 2007, edition of the *New York Times* went on to report glowingly that Ratchet and Clank Future was "so lushly compelling that you find yourself just staring at the screen, as if it were a movie."

PG. 191   Brilliant game designer Warren Spector also worked on Thief: The Dark Project.

13.

THOSE MOVIES SUCK

Based on older interviews with Hironobi Sakaguchi, Frank Darabont, and John Milius, as well as recent interviews with members of Blizzard Entertainment, M. Night Shyamalan, and members of the game and movie industries who wished to remain anonymous.

PG. 210   Kenneth Turan's *Los Angeles Times* review of *Final Fantasy: The Spirits Within* was published on July 11, 2001.

14.

UNDER THE GUN: THE KIDS IN THE SANDBOX

AND

15.
ROCKSTAR GETS PILLORIED

Both are based in large part on interviews with Sam Houser.

It was difficult to get to Rockstar. Four months of requests to the PR department went unnoticed. It sends a clear message: Rockstar prefers to make games, not talk about them. But they needed to be in this book, so I kept trying. I sent my last book, *My Life Among the Serial Killers,* to Sam and Dan Houser, who passed it on to Rockstar's terrific Jennifer Kolbe, who became my champion. After some months of postponement during the crunch time for Red Dead Redemption, a very gracious Sam Houser came through with seven hours of interviews.

These chapters are also based on conversations with others who have worked with Rockstar, and members of the Halo team and the original Doom team.

PG. 231   Sam Houser was right to be annoyed about State of Emergency. According to PSXextreme, the game did garner the most buzz and awards at E3, 2001. When it was released, however, it garnered middling reviews and was often returned to stores because of bugs. http://www.psxextreme.com/scripts/reviews2/review. asp?revID=128

PG. 233   Truman Capote, *In Cold Blood* (Random House, 1965), page 5.

PG. 234   Senator Lieberman's quote is from *Forbes* via Reuters, "Lieberman Denounces 'Grand Theft Auto' Video Game," January 25, 2004.

PG. 238   Senator Clinton announced her stance regarding the game on July 13, 2005. The words reverberated throughout the media and on videogame sites like GameSpot. http://www.gamespot.com/ news/2005/07/13/news_6129021.html.

PG. 241   The Coke commercial is utterly brilliant and worth watching a few times. http://www.youtube.com/watch?v=7wt5FiZQrgM

16.
THE POPCAP GUYS AND THE FAMILY JEWELS

This chapter is based on interviews with Jason Kapulka, John Vechey, and Brian Fiete and a conversation with David Roberts, along with others at PopCap.

17.
THE THEORIST GOES GLOBAL

The chapter is based in large part on interviews with Will Wright and Jeff Braun, who were very generous with their time. It also draws from interviews with Shigeru Miyamoto, various members of the Sims and Spore teams, an older conversation with Peter Molyneaux, and an e-mail conversation with Bill Barol.

PG. 2 6 6   Bill Barol, "Big Fun in a Small Town," *Newsweek,* May 29, 1989, pg. 64.

PG. 2 7 0   Martin Gardner's "Mathematical Games" columns from *Scientific American* from 1956 to 1980 are collected on a 4,500-page CD-ROM that consolidates his fifteen books, published by the Mathematical Association of America (May 2005).

18.
WII NATION

Based on three interviews over the years with Shigeru Miyamoto, interviews with Howard Phillips, Trip Hawkins, and Will Wright, a conversation with Reggie Fils-Aime, older interviews with Perrin Kaplan and George Harrison, and a brief personal encounter with Lindsay Lohan. I also had conversations with other members of Nintendo of America who prefer to remain anonymous, and spoke with some people who worked with Nintendo as third-party licensees.

PG. 2 8 3   Dean Takahashi's groundbreaking VentureBeat series on the Microsoft console is called "Xbox 360 Defects: An Inside History of Microsoft's Video Game Console Woes," and it began online on September 5, 2008.

PG. 285   The Nintendo statistics are from Nintendo of America.

19.
THE FUTURE

Based on interviews with Donald Mustard, Laura Mustard, Mike Capps, Mark Coates, analyst Billy Pidgeon, Cevat Yerli, Sam Houser, Will Wright, Hermen Hulst, members of the New York Videogame Critics Circle, and older interviews with game executives Peter Moore, Shane Kim, Ed Fries, and J. Allard, and writer/game director Amy Hennig.

SELECTED BIBLIOGRAPHY

Baer, Ralph. *Videogames: In the Beginning* (Rolenta Press, 2005).

Bogost, Ian. *Persuasive Games: The Expressive Power of Videogames* (MIT Press, 2007).

Bruck, Connie. *Master of the Game: Steve Ross and the Invention of Time Warner* (Penguin, 1995).

Burnham, Van. *Supercade* (MIT Press, 2001).

Chaplin, Heather, and Aaron Ruby. *Smartbomb* (Algonquin Press, 2005).

Cohen, Scott. *Zap: The Rise and Fall of Atari* (McGraw-Hill, 1987).

Compton, Shanna. *Gamers: Writers, Artists and Programmers on the Pleasures of Pixels* (Soft Skull Press, 2004).

DeMaria, Rusel, and Johnny L. Wilson. *High Score* (McGraw-Hill, 2002).

DeMaria, Rusel, and Paul Lipscombe. *EverQuest: The 10th Anniversary Collector's Edition* (BradyGames, 2009).

Fawcett, Bill. *The Battle for Azeroth* (SmartPop, 2006).

Fell, John L. *A History of Films* (Holt, Rinehart, Winston, 1979).

Funk, Joe. *EA: Celebrating 25 Years of Interactive Entertainment* (Prime, 2007).

Gibson, John M. *I Am 8-Bit* (Chronicle, 2006).

Guinness. *Guinness World Records Gamer's Edition* (Guinness, 2008).

Halter, Ed. *From Sun Tzu to Xbox: War and Videogames* (Public Affairs, 2006).

Herman, Leonard. *Phoenix, The Rise & Fall of Videogames* (Rolenta Press, 2001).

Kane, Mitchell. *Game Boys* (Viking Adult, 2008).

Kent, Steven L. *The Ultimate History of Video Games* (Three Rivers Press, 2001).

King, Stephen. *Danse Macabre* (Everest House, 1981).

Kohler, Chris. *Retro Gaming Hacks* (O'Reilly Media, 2005).

Kushner, David. *Masters of Doom* (Random House, 2003).

Levy, Steve. *Hackers: Heroes of the Computer Revolution* (Doubleday, 1984).

Manguel, Alberto. *A History of Reading* (Viking, 1996).

Poole, Steve. *Trigger Happy* (Arcade Publishing, 2000).

Saltzman, Marc. *Game Design Secrets of the Sages* (Brady, 2000).

Sheff, David. *Game Over* (Random House, 1993).

Smith, Rob. *Rogue Leaders: The Story of LucasArts* (Chronicle, 2008).

INDEX

ABOUT THE AUTHOR

HAROLD GOLDBERG has reviewed videogames for fifteen years for such publications as *Wired, Entertainment Weekly, Boys' Life, The Village Voice,* and *Radar,* and for three years penned a widely syndicated gaming column. He has also written on a variety of other subjects for the *New York Times, Vanity Fair, Esquire, New York,* and *Rolling Stone.* In addition, Goldberg served as editor in chief of Sony Online Entertainment during the launch of EverQuest. His other books include *My Life Among the Serial Killers,* cowritten with Dr. Helen Morrison, and *Sidney Lumet: Interviews.*